NIST Special Publication 800-160
Volume 2

# Developing Cyber Resilient Systems:
## A Systems Security Engineering Approach

RON ROSS
VICTORIA PILLITTERI
RICHARD GRAUBART
DEBORAH BODEAU
ROSALIE MCQUAID

This publication is available free of charge from:
https://doi.org/10.6028/NIST.SP.800-160v2

# COMPUTER SECURITY

National Institute of
Standards and Technology
U.S. Department of Commerce

NIST Special Publication 800-160
Volume 2

# Developing Cyber Resilient Systems:
## A Systems Security Engineering Approach

**RON ROSS**
**VICTORIA PILLITTERI**
*Computer Security Division*
*National Institute of Standards and Technology*

**RICHARD GRAUBART**
**DEBORAH BODEAU**
**ROSALIE MCQUAID**
*Cyber Resiliency and Innovative*
*Mission Engineering Department*
*The MITRE Corporation*

This publication is available free of charge from:
https://doi.org/10.6028/NIST.SP.800-160v2

**November 2019**

U.S. Department of Commerce
*Wilbur L. Ross, Jr., Secretary*

National Institute of Standards and Technology
*Walter Copan, NIST Director and Under Secretary of Commerce for Standards and Technology*

# Authority

This publication has been developed by NIST to further its statutory responsibilities under the Federal Information Security Modernization Act (FISMA), 44 U.S.C. § 3551 *et seq.*, Public Law (P.L.) 113-283. NIST is responsible for developing information security standards and guidelines, including minimum requirements for federal information systems. Such information security standards and guidelines shall not apply to national security systems without the express approval of the appropriate federal officials exercising policy authority over such systems. This guideline is consistent with the requirements of the Office of Management and Budget (OMB) Circular A-130.

Nothing in this publication should be taken to contradict the standards and guidelines made mandatory and binding on federal agencies by the Secretary of Commerce under statutory authority. Nor should these guidelines be interpreted as altering or superseding the existing authorities of the Secretary of Commerce, OMB Director, or any other federal official. This publication may be used by nongovernmental organizations on a voluntary basis, and is not subject to copyright in the United States. Attribution would, however, be appreciated by NIST.

National Institute of Standards and Technology Special Publication 800-160, Volume 2
Natl. Inst. Stand. Technol. Spec. Publ. 800-160, Volume 2, 229 pages (November 2019)

CODEN: NSPUE2

This publication is available free of charge from:
https://doi.org/10.6028/NIST.SP.800-160v2

Certain commercial entities, equipment, or materials may be identified in this document to describe an experimental procedure or concept adequately. Such identification is not intended to imply recommendation or endorsement by NIST, nor is it intended to imply that the entities, materials, or equipment are necessarily the best available for the purpose.

There may be references in this publication to other publications currently under development by NIST in accordance with its assigned statutory responsibilities. The information in this publication, including concepts, practices, and methodologies may be used by federal agencies even before the completion of such companion publications. Thus, until each publication is completed, current requirements, guidelines, and procedures, where they exist, remain operative. For planning and transition purposes, federal agencies may wish to closely follow the development of these new publications by NIST.

Organizations are encouraged to review draft publications during the designated public comment periods and provide feedback to NIST. Many NIST publications, other than the ones noted above, are available at https://csrc.nist.gov/publications.

## Comments on this publication may be submitted to:

National Institute of Standards and Technology
Attn: Computer Security Division, Information Technology Laboratory
100 Bureau Drive (Mail Stop 8930) Gaithersburg, MD 20899-8930
Email: sec-cert@nist.gov

All comments are subject to release under the Freedom of Information Act (FOIA) [FOIA96].

## Reports on Computer Systems Technology

The National Institute of Standards and Technology (NIST) Information Technology Laboratory (ITL) promotes the U.S. economy and public welfare by providing technical leadership for the Nation's measurement and standards infrastructure. ITL develops tests, test methods, reference data, proof of concept implementations, and technical analyses to advance the development and productive use of information technology (IT). ITL's responsibilities include the development of management, administrative, technical, and physical standards and guidelines for the cost-effective security of other than national security-related information in federal information systems. The Special Publication 800-series reports on ITL's research, guidelines, and outreach efforts in information systems security and privacy and its collaborative activities with industry, government, and academic organizations.

# Abstract

This publication is used in conjunction with ISO/IEC/IEEE 15288:2015, *Systems and software engineering—Systems life cycle processes*, NIST Special Publication 800-160, Volume 1, *Systems Security Engineering—Considerations for a Multidisciplinary Approach in the Engineering of Trustworthy Secure Systems*, and NIST Special Publication 800-37, *Risk Management Framework for Information Systems and Organizations—A System Life Cycle Approach for Security and Privacy*. It can be viewed as a handbook for achieving the identified cyber resiliency outcomes based on a systems engineering perspective on system life cycle processes in conjunction with risk management processes, allowing the experience and expertise of the organization to help determine what is correct for its purpose. Organizations can select, adapt, and use some or all of the cyber resiliency constructs (i.e., objectives, techniques, approaches, and design principles) described in this publication and apply the constructs to the technical, operational, and threat environments for which systems need to be engineered. The system life cycle processes and cyber resiliency constructs can be used for new systems, system upgrades, or repurposed systems; can be employed at any stage of the system life cycle; and can take advantage of any system or software development methodology including, for example, waterfall, spiral, or agile. The processes and associated cyber resiliency constructs can also be applied recursively, iteratively, concurrently, sequentially, or in parallel and to any system regardless of its size, complexity, purpose, scope, environment of operation, or special nature. The full extent of the application of the content in this publication is guided and informed by stakeholder protection needs, mission assurance needs, and concerns with cost, schedule, and performance. The tailorable nature of the engineering activities and tasks and the system life cycle processes ensure that systems resulting from the application of the security and cyber resiliency design principles, among others, have the level of trustworthiness deemed sufficient to protect stakeholders from suffering unacceptable losses of their assets and associated consequences. Trustworthiness is made possible, in part, by the rigorous application of the security and cyber resiliency design principles, constructs, and concepts within a structured set of systems life cycle processes that provides the necessary traceability of requirements, transparency, and evidence to support risk-informed decision-making and trades.

# Keywords

Advanced persistent threat; controls; cyber resiliency; cyber resiliency approaches; cyber resiliency design principles; cyber resiliency engineering framework; cyber resiliency goals; cyber resiliency objectives; cyber resiliency techniques; risk management strategy; system life cycle; systems security engineering; trustworthiness.

# Trademark Information

# Acknowledgements

The authors gratefully acknowledge and appreciate the contributions from DJ Anand, Jon Boyens, Nicolas Chaillan, Ed Custeau, Holly Dunlap, Avi Gopstein, Suzanne Hassell, Bill Heinbockel, Daryl Hild, Scott Jackson, Lauren Knausenberger, Ellen Laderman, Logan Mailloux, Jeff Marron, Cory Ocker, Rebecca Onuskanich, James Reilly, Thom Schoeffling, Martin Stanley, Shane Steiger, Mike Thomas, Beth Wilson, and David Wollman whose thoughtful comments improved the overall quality, thoroughness, and usefulness of this publication. The authors would also like to acknowledge the INCOSE Systems Security Engineering and Resiliency Working Groups, the Air Force Research Laboratory (AFRL), and the National Defense Industrial Association (NDIA) Systems Security Engineering Committee for their feedback on the initial drafts of this publication.

In addition to the above acknowledgments, a special note of thanks goes to Jeff Brewer, Jim Foti, Jeff Marron, Isabel Van Wyk, Eduardo Takamura, and the NIST web services team for their outstanding administrative support. The authors also wish to recognize the professional staff from the NIST Computer Security Division and the Applied Cybersecurity Division for their contributions in helping to improve the technical content of the publication. Finally, the authors gratefully acknowledge the significant contributions from individuals and organizations in the public and private sectors, nationally and internationally, whose insightful, thoughtful, and constructive comments improved the quality, thoroughness, and usefulness of this publication.

# Patent Disclosure Notice

*NOTICE: The Information Technology Laboratory (ITL) has requested that holders of patent claims whose use may be required for compliance with the guidance or requirements of this publication disclose such patent claims to ITL. However, holders of patents are not obligated to respond to ITL calls for patents and ITL has not undertaken a patent search in order to identify which, if any, patents may apply to this publication.*

*As of the date of publication and following call(s) for the identification of patent claims whose use may be required for compliance with the guidance or requirements of this publication, no such patent claims have been identified to ITL.*

*No representation is made or implied by ITL that licenses are not required to avoid patent infringement in the use of this publication.*

# Table of Contents

**CHAPTER ONE   INTRODUCTION** ......................................................................................................1

    1.1 PURPOSE AND APPLICABILITY ........................................................................................ 3

    1.2 TARGET AUDIENCE............................................................................................................ 4

    1.3 PUBLICATION ORGANIZATION ....................................................................................... 5

**CHAPTER TWO   THE FUNDAMENTALS** ....................................................................................**6**

    2.1 CYBER RESILIENCY ENGINEERING FRAMEWORK ........................................................ 7

        *2.1.1  CYBER RESILIENCY GOALS* ................................................................................... 8

        *2.1.2  CYBER RESILIENCY OBJECTIVES* .......................................................................... 9

        *2.1.3  CYBER RESILIENCY TECHNIQUES AND APPROACHES* ........................................ 10

        *2.1.4  CYBER RESILIENCY DESIGN PRINCIPLES* ........................................................... 13

        *2.1.5  RELATIONSHIP AMONG CYBER RESILIENCY CONSTRUCTS* ................................ 14

    2.2 CYBER RESILIENCY IN THE SYSTEM LIFE CYCLE .......................................................... 15

    2.3 RISK MANAGEMENT AND CYBER RESILIENCY ............................................................ 19

**CHAPTER THREE   CYBER RESILIENCY IN PRACTICE** ...........................................................**20**

    3.1 SELECTING AND PRIORITIZING CYBER RESILIENCY CONSTRUCTS ............................. 20

        *3.1.1  ACHIEVEMENT OF GOALS AND OBJECTIVES* ..................................................... 20

        *3.1.2  CYBER RISK MANAGEMENT STRATEGY* .............................................................. 20

        *3.1.3  TYPE OF SYSTEM* ................................................................................................. 21

        *3.1.4  CYBER RESLIENCY CONFLICTS AND SYNERGIES* ................................................ 23

        *3.1.5  OTHER DISCIPLINES AND EXISTING INVESTMENTS* ........................................... 24

        *3.1.6  ARCHITECTURAL LOCATIONS* .............................................................................. 26

        *3.1.7  EFFECTS ON ADVERSARIES, THREATS, AND RISKS* ............................................ 26

        *3.1.8  MATURITY AND POTENTIAL ADOPTION* ............................................................ 27

    3.2 ANALYTIC PRACTICES AND PROCESSES ....................................................................... 28

        *3.2.1  UNDERSTAND THE CONTEXT* .............................................................................. 30

        *3.2.2  ESTABLISH THE INITIAL CYBER RESILIENCY BASELINE* ...................................... 35

        *3.2.3  ANALYZE THE SYSTEM* ........................................................................................ 37

        *3.2.4  DEFINE AND ANALYZE SPECIFIC ALTERNATIVES* ............................................... 40

        *3.2.5  DEVELOP RECOMMENDATIONS* .......................................................................... 42

**APPENDIX A   REFERENCES** .......................................................................................................**44**

**APPENDIX B   GLOSSARY** .........................................................................................................**56**

**APPENDIX C   ACRONYMS**........................................................................................................**67**

**APPENDIX D   BACKGROUND** ..................................................................................................**71**

    D.1 DEFINING CYBER RESILIENCY ...................................................................................... 71

    D.2 DISTINGUISHING CHARACTERISTICS OF CYBER RESILIENCY ..................................... 72

    D.3 RELATIONSHIP WITH OTHER SPECIALITY ENGINEERING DISCIPLINES ...................... 74

    D.4 RELATIONSHIP BETWEEN CYBER RESILIENCY AND RISK ........................................... 78

**APPENDIX E   CYBER RESILIENCY CONSTRUCTS** ...................................................................**81**

    E.1 CYBER RESILIENCY GOALS ............................................................................................ 81

    E.2 CYBER RESILIENCY OBJECTIVES ................................................................................... 82

    E.3 CYBER RESILIENCY TECHNIQUES .................................................................................. 85

    E.4 CYBER RESILIENCY IMPLEMENTATION APPROACHES .................................................. 87

E.5   CYBER RESILIENCY DESIGN PRINCIPLES ............................................................... 98
    *E.5.1   STRATEGIC DESIGN PRINCIPLES* ....................................................................... 98
    *E.5.2   STRUCTURAL DESIGN PRINCIPLES* ................................................................... 105
E.6   RELATIONSHIPS AMONG CYBER RESILIENCY CONSTRUCTS ........................................ 118

**APPENDIX F   CYBER RESILIENCY IN THE SYSTEM LIFE CYCLE ...................................122**

F.1   CYBER RESILIENCY AND SSE TERMINOLOGY ............................................................. 122
    *F.1.1   SECURITY AND CYBER RESILIENCY ASPECTS* ..................................................... 122
    *F.1.2   SECURITY AND CYBER RESILIENCY CRITERIA* ..................................................... 123
    *F.1.3   SECURITY AND CYBER RESILIENCY REQUIREMENTS AND CHARACTERISTICS* ........................ 124
    *F.1.4   CYBER RESILIENCY AND SECURITY FUNCTION, VIEWS, AND MODELS* .............................. 125
F.2   CYBER RESILIENCY IN SYSTEM LIFE CYCLE PROCESSES ............................................ 126
    *F.2.1   BUSINESS OR MISSION ANALYSIS* .................................................................... 126
    *F.2.2   STAKEHOLDER NEEDS AND REQUIREMENTS DEFINITION* ............................................ 128
    *F.2.3   SYSTEM REQUIREMENTS DEFINITION* .................................................................. 129
    *F.2.4   ARCHITECTURE DEFINITION* ............................................................................ 130
    *F.2.5   DESIGN DEFINITION* .................................................................................... 132
    *F.2.6   SYSTEM ANALYSIS* ..................................................................................... 133
    *F.2.7   IMPLEMENTATION* ...................................................................................... 135
    *F.2.8   INTEGRATION* ........................................................................................... 135
    *F.2.9   VERIFICATION* ........................................................................................... 135
    *F.2.10   TRANSITION* ........................................................................................... 136
    *F.2.11   VALIDATION* ........................................................................................... 137
    *F.2.12   OPERATION* ........................................................................................... 138
    *F.2.13   MAINTENANCE* ........................................................................................ 139
    *F.2.14   DISPOSAL* ............................................................................................. 139

**APPENDIX G   CONTROLS SUPPORTING CYBER RESILIENCY ...................................141**

**APPENDIX H   ADVERSARY-ORIENTED ANALYSIS ...............................................154**

H.1   POTENTIAL EFFECTS ON THREAT EVENTS ................................................................ 154
H.2   COVERAGE ANALYSIS FOR CYBER RESILIENCY APPROACHES ...................................... 160
    *H.2.1   UTILITY OF THE TABLES* ............................................................................... 162
    *H.2.2   ORGANIZATION OF THE TABLES* ...................................................................... 162
    *H.2.3   ASSUMPTIONS AND CAVEATS* ........................................................................ 162

**APPENDIX I   CYBER RESILIENCY USE CASES ...................................................174**

I.1   SELF-DRIVING CAR ............................................................................................ 174
    *I.1.1   MOTIVATING THREAT SCENARIO* ..................................................................... 175
    *I.1.2   APPLICABILITY OF CYBER RESILIENCY CONSTRUCTS* ............................................. 175
    *I.1.3   SOLUTIONS CONSIDERED* ............................................................................. 175
    *I.1.4   CONTEXT DETAILS* ..................................................................................... 176
    *I.1.5   RESTATEMENT AND APPLICATION OF CYBER RESILIENCY CONSTRUCTS* ........................ 178
    *I.1.6   DEFINITION AND ANALYSIS OF SOLUTION CHARACTERISTICS* ..................................... 181
I.2   ENTERPRISE IT SYSTEM ...................................................................................... 182
    *I.2.1   MOTIVATING THREAT SCENARIO* ..................................................................... 183
    *I.2.2   APPLICABILITY OF CYBER RESILIENCY CONSTRUCTS* ............................................. 183
    *I.2.3   SOLUTIONS CONSIDERED* ............................................................................. 183
    *I.2.4   CONTEXT DETAILS* ..................................................................................... 185
    *I.2.5   RESTATEMENT AND APPLICATION OF CYBER RESILIENCY CONSTRUCTS* ........................ 186
    *I.2.6   DEFINITION AND ANALYSIS OF SOLUTION CHARACTERISTICS* ..................................... 192
I.3   CAMPUS MICROGRID .......................................................................................... 192

*I.3.1  MOTIVATING THREAT SCENARIO* ........................................................................................ *193*
*I.3.2  APPLICABILITY OF CYBER RESILIENCY CONSTRUCTS* ............................................................. *193*
*I.3.3  SOLUTIONS CONSIDERED* ................................................................................................... *193*
*I.3.4  CONTEXT DETAILS* ............................................................................................................ *194*
*I.3.5  RESTATEMENT AND APPLICATION OF CYBER RESILIENCY CONSTRUCTS* ............................... *196*
*I.3.6  DEFINITION AND ANALYSIS OF SOLUTION CHARACTERISTICS* ................................................ *199*

**APPENDIX J  CYBER RESILIENCY IN A REAL-WORLD EXAMPLE**................................................**201**

J.1  POWER GRID ATTACK—2015 ................................................................................................ 201
J.2  POWER GRID ATTACK—2016 ................................................................................................ 203

## DISCLAIMER

This publication is intended to be used in conjunction with and as a supplement to ISO/IEC/IEEE 15288:2015, *Systems and software engineering — System life cycle processes*. It is recommended that organizations using this publication obtain [ISO 15288] to fully understand the context of the security-related activities and tasks in each of the system life cycle processes. Content from the international standard that is referenced in this publication is reprinted with permission from the Institute of Electrical and Electronics Engineers and is noted as follows:

*ISO/IEC/IEEE 15288-2015. Reprinted with permission from IEEE, Copyright IEEE 2015, All rights reserved.*

## HOW TO USE THIS PUBLICATION

This publication is intended to be used in conjunction with NIST Special Publication 800-160 Volume 1, *Systems Security Engineering – Considerations for a Multidisciplinary Approach in the Engineering of Trustworthy Secure Systems*. This publication is designed to be flexible in its application to meet the diverse and changing needs of organizations. It is not intended to provide a specific recipe for execution. Rather, it can be viewed as a catalog or handbook for achieving the identified cyber resiliency outcomes from a systems engineering perspective on system life cycle processes, leveraging the experience and expertise of the engineering organization to determine what is correct for its purpose. Stakeholders choosing to use this guidance can employ some or all of the cyber resiliency constructs (goals, objectives, techniques, approaches, and design principles) as well as the analytic and life cycle processes, tailoring them as appropriate to the technical, operational, and threat environments for which systems need to be engineered. In addition, organizations choosing to use this guidance for their systems security engineering efforts can select and employ some or all of the thirty processes in [ISO 15288] and some or all of the security-related activities and tasks defined for each process. Note that there are process dependencies in [ISO 15288]. The successful completion of some activities and tasks invokes other processes or leverages the results of other processes.

The system life cycle processes can be used for new systems, system upgrades, or systems that are being repurposed; can be employed at any stage of the system life cycle; and can take advantage of any system and/or software development methodology including, for example, waterfall, spiral, or agile. The processes can also be applied recursively, iteratively, concurrently, sequentially, or in parallel and to any system regardless of its size, complexity, purpose, scope, environment of operation, or special nature.

The full extent of the application of the content in this publication is informed by stakeholder needs, organizational capability, and cyber resiliency goals and objectives—as well as concerns for cost, schedule, and performance. The tailorable nature of the engineering activities and tasks and the system life cycle processes help to ensure that the specific systems resulting from the application of the security design principles and concepts have the level of trustworthiness deemed sufficient to protect stakeholders from suffering unacceptable losses of their assets and the associated consequences. Such trustworthiness is made possible by the rigorous application of those cyber resiliency design principles, constructs, and concepts within a disciplined and structured set of processes that provides the necessary evidence and transparency to support risk-informed decision making and trades.

# Foreword

The United States has developed incredibly powerful and complex systems that include cyber resources—systems that are inexorably linked to the economic and national security interests of the Nation. The complete dependence on those systems for mission and business success in the public and private sectors, including the critical infrastructure, has left the Nation extremely vulnerable to hostile cyber-attacks and other serious threats, including natural disasters, structural/component failures, and errors of omission and commission. The susceptibility to such threats was described in the Defense Science Board Task Force Report entitled *Resilient Military Systems and the Advanced Cyber Threat* [DSB13]. The reported concluded that,

> "...the cyber threat is serious and that the United States cannot be confident that our critical Information Technology systems will work under attack from a sophisticated and well-resourced opponent utilizing cyber capabilities in combination with all of their military and intelligence capabilities (a full spectrum adversary) ..."

The Defense Science Board Task Force stated that the susceptibility to the advanced cyber threat by the Department of Defense is also a concern for public and private networks, and recommended that steps be taken immediately to build an effective response to measurably increase confidence in the systems we depend on (in the public and private sectors) and at the same time, decrease a would-be attacker's confidence in the effectiveness of their capabilities to compromise those systems. This conclusion was based on the following facts:

- The adversaries have successfully penetrated our critical systems and networks;

- The relative ease that our Red Teams have in disrupting or completely defeating our forces in exercises using exploits available on the Internet; and

- The weak security posture of our systems and networks.

The Task Force also described several tiers of vulnerabilities within organizations, including known vulnerabilities, unknown vulnerabilities, and adversary-created vulnerabilities. The important and sobering message is that the top two tiers of vulnerabilities (i.e., the unknown vulnerabilities and adversary-created vulnerabilities) are, for the most part, totally invisible to most organizations. Sound systems security engineering approaches will produce systems that are less susceptible to these tiers of vulnerabilities, while increasing confidence that systems providing critical mission and business operations can withstand and survive well-resourced, sophisticated cyber-attacks.

To begin to address the challenges of the 21st century, organizations must:

- Understand the modern threat space (i.e., adversary capabilities and intentions revealed by the targeting actions of those adversaries);

- Identify stakeholder assets and protection needs and provide protection commensurate with the criticality of those assets and needs and the consequences of asset loss;

- Increase understanding of the growing complexity of systems to effectively reason about, manage, and address the uncertainty associated with that complexity;

- Integrate security requirements, functions, and services into the mainstream management and technical processes within the system development life cycle; and

- Prioritize, design, and build trustworthy secure systems capable of protecting stakeholder assets.

This publication addresses the engineering-driven actions necessary to develop defensible and survivable systems that include cyber resources, including other systems that depend on those systems. It starts from NIST Special Publication 800-160, Volume 1, which is based on a set of well-established International Standards for systems engineering published by the International Organization for Standardization (ISO), the International Electrotechnical Commission (IEC), and the Institute of Electrical and Electronics Engineers (IEEE) [ISO 15288] and incorporates systems security engineering approaches into the foundational standard. The objective of the NIST Systems Security Engineering initiative is to address security, safety, and resiliency issues from a stakeholder requirements and protection needs perspective, and to use established engineering processes to help ensure that such requirements and needs are addressed with the appropriate fidelity and rigor across the entire system life cycle.

In addition to the systems engineering community, this publication can also serve the needs of organizations responsible for developing, acquiring, and using systems to support essential missions and functions. As such, references to risk management and risk management strategies can have multiple interpretations, including managing the risk associated with developing a system (i.e., programmatic risk or risk viewed from a project-related, systems engineering perspective); managing the mission or business function risk associated with depending on a system (i.e., operational risk); managing the organizational risk of depending on systems which are part of cyberspace (i.e., enterprise cyber risks); or managing the security risks associated with requirements arising from legislation, regulations, policies, standards, or the organization's mission or business activities. The cyber resiliency engineering framework is sufficiently flexible to be able to support multiple perspectives by tailoring and applying the content appropriately to either an engineering-focused systems life cycle process or to an installed base of existing systems as part of an enterprise-wide information security or risk management program. The objective is to obtain trustworthy secure systems that are fully capable of supporting critical missions and business functions while protecting stakeholder assets and to do so with a level of assurance that is consistent with the risk tolerance of those stakeholders.

-- Ron Ross
**National Institute of Standards and Technology**

## DEFENDING THE NATION IN THE 21ST CENTURY

*"Among the forces that threaten the United States and its interests are those that blend the lethality and high-tech capabilities of modern weaponry with the power and opportunity of asymmetric tactics such as terrorism and cyber warfare. We are challenged not only by novel employment of conventional weaponry, but also by the hybrid nature of these threats. We have seen their effects on the American homeland. Moreover, we must remember that we face a determined and constantly adapting adversary."*

**Quadrennial Homeland Security Review Report**
February 2010

## CYBER RESILIENCY—AN INCREASINGLY NECESSARY SYSTEM PROPERTY

Increasingly, most engineered systems incorporate or depend on cyber resources, and hence are susceptible to adversity that affects such resources and particularly to cyber-attacks. Harms resulting from cyber-attacks and from the effects of faults, failures, and human errors, which adversaries can leverage and emulate are experienced at the organizational level, mission or business process level, and the system level [SP 800-39]. The management of cyber risks is thus an increasingly crucial aspect of any risk management program.

Cyber resiliency is defined as "the ability to anticipate, withstand, recover from, and adapt to adverse conditions, stresses, attacks, or compromises on systems that use or are enabled by cyber resources." (See Appendix D.1 for information on how this definition relates to other resilience-related definitions.) Systems with this property are characterized by having security measures "built in" as a foundational part of the architecture and design. Moreover, these systems can withstand cyber-attacks, faults, and failures and can continue to operate even in a degraded or debilitated state, carrying out mission-essential functions, and ensuring that the other aspects of trustworthiness (in particular, safety and information security) are preserved.

Cyber resiliency must be provided in a cyber-contested environment that includes the Advanced Persistent Threat (APT). Therefore, any discussion of cyber resiliency is predicated on the assumption that adversaries will breach defenses and that, whether via breaches or via supply chain attacks, adversaries will establish a long-term presence in organizational systems. (See Appendix D.2 for more information on the characteristics of cyber resiliency.) The assumption of a sophisticated, well-resourced, and persistent adversary whose presence in systems can go undetected for extended periods is a key differentiator between cyber resiliency and other aspects of trustworthiness.

## SYSTEM RESILIENCE AND CYBER RESILIENCY
### *COMPARING AND CONTRASTING*

This publication focuses on cyber resiliency engineering as an emerging specialty systems engineering discipline applied in conjunction with resilience engineering and systems security engineering. The relationship between these disciplines can be seen in the example of an automobile. An automobile contains many cyber resources including, for example, embedded control units for acceleration, braking, and engine control and entertainment and cellular communications systems. The automobile and its human operator can be viewed as a *system-of-interest* from the systems security engineering perspective. The system-of-interest has an assumed environment of operation (including, for example, the countries in which the vehicle is sold), which includes assumptions about the distribution of fuel or charging stations.

As a system element, the fuel or battery system includes cyber resources (e.g., to perform fuel consumption or battery use analysis and predict the remaining travel range). A *system resilience engineering analysis* considers whether and how easily the operator could fail to notice a low-fuel or low-battery indicator. A system resilience engineering analysis also considers whether the expected travel range of the vehicle is shorter than the expected maximum distance between fuel or charging stations in the intended operational environment.

A *cyber resiliency engineering analysis* considers ways in which false information about the fuel level could be presented to the operator or to other system elements (e.g., an engine fail-safe which cuts off or deactivates if no fuel is being supplied) because of malware introduced into fuel consumption analysis. A cyber resiliency engineering analysis also considers ways in which other system elements could detect or compensate for the resulting misbehavior or prevent the malware from being introduced. While such an analysis could be made part of a general system resilience engineering analysis, it requires specialized expertise about how the APT can find and exploit vulnerabilities in the cyber resources, as well as about techniques that could be used to reduce the associated risks.

## CYBER RESILIENT SYSTEMS

_Cyber resilient systems_ operate more like the human body than a finite-state computer. The human body has a powerful immune system that absorbs a constant barrage of environmental hazards and provides the necessary defense mechanisms to maintain a healthy state. The human body also has self-repair systems to recover from illness and injury when defenses are breached. But cyber resilient systems, like the human body, cannot defend against all hazards at all times. While the body cannot always recover to the same state of health as before an injury or illness, it can adapt; similarly, cyber resilient systems can recover at least minimal essential functionality. Understanding the limitations of both humans and machines is a fundamental _risk management_ activity.

## RELATIONSHIP BETWEEN ISO 15288 AND OPERATIONAL/CYBER RESILIENCY

Though the focus of [ISO 15288] is the systems and software engineering processes, operational resiliency is addressed indirectly through requiring enterprise-wide commitment, resources, and processes. The interacting elements in the definition of a *system* include layers of resilience in hardware, software, data, information, humans, processes, facilities, materials, and naturally occurring physical entities. This is important because if the organization's mission or its business requires sustainability during perturbations, disturbances, or cyber-attacks, then the operational resiliency procedures must be applied to all of the system's assets. It would be of limited value to have resiliency measures implemented in the software architecture if there is no redundancy and survivability in the hardware; if the communications networks are fragile; if critical personnel are not available—as in a natural disaster or inclement weather—to operate and maintain the system; or if there are no facilities available for producing the organization's products and/or services.

## SECONDARY EFFECTS OF APPLYING CYBER RESILIENCY CONSTRUCTS

In addition to the first-order effects realized by organizations due to the application of individual cyber resiliency techniques (or combination of techniques) defined in this publication, there may also be beneficial second-order effects. For example, the "noise" (i.e., distracting information) created by organizations that implement the cyber resiliency techniques of Diversity, Deception, and Unpredictability can help improve their detection capabilities and potentially reveal the presence of adversaries. Second-order effects are beyond the scope of this publication.

## APPLICATION OF CYBER RESILIENCY IN THE SYSTEM DEVELOPMENT LIFE CYCLE

*Use Case in Partnership with the US Air Force and AFRL*

NIST is working with the United States Air Force and the Air Force Research Laboratory (AFRL) to explore ways in which to incorporate the cyber resiliency constructs in this publication into the system development life cycle through the use of automated support tools. The use of such tools can help ensure that cyber resiliency requirements are clearly defined and can be more easily integrated into the system development life cycle. Automated tools can provide an efficient and effective vehicle for incorporating cyber resiliency capabilities into a variety of systems (e.g., weapons systems, space systems, command and control systems, industrial control systems, enterprise IT systems) using any established life cycle development process or approach (e.g., agile, waterfall, spiral, DevOps, DevSecOps). Automation can also support the rapid testing and evaluation of cyber resiliency capabilities in critical systems to reduce the time to operational deployment.

# Executive Summary

The goal of the NIST Systems Security Engineering initiative is to address security, safety, and resiliency issues from a stakeholder requirements and protection needs perspective, using established engineering processes to ensure that those requirements and needs are addressed across the entire system life cycle to develop more trustworthy systems.[1] To that end, NIST Special Publication 800-160, Volume 2, focuses on cyber resiliency engineering, an emerging specialty systems engineering discipline applied in conjunction with resilience engineering and systems security engineering to develop more survivable, trustworthy systems. Cyber resiliency engineering aims to design, architect, and develop systems with the ability to anticipate, withstand, recover from, and adapt to adverse conditions, stresses, attacks, or compromises that use or are enabled by cyber resources. From a risk management perspective, cyber resiliency is intended to reduce the mission, business, organizational, or sector risk of depending on cyber resources.

This publication is intended to be used in conjunction with ISO/IEC/IEEE 15288:2015, *Systems and software engineering—Systems life cycle processes*, NIST Special Publication 800-160, Volume 1, *Systems Security Engineering—Considerations for a Multidisciplinary Approach in the Engineering of Trustworthy Secure Systems*, and NIST Special Publication 800-37, *Risk Management Framework for Information Systems and Organizations—A System Life Cycle Approach for Security and Privacy*. The application of the principles in this publication, in combination with the system life cycle processes in Special Publication 800-160, Volume 1, and the risk management methodology in Special Publication 800-37, can be viewed as a handbook for achieving the cyber resiliency outcomes. Guided and informed by stakeholder protection needs, mission/business assurance needs, and stakeholder concerns with cost, schedule, and performance, the cyber resiliency constructs, principles, and approach can be applied to critical systems to identify, prioritize, and implement solutions to meet the unique cyber resiliency needs of organizations.

NIST Special Publication 800-160, Volume 2, presents a cyber resiliency engineering framework (i.e., conceptual framework) for understanding and applying cyber resiliency, a concept of use for the conceptual framework, and specific engineering considerations for implementing cyber resiliency in the system life cycle. The cyber resiliency engineering framework constructs include cyber resiliency goals, objectives, techniques, approaches, and design principles. Organizations can select, adapt, and use some or all of the cyber resiliency constructs described in this publication and apply the constructs to the technical, operational, and threat environments for which systems need to be engineered.

Building off the conceptual framework, this publication also identifies considerations for determining which cyber resiliency constructs are most relevant to a system-of-interest and a tailorable cyber resiliency analysis process to apply the selected cyber resiliency concepts,

---

[1] In the context of systems engineering, trustworthiness means "worthy of being trusted to fulfill whatever critical requirements may be needed for a particular component, subsystem, system, network, application, mission, enterprise, or other entity. Trustworthiness requirements can include, for example, attributes of safety, security, reliability, dependability, performance, resilience, and survivability under a wide range of potential adversity in the form of disruptions, hazards, and threats."

constructs, and practices to a system. The cyber resiliency analysis is intended to determine whether the cyber resiliency properties and behaviors of a system-of-interest, wherever it is in the life cycle, are sufficient for the organization using that system to meet its mission assurance, business continuity, or other security requirements in a threat environment that includes the advanced persistent threat (APT). A cyber resiliency analysis is performed with the expectation that such analysis will support engineering and risk management decisions about the system-of-interest.

The conceptual framework is supplemented by several technical appendices that provide additional information to support its application, including:

- Background and contextual information on cyber resiliency;

- Detailed descriptions of the individual cyber resiliency constructs (i.e., goals, objectives, techniques, implementation approaches, design principles) that are part of the cyber resiliency engineering framework;

- How cyber resiliency concerns can be addressed as part of the life cycle processes in systems security engineering [SP 800-160 v1];

- Controls in [SP 800-53] which directly support cyber resiliency (including the questions used to determine if controls support cyber resiliency, the relevant controls, and resiliency techniques and approaches);

- An approach for adversary-oriented analysis of a system and applications of cyber resiliency, a vocabulary to describe the current or potential effects of a set of mitigations, and a representative cyber threat coverage analysis for cyber resiliency approaches;

- Cyber resiliency use cases that describe three representative situations (e.g., self-driving car, enterprise IT system, campus microgrid) in which cyber resiliency can be considered by systems security engineering and security risk management; and

- An example of how cyber resiliency could be applied in the critical infrastructure based on publicly available descriptions of the cyber-attacks on the Ukrainian power grid in 2015 and 2016.

# Errata

This table contains changes that have been incorporated into Special Publication 800-160, Volume 2. Errata updates can include corrections, clarifications, or other minor changes in the publication that are either *editorial* or *substantive* in nature.

| DATE | TYPE | REVISION | PAGE |
|------|------|----------|------|
|  |  |  |  |
|  |  |  |  |
|  |  |  |  |
|  |  |  |  |
|  |  |  |  |
|  |  |  |  |
|  |  |  |  |
|  |  |  |  |
|  |  |  |  |
|  |  |  |  |
|  |  |  |  |
|  |  |  |  |
|  |  |  |  |
|  |  |  |  |
|  |  |  |  |
|  |  |  |  |
|  |  |  |  |
|  |  |  |  |
|  |  |  |  |
|  |  |  |  |
|  |  |  |  |
|  |  |  |  |
|  |  |  |  |
|  |  |  |  |
|  |  |  |  |
|  |  |  |  |
|  |  |  |  |
|  |  |  |  |
|  |  |  |  |
|  |  |  |  |
|  |  |  |  |
|  |  |  |  |
|  |  |  |  |
|  |  |  |  |
|  |  |  |  |
|  |  |  |  |

CHAPTER ONE

# INTRODUCTION

THE NEED FOR CYBER RESILIENT SYSTEMS

The need for trustworthy secure _systems_[2] stems from a variety of _stakeholder_ needs that are driven by mission, business, and other objectives and concerns. The principles, concepts, and practices for engineering trustworthy secure systems can be expressed in various ways, depending on which aspect of trustworthiness is of concern to stakeholders. NIST Special Publication 800-160, Volume 1 [SP 800-160 v1], provides guidance on systems security engineering with an emphasis on protection against _asset_ loss.[3] In addition to security, other aspects of trustworthiness include, for example, reliability, safety, and resilience. Specialty engineering disciplines address different aspects of trustworthiness. While each specialty discipline frames the problem domain and the potential solution space for its aspect of trustworthiness somewhat differently, [SP 800-160 v1] includes systems engineering processes to align the concepts, frameworks, and analytic processes from multiple disciplines to make trade-offs within and between the various aspects of trustworthiness applicable to a _system-of-interest_.[4]

NIST Special Publication 800-160, Volume 2, focuses on the property of _cyber resiliency_, which has a strong relationship to security and resilience, but which provides a distinctive framework for its identified problem domain and solution space. Cyber resiliency is the ability to anticipate, withstand, recover from, and adapt to adverse conditions, stresses, attacks, or compromises on systems that use or are enabled by cyber resources.[5]

Cyber resiliency can be sought at multiple levels, including for system elements, systems, missions or business functions and the system-of-systems which support those functions, organizations, sectors, regions, the Nation, or transnational missions/business functions. From an engineering perspective, cyber resiliency is an emergent quality property of an engineered system, where an "engineered system" can be a system element made up of constituent components, a system, or a system-of-systems. Cyber resilient systems are those systems that have security measures or safeguards "built in" as a foundational part of the architecture and

---

[2] A _system_ is a combination of interacting elements organized to achieve one or more stated purposes. The interacting elements that compose a system include hardware, software, data, humans, processes, procedures, facilities, materials, and naturally occurring entities [ISO 15288].

[3] An _asset_ refers to an item of value to stakeholders. Assets may be tangible (e.g., a physical item, such as hardware, firmware, computing platform, network device, or other technology component, or individuals in key or defined roles in organizations) or intangible (e.g., data, information, software, trademark, copyright, patent, intellectual property, image, or reputation). Refer to [SP 800-160 v1] for the system security perspective on assets.

[4] A _system-of-interest_ is a system whose life cycle is under consideration in the context of [ISO 15288]. A system-of-interest can also be viewed as the system that is the focus of the systems engineering effort. The system-of-interest contains system elements, system element interconnections, and the environment in which they are placed.

[5] The term _adversity_ is used in this publication to mean adverse conditions, stresses, attacks, or compromises and is consistent with the use of the term in [SP 800-160 v1] as disruptions, hazards, and threats. Adversity in the context of the definition of cyber resiliency specifically includes, but is not limited to, cyber-attacks. For example, cyber resiliency engineering analysis considers the potential consequences of physical destruction of a cyber resource to the system-of-interest of which that resource is a system element.

design and that display a high level of resiliency. Thus, cyber resilient systems can withstand cyber-attacks, faults, and failures and continue to operate in a degraded or debilitated state carrying out the mission-essential functions of the organization. From an enterprise risk management perspective, cyber resiliency is intended to reduce the mission, business, organizational, or sector risk of depending on cyber resources.

Cyber resiliency supports mission assurance in a contested environment for missions that depend on systems which include cyber resources. A *cyber resource* is an information resource which creates, stores, processes, manages, transmits, or disposes of information in electronic form and which can be accessed via a network or using networking methods. However, some information resources are specifically designed to be accessed using a networking method only intermittently (e.g., via a low-power connection to check the status of an insulin pump, via a wired connection to upgrade software in an embedded avionic device). These cyber resources are characterized as operating primarily in a disconnected or non-networked mode.[6]

Systems increasingly incorporate cyber resources as *system elements*. As a result, systems are susceptible to harms resulting from the effects of adversity on cyber resources and, particularly to harms resulting from cyber-attacks. The cyber resiliency problem is defined as how to achieve adequate mission resilience by providing: (1) adequate *system resilience*[7] and (2) adequate mission/business function and operational/organizational resilience in the presence of possible adversity affecting cyber resources. The cyber resiliency problem domain overlaps with the security problem domain since a system should be *securely resilient*.[8] The cyber resiliency problem domain is guided and informed by an understanding of the threat landscape and, in particular, the *advanced persistent threat* (APT).[9] All discussions of cyber resiliency focus on assuring the mission or business functions and are predicated on the assumption that the adversary will breach defenses and establish a long-term presence in organizational systems. A *cyber resilient system* is a system that provides a degree of cyber resiliency commensurate with

---

[6] Some information resources, which include computing hardware, software, and stored information, are designed to be inaccessible via networking methods but can be manipulated physically or electronically to yield information or to change behavior (e.g., side-channel attacks on embedded cryptographic hardware). Such system elements may also be considered cyber resources for purposes of cyber resiliency engineering analysis.

[7] *System resilience* is defined by the INCOSE Resilient Systems Working Group (RSWG) as "the capability of a system with specific characteristics before, during, and after a disruption to absorb the disruption, recover to an acceptable level of performance, and sustain that level for an acceptable period of time [INCOSE11]."

[8] The term *securely resilient* refers to the system's ability to preserve a secure state despite disruption, including the system transitions between normal and degraded modes. System resiliency is a primary objective of systems security engineering [SP 800-160 v1].

[9] The Advanced Persistent Threat (APT) is an adversary that possesses sophisticated levels of expertise and significant resources which allow it to create opportunities to achieve its objectives by using multiple attack vectors including, for example, cyber, physical, and deception. These objectives typically include establishing and extending footholds within the systems of the targeted organizations for the express purposes of exfiltrating information; undermining or impeding critical aspects of a mission, program, or organization; or positioning itself to carry out these objectives in the future. The APT pursues its objectives repeatedly over an extended period, adapts to defenders' efforts to resist it, and is determined to maintain the level of interaction needed to execute its objectives [SP 800-39] [CNSSI 4009]. While some sources define the APT to be an adversary at Tier V or Tier VI in the threat model in [DSB13], in particular, to be a state actor, the definition used in this publication includes any actors with the characteristics described above. The above definition also includes adversaries that subvert the supply chain to compromise cyber resources, which are subsequently made part of the system-of-interest. As discussed in Chapter Two and Appendix D.2, the APT is a crucial aspect of the threat landscape for cyber resiliency engineering.

the system's criticality, treating cyber resiliency as one aspect of trustworthiness which requires assurance in conjunction with other aspects such as security, reliability, and safety.

---

### SYSTEM SECURITY AS A DESIGN PROBLEM

"A combination of hardware, software, communications, physical, personnel and administrative-procedural safeguards is required for comprehensive security. In particular, software safeguards alone are not sufficient."

-- The Ware Report
*Defense Science Board Task Force on Computer Security, 1970.*

---

## 1.1 PURPOSE AND APPLICABILITY

The purpose of this document is to supplement [SP 800-160 v1] and [SP 800-37] (or other risk management processes or methodologies) with guidance on how to apply cyber resiliency concepts, constructs, and engineering practices as part of systems security engineering and risk management for systems and organizations. This document identifies considerations towards the engineering of systems that include the following circumstances, or systems that depend on cyber resources. Circumstances or types of systems to which this document applies include:[10]

- **Circumstances:** New systems, reactive modifications to fielded systems, planned upgrades to fielded systems while continuing to sustain day-to-day operations, evolution of systems, retirement of systems; and

- **Types of systems:**

    - Dedicated or special-purpose systems (e.g., security-dedicated or security-purposed systems, cyber-physical systems [CPS],[11] Internet of Things [IoT] or Network of Things [NoT][12]); high-confidence, dedicated-purpose systems; or large-scale processing environments;

    - General-purpose or multi-use systems (e.g., enterprise information technology [EIT]), shared services, or common infrastructures; and

    - Systems-of-systems (e.g., critical infrastructure systems [CIS]).

---

[10] Note that this list is not intended to be exhaustive or mutually exclusive. Circumstances and types of systems are discussed in more detail in Sections 2.2 and 3.1.3.

[11] A cyber-physical system (CPS) is a system that includes engineered interacting networks of computational and physical components. CPSs range from simple devices to complex systems-of-systems. A CPS device is a device that has an element of computation and interacts with the physical world through sensing and actuation [SP 1500-201].

[12] A Network of Things (NoT) is a system consisting of devices that include a sensor and a communications capability, a network, software that aggregates sensor data, and an external utility (i.e., a software or hardware product or service that executes processes or feeds data into the system) [SP 800-183]. While "things" may be cyber-physical devices, they may not be intended to be part of CPS. The Internet of Things (IoT) is a NoT in which the "things" are tethered to the Internet. Such systems face trustworthiness challenges related to scalability, heterogeneity, data integrity, composability, predictability, confidentiality, accountability, ownership, and visibility [SP 800-183] [IR 8259].

## 1.2 TARGET AUDIENCE

This publication is intended for systems security engineering and other professionals who are responsible for the activities and tasks related to the system life cycle processes in [SP 800-160 v1], the risk management processes in [SP 800-39], or the Risk Management Framework (RMF) in [SP 800-37].[13] The term *systems security engineer* is used in this publication to include those security professionals who perform any of the activities and tasks in [SP 800-160 v1]. This publication can also be used by professionals who perform other system life cycle activities that impact trustworthiness or who perform activities related to the education or training of systems engineers and systems security engineers. These include but are not limited to:

- Individuals with systems engineering, architecture, design, development, and integration responsibilities;

- Individuals with software engineering, architecture, design, development, integration, and software maintenance responsibilities;

- Individuals with security governance, risk management, and oversight responsibilities, particularly those defined in [SP 800-37];

- Individuals with independent security verification, validation, testing, evaluation, auditing, assessment, inspection, and monitoring responsibilities;

- Individuals with system security administration, operations, maintenance, sustainment, logistics, and support responsibilities;

- Individuals with acquisition, budgeting, and project management responsibilities;

- Providers of technology products, systems, or services; and

- Academic institutions offering systems security engineering and related programs.

This special publication assumes that systems security engineering activities in [SP 800-160 v1] and risk management processes in [SP 800-37] are performed under the auspices of or within an organization (referred to as "the organization" in this document).[14] The activities and processes take into consideration the concerns of a variety of stakeholders, within and external to the organization. The organization, through systems security engineering and risk management activities, identifies stakeholders, elicits their concerns, and represents those concerns in the systems security engineering and risk management activities.

---

[13] This includes security and risk management practitioners with significant responsibilities for the protection of existing systems, information, and the information technology infrastructure within enterprises (i.e., the installed base). Such practitioners may use the cyber resiliency content in this publication in other than engineering-based system life cycle processes. These application areas may include use of the *Risk Management Framework* [SP 800-37], the controls in [SP 800-53], or the *Framework for Improving Critical Infrastructure Cybersecurity* [NIST CSF] where such applications have cyber resiliency-related concerns.

[14] Systems security engineering and risk management apply to systems-of-systems in which multiple organizations are responsible for constituent systems. In such situations, systems security engineering and risk management activities are performed within individual organizations (each an instance of "the organization") and supported by cooperation or coordination across those organizations.

## 1.3  PUBLICATION ORGANIZATION

The remainder of this special publication is organized as follows:

- <u>Chapter Two</u> describes the conceptual framework for cyber resiliency engineering.

- <u>Chapter Three</u> describes considerations for selecting and prioritizing cyber resiliency techniques and implementation approaches, and presents a tailorable process for applying cyber resiliency concepts, constructs, and practices to a system.

- **Supporting appendices** provide additional cyber resiliency-related information including:

  - <u>Appendix A</u>: References;[15]

  - <u>Appendix B</u>: Glossary;

  - <u>Appendix C</u>: Acronyms;

  - <u>Appendix D</u>: Background;

  - <u>Appendix E</u>: Cyber Resiliency Constructs;

  - <u>Appendix F</u>: Cyber Resiliency in System Life Cycle;

  - <u>Appendix G</u>: Controls Supporting Cyber Resiliency;

  - <u>Appendix H</u>: Adversary-Oriented Analysis;

  - <u>Appendix I</u>: Cyber Resiliency Use Cases; and

  - <u>Appendix J</u>: Cyber Resiliency Real-World Example.

---

[15] Unless otherwise stated, all references to NIST publications refer to the most recent version of those publications.

CHAPTER TWO

# THE FUNDAMENTALS

BASIC CONCEPTS ASSOCIATED WITH CYBER RESILIENCY

As described previously, cyber resiliency is the ability to anticipate, withstand, recover from, and adapt to adverse conditions, stresses, attacks, or compromises on systems that use or are enabled by cyber resources. This section presents a conceptual framework for understanding and applying cyber resiliency, a concept of use for the conceptual framework, and specific engineering considerations for implementing cyber resiliency in the system life cycle. The discussion relies on several terms as described in the following paragraphs: cyber resiliency concepts, constructs, engineering practices, and solutions.

Cyber resiliency *concepts* are related to the problem domain and the solution set for cyber resiliency. The concepts are represented in cyber resiliency risk models and by cyber resiliency constructs.[16] The *constructs* are the basic elements of the conceptual framework and include goals, objectives, techniques, implementation approaches, and design principles.[17] The framework provides a way to understand the cyber resiliency problem and solution domain. Cyber resiliency goals and objectives identify the "what" of cyber resiliency—that is, what properties and behaviors are integral to cyber resilient systems. Cyber resiliency techniques, implementation approaches, and design principles characterize ways of achieving or improving resilience in the face of threats to systems and system components (i.e., the "how" of cyber resiliency). Cyber resiliency constructs address adversarial and non-adversarial threats from cyber and non-cyber sources. The concern for cyber resiliency focuses on aspects of trustworthiness—in particular, security and resilience—and risk from the perspective of mission assurance against determined adversaries (e.g., the advanced persistent threat).

Cyber resiliency *engineering practices* are the methods, processes, modeling, and analytical techniques used to identify and analyze proposed cyber resiliency solutions. The application of cyber resiliency engineering practices in system life cycle processes ensures that cyber resiliency *solutions* are driven by stakeholder requirements and protection needs, which, in turn, guide and inform the development of system requirements for the system-of-interest [ISO 15288, SP 800-160 v1]. Such solutions consist of combinations of technologies, architectural decisions, systems engineering processes, and operational policies, processes, procedures, or practices which solve problems in the cyber resiliency domain. That is, they provide a sufficient level of cyber resiliency to meet stakeholder needs and to reduce risks to organizational mission or business capabilities in the presence of a variety of threat sources, including the APT.

Cyber resiliency *solutions* use cyber resiliency techniques and approaches to implementing those techniques, as described in Section 2.1.3. Cyber resiliency solutions apply the design principles described in Section 2.1.4. Cyber resiliency solutions typically implement mechanisms (e.g., controls and control enhancements defined in [SP 800-53]) which apply one or more cyber

---

[16] As discussed in Appendix D.1, cyber resiliency concepts and constructs are informed by definitions and frameworks related to other forms of resilience as well as system survivability. A reader unfamiliar with the concept of resilience may benefit from reading that appendix before this section.

[17] Additional constructs (e.g., sub-objectives, capabilities) may be used in some modeling and analytic practices.

resiliency techniques or approaches or which are intended to achieve one or more cyber resiliency objectives. These mechanisms are selected in response to the security and cyber resiliency requirements defined as part of the system life cycle requirements engineering process described in [SP 800-160 v1], or to mitigate security and cyber resiliency risks that arise from architectural or design decisions.

## 2.1 CYBER RESILIENCY ENGINEERING FRAMEWORK

The following sections provide a description of the conceptual framework for cyber resiliency engineering.[18] The framework constructs include cyber resiliency goals, objectives, techniques, approaches, and design principles. The relationship among constructs is also described. These constructs, like cyber resiliency, can be applied at levels beyond the system (e.g., mission or business function level, organizational level, or sector level). Table 1 summarizes the definition and purpose of each construct and how each construct is applied at the system level.

### TABLE 1: CYBER RESILIENCY CONSTRUCTS

| CONSTRUCT | DEFINITION, PURPOSE, AND APPLICATION AT THE SYSTEM LEVEL | | |
|---|---|---|---|
| Goal | **Definition**: A high-level statement supporting (or focusing on) each aspect (i.e., anticipate, withstand, recover, adapt) in the definition of cyber resiliency.<br>**Purpose**: Align the definition of cyber resiliency with definitions of other types of resilience.<br>**Application**: Can be used to express high-level stakeholder concerns, goals, or priorities. | | |
| Objective | **Definition**: A high-level statement (designed to be restated in system-specific and stakeholder-specific terms) of what a system must achieve in its operational environment and throughout its life cycle to meet stakeholder needs for mission assurance and resilient security; the objectives are more specific than goals and more relatable to threats.<br>**Purpose**: Enable stakeholders and systems engineers to reach a common understanding of cyber resiliency concerns and priorities; facilitate definition of metrics or measures of effectiveness (MOEs).<br>**Application**: Used in scoring methods or summaries of analyses (e.g., cyber resiliency posture assessments). | | |
| | Sub-Objective | **Definition**: A statement, subsidiary to a cyber resiliency objective, which emphasizes different aspects of that objective or identifies methods to achieve that objective.<br>**Purpose**: Serve as a step in the hierarchical refinement of an objective into activities or capabilities for which performance measures can be defined.<br>**Application**: Used in scoring methods or analyses; may be reflected in system functional requirements. | |
| | | Activity or Capability | **Definition**: A statement of a capability or action which supports the achievement of a sub-objective and hence, of an objective.<br>**Purpose**: Facilitate the definition of metrics or MOEs. While a representative set of activities or capabilities have been identified in [Bodeau18b], these are intended solely as a starting point for selection, tailoring, and prioritization.<br>**Application**: Used in scoring methods or analyses; reflected in system functional requirements. |

---

[18] The conceptual cyber resiliency engineering framework described in this publication is based on and consistent with the _Cyber Resiliency Engineering Framework_ developed by The MITRE Corporation [Bodeau11].

**TABLE 1: CYBER RESILIENCY CONSTRUCTS**

| CONSTRUCT | DEFINITION, PURPOSE, AND APPLICATION AT THE SYSTEM LEVEL |
|---|---|
| Strategic Design Principle | **Definition:** A high-level statement which reflects an aspect of the risk management strategy that informs systems security engineering practices for an organization, mission, or system. <br> **Purpose:** Guide and inform engineering analyses and risk analyses throughout the system life cycle. Highlight different structural design principles, cyber resiliency techniques and implementation approaches. <br> **Application:** Included, cited, or restated in system non-functional requirements (e.g., Statement of Work [SOW] requirements for analyses or documentation). |
| Structural Design Principle | **Definition:** A statement which captures experience in defining system architectures and designs. <br> **Purpose:** Guide and inform design and implementation decisions throughout the system life cycle. Highlight different cyber resiliency techniques and implementation approaches. <br> **Application:** Included, cited, or restated in system non-functional requirements (e.g., Statement of Work [SOW] requirements for analyses or documentation); used in systems engineering to guide the use of techniques, implementation approaches, technologies, and practices. |
| Technique | **Definition**: A set or class of technologies, processes, or practices providing capabilities to achieve one or more cyber resiliency objectives. <br> **Purpose:** Characterize technologies, practices, products, controls, or requirements, so that their contribution to cyber resiliency can be understood. <br> **Application:** Used in engineering analysis to screen technologies, practices, products, controls, solutions, or requirements; used in the system by implementing or integrating technologies, practices, products, or solutions. |
| Implementation Approach | **Definition**: A subset of the technologies and processes of a cyber resiliency technique, defined by how the capabilities are implemented. <br> **Purpose:** Characterize technologies, practices, products, controls, or requirements so that their contribution to cyber resiliency and their potential effects on threat events can be understood. <br> **Application:** Used in engineering analysis to screen technologies, practices, products, controls, solutions, or requirements; used in the system by implementing or integrating technologies, practices, products, or solutions. |
| Solution | **Definition**: A combination of technologies, architectural decisions, systems engineering processes, and operational processes, procedures, or practices which solves a problem in the cyber resiliency domain. <br> **Purpose:** Provide a sufficient level of cyber resiliency to meet stakeholder needs and to reduce risks to mission or business capabilities in the presence of advanced persistent threats. <br> **Application:** Integrated into the system or its operational environment. |

## 2.1.1 CYBER RESILIENCY GOALS

Cyber resiliency, like security, is a concern at multiple levels in an organization. The four cyber resiliency goals, which are common to many resilience definitions, are included in the definition and the conceptual framework to provide linkage between risk management decisions at the mission/business process level and at the system level with those at the organizational level. Organizational risk management strategies can use the cyber resiliency goals and associated strategies to incorporate cyber resiliency.[19] For cyber resiliency engineering analysis, cyber resiliency objectives,[20] rather than goals, are the starting point. The term *adversity*, as used in the cyber resiliency goals in Table 2, specifically includes stealthy, persistent, sophisticated, and

---

[19] See Appendix D.

[20] See Section 2.1.2.

well-resourced adversaries (i.e., the APT) who may have compromised system components and established a foothold within an organization's systems.

**TABLE 2: CYBER RESILIENCY GOALS**

| GOAL | DESCRIPTION |
|------|-------------|
| **Anticipate** | Maintain a state of informed preparedness for adversity. |
| **Withstand** | Continue essential mission or business functions despite adversity. |
| **Recover** | Restore mission or business functions during and after adversity. |
| **Adapt** | Modify mission or business functions and/or supporting capabilities to predicted changes in the technical, operational, or threat environments. |
|  |  |

## 2.1.2 CYBER RESILIENCY OBJECTIVES

Cyber resiliency objectives are more specific statements of what a system must achieve in its operational environment and throughout its life cycle to meet stakeholder needs for mission assurance and resilient security. Cyber resiliency objectives[21] as described in Table 3 support interpretation and facilitate prioritization and assessment, making it straightforward to develop questions such as:

- What does each cyber resiliency objective mean in the context of the organization and of the mission or business process the system is intended to support?

- Which cyber resiliency objectives are most important to a given stakeholder?

- To what degree can each cyber resiliency objective be achieved?

- How quickly and cost-effectively can each cyber resiliency objective be achieved?

- With what degree of confidence or trust can each cyber resiliency objective be achieved?

**TABLE 3: CYBER RESILIENCY OBJECTIVES[22]**

| OBJECTIVE | DESCRIPTION |
|-----------|-------------|
| **Prevent or Avoid** | Preclude the successful execution of an attack or the realization of adverse conditions. |
| **Prepare** | Maintain a set of realistic courses of action that address predicted or anticipated adversity. |
| **Continue** | Maximize the duration and viability of essential mission or business functions during adversity. |
| **Constrain** | Limit damage[23] from adversity. |

---

[21] The term *objective* is defined and used in multiple ways. In this document, uses are qualified (e.g., cyber resiliency objectives, security objectives [FIPS 199], adversary objectives [NSA18], engineering objectives or purposes [ISO 24765]) for clarity. Cyber resiliency goals and objectives can be viewed as two levels of fundamental objectives, as used in Decision Theory [Clemen13]. Alternately, cyber resiliency goals can be viewed as fundamental objectives and cyber resiliency objectives as enabling objectives [Brtis16]. By contrast, cyber resiliency techniques can be viewed as means objectives [Clemen13].

[22] See Appendix E for specific relationships between objectives and goals.

[23] From the perspective of cyber resiliency, *damage* can be to the organization (e.g., loss of reputation, increased existential risk), to missions or business functions (e.g., decrease in the ability to complete the current mission and to accomplish future missions), to security (e.g., decrease in the ability to achieve the security objectives of integrity, availability, and confidentiality or decrease in the ability to prevent, detect, and respond to cyber incidents), to the system (e.g., decrease in the ability to meet system requirements or unauthorized use of system resources), or to specific system elements (e.g., physical destruction; corruption, modification, or fabrication of information).

**TABLE 3: CYBER RESILIENCY OBJECTIVES**

| OBJECTIVE | DESCRIPTION |
|---|---|
| Reconstitute | Restore as much mission or business functionality as possible after adversity. |
| Understand | Maintain useful representations of mission and business dependencies and the status of resources with respect to possible adversity. |
| Transform | Modify mission or business functions and supporting processes to handle adversity and address environmental changes more effectively. |
| Re-Architect | Modify architectures to handle adversity and address environmental changes more effectively. |

Because stakeholders may find the statements of cyber resiliency objectives difficult to relate to their specific concerns, the objectives can be tailored or restated in terms of mission or business functions. Cyber resiliency objectives can be hierarchically refined to emphasize the different aspects of an objective or the methods to achieve an objective, thus creating sub-objectives. Cyber resiliency objectives (and, as needed to help stakeholders interpret objectives for their concerns, sub-objectives) enable stakeholders to assert their different resiliency priorities based on mission or business functions.[24]

---

**TAILORING CYBER RESILIENCY OBJECTIVES**

Cyber resiliency objectives can be tailored to reflect the organization's missions and business functions or operational concept for the system-of-interest. Tailoring objectives can also help stakeholders determine which objectives apply and the priority to assign to each objective. The examples below illustrate the tailoring concept for cyber resiliency objectives:

- For an implantable medical device, the Continue objective can be tailored as follows: *Enable the patient or healthcare provider to engage fail-safe mechanisms*. The Constrain objective can be tailored as follows: *Ensure that the device can fail safely despite cyber-attacks, disruptions, or interference.*

- For a workflow system which is a constituent system of an organization's enterprise architecture, the Continue objective can be tailored by identifying critical business functions. The Constrain objective can be tailored as follows: *Limit damage from disruption and erroneous information.*

---

## 2.1.3 CYBER RESILIENCY TECHNIQUES AND APPROACHES

Cyber resiliency goals and objectives provide a vocabulary for describing what properties and capabilities are needed. Cyber resiliency techniques, approaches, and design principles (discussed in Section 2.1.4) provide a vocabulary for discussing how a system can achieve its cyber resiliency goals and objectives. A cyber resiliency technique is a set or class of practices and technologies intended to achieve one or more goals or objectives by providing capabilities. Fourteen techniques are part of the cyber resiliency engineering framework as follows:

- **Adaptive Response:** Implement agile courses of action to manage risks;

---

[24] Table E-1 in Appendix E provides representative examples cf sub-objectives.

- **Analytic Monitoring:** Monitor and analyze a wide range of properties and behaviors on an ongoing basis and in a coordinated way;

- **Contextual Awareness:** Construct and maintain current representations of the posture of missions or business functions considering threat events and courses of action;

- **Coordinated Protection:** Ensure that protection mechanisms operate in a coordinated and effective manner;

- **Deception:** Mislead, confuse, hide critical assets from, or expose covertly tainted assets to the adversary;

- **Diversity:** Use heterogeneity to minimize common mode failures, particularly threat events exploiting common vulnerabilities;

- **Dynamic Positioning:** Distribute and dynamically relocate functionality or system resources;

- **Non-Persistence:** Generate and retain resources as needed or for a limited time;

- **Privilege Restriction:** Restrict privileges based on attributes of users and system elements as well as on environmental factors;

- **Realignment:** Align system resources with current organizational mission or business function needs to reduce risk;

- **Redundancy:** Provide multiple protected instances of critical resources;

- **Segmentation:** Define and separate system elements based on criticality and trustworthiness;

- **Substantiated Integrity:** Ascertain whether critical system elements have been corrupted; and

- **Unpredictability:** Make changes randomly or unpredictably.

The cyber resiliency techniques are described in Appendix E. Each technique is characterized by both the capabilities it provides and the intended consequences of using the technologies or the processes it includes. The cyber resiliency techniques reflect an understanding of the threats as well as the technologies, processes, and concepts related to improving cyber resiliency to address the threats. The cyber resiliency engineering framework assumes that the cyber resiliency techniques will be selectively applied to the architecture or design of organizational mission or business functions and their supporting system resources. Since natural synergies and conflicts exist among the cyber resiliency techniques, engineering trade-offs must be made. Cyber resiliency techniques are expected to change over time as threats evolve, advances are made based on research, security practices evolve, and new ideas emerge.

Twelve of the fourteen cyber resiliency techniques can be applied to either adversarial or non-adversarial threats (including both cyber-related and non-cyber-related threats). The two cyber resiliency techniques that only address adversarial threats are Deception and Unpredictability. The cyber resiliency techniques are also interdependent. For example, the Analytic Monitoring technique supports Contextual Awareness. The Unpredictability technique, however, is different from the other techniques in that it is always applied in conjunction with some other technique (e.g., working with the Dynamic Positioning technique to establish unpredictable times for repositioning of potential targets of interest).

The definitions of cyber resiliency techniques are intentionally broad to insulate the definitions from changing technologies and threats, thus limiting the need for frequent changes to the set of techniques.[25]

To support detailed engineering analysis, multiple representative approaches to implementing each technique are identified. As illustrated in Figure 1, an *implementation approach* (or, for brevity, an *approach*) is a subset of the technologies and processes included in a technique, defined by how the capabilities are implemented or how the intended outcomes are achieved. Table E-4 in Appendix E defines representative approaches and gives representative examples of technologies and practices. The set of approaches for a specific technique is not exhaustive and represents relatively mature technologies and practices. Thus, technologies emerging from research can be characterized in terms of the techniques they apply while not being covered by any of the representative approaches.[26]

**FIGURE 1: CYBER RESILIENCY TECHNIQUES AND IMPLEMENTATION APPROACHES**

---

[25] In fact, the definitions of the cyber resiliency goals, objectives, and techniques are generally defined so that they can be applied to all types of threats (not solely cyber threats) and all types of systems (not solely those systems that include or are enabled by cyber resources). However, the motivation for these definitions and for the selection of objectives and techniques for inclusion in the cyber resiliency engineering framework is the recognition of dependence on systems involving cyber resources in a threat environment that includes the APT.

[26] Decisions about whether and how to apply less-mature technologies and practices are strongly influenced by the organization's risk management strategy. See [SP 800-39].

---

**APPLY TECHNIQUES AND APPROACHES SELECTIVELY**

Applying a cyber resiliency technique typically will not require the use of all approaches which are representative of it, and not all techniques will be applied to a given system-of-interest. The following examples illustrate the application of cyber resiliency techniques and approaches:

- In a microgrid supplying and managing power for an organization, the cyber resiliency technique of Deception can be applied sparingly. The Tainting approach will almost certainly not be applied because of the potential detrimental impact to serving the mission/business function and delivery of the critical service. Whether the Disinformation and Misdirection implementation approaches are applied will depend on the organization's risk management strategy, and while encryption of control messages may be viewed as an application of Obfuscation, its primary intention in this case would be to apply the Integrity Checks approach to Substantiated Integrity. Unpredictability will almost certainly not be applied to the campus microgrid system.

- By contrast, an organization which interacts routinely with consumers via Internet-facing services can use all approaches to Deception, investing time and effort in maintaining a deception environment and analyzing interactions with adversaries from that environment. In addition, the organization can apply Unpredictability in conjunction with Deception and possibly with other techniques, such as Non-Persistence, Dynamic Positioning, and Privilege Restriction.

---

### 2.1.4 CYBER RESILIENCY DESIGN PRINCIPLES

A *design principle* refers to a distillation of experience designing, implementing, integrating, and upgrading systems that systems engineers and architects can use to guide and inform design decisions and analysis. A design principle takes the form of a terse statement or a phrase identifying a key concept accompanied by one or more statements that describe how that concept applies to system design (where "system" is construed broadly to include operational processes and procedures and may also include development and maintenance environments). Design principles are defined for many specialty engineering disciplines using the terminology, experience, and research results that are specific to the specialty.

Cyber resiliency design principles, like design principles from other specialty disciplines, can be applied in different ways at multiple stages in the system life cycle, including the operations and maintenance stage. The design principles can also be used in a variety of system development models, including agile and spiral development. The cyber resiliency design principles identified in this publication can serve as a starting point for systems engineers and architects. For any given situation, only a subset of the design principles are selected, and those principles are tailored or "re-expressed" in terms more meaningful to the program, system, or system-of-systems to which they apply.

The cyber resiliency design principles are strongly informed by and can be aligned with design principles from other specialty disciplines, such as the security design principles in [SP 800-160 v1]. Many of the cyber resiliency design principles are based on design principles for security, resilience engineering, or both. Design principles can be characterized as *strategic* (i.e., applied throughout the systems engineering process, guiding the direction of engineering analyses) or *structural* (i.e., directly affecting the architecture and design of the system or system elements) [Ricci14]. Both strategic and structural cyber resiliency design principles can be reflected in security-related systems engineering artifacts. A complete list of strategic and structural cyber resiliency design principles is provided in Appendix E.

---

**TAILOR DESIGN PRINCIPLES AND APPLY SELECTIVELY**

Cyber resiliency design principles are used to guide analysis and engineering decisions and to help stakeholders understand the rationale for those decisions. Therefore, design principles can be tailored in terms meaningful to the purpose and architecture of the _system-of-interest_. For example, the Support agility and architect for adaptability strategic design principle might be tailored for a microgrid supplying and managing power for a campus as follows:

_Design microgrid constituent systems in a modular way to accommodate technology and usage concepts, which change at different rates._

The design principle might not be directly applicable to an implantable medical device, but it can be applied to a system-of-systems of which the device is a constituent system element in conjunction with the security design principle of _secure evolvability_.

Descriptions of how structural design principles apply will reflect the underlying architecture of the system-of-interest. For example, how the Make resources location-versatile design principle applies to a workflow system might depend on how the enterprise architecture incorporates virtualization and cloud services as well as how it provides off-site backup. Alternatively, the description of how the same design principle applies to a satellite constellation might refer to satellite maneuverability.

---

## 2.1.5 RELATIONSHIP AMONG CYBER RESILIENCY CONSTRUCTS

Cyber resiliency constructs in the form of goals, objectives, techniques, implementation approaches, and design principles enable systems engineers to express cyber resiliency concepts and the relationships among them. In addition, the cyber resiliency constructs also relate to risk management. That relationship leads systems engineers to analyze cyber resiliency solutions in terms of their potential effects on risk and on specific threat events or types of malicious cyber activities. The selection and relative priority of these cyber resiliency constructs is determined by the organization's strategy for managing the risks of depending on systems which include cyber resources—in particular, by the organization's risk framing.[27] The relative priority of the cyber resiliency goals and objectives and relevance of the cyber resiliency design principles are determined by the risk management strategy of the organization, which takes into consideration the concerns of, constraints on, and equities of all stakeholders (including those who are not part of the organization). Figure 2 illustrates the relationships among the cyber resiliency constructs. These relationships are represented by specific mapping tables in Appendix E.

---

[27] The first component of risk management addresses how organizations _frame_ risk or establish a risk context—that is, describing the environment in which risk-based decisions are made. The purpose of the risk-framing component is to produce a _risk management strategy_ that addresses how organizations intend to assess risk, respond to risk, and monitor risk—making explicit and transparent the risk perceptions that organizations routinely use in making both investment and operational decisions [SP 800-39]. The risk management strategy addresses how the organization manages the risks of depending on systems that include cyber resources; and is part of a comprehensive, enterprise-wide risk management strategy; and reflects stakeholder concerns and priorities.

As Figure 2 illustrates, a cyber resilient system (i.e., cyber resiliency solution) is the result of the engineering selection, prioritization, and application of cyber resiliency design principles, techniques, and implementation approaches. The organization's risk management strategy is translated into interpretations and prioritizations of cyber resiliency goals and objectives, which guide and inform trade-offs among different forms of risk mitigation.

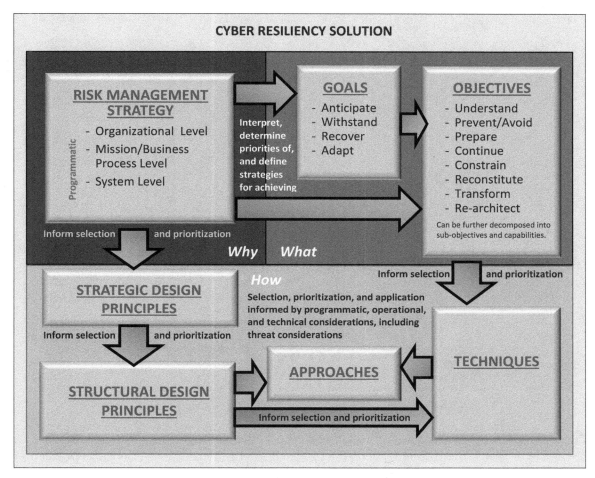

**FIGURE 2: RELATIONSHIPS AMONG CYBER RESILIENCY CONSTRUCTS**

## 2.2 CYBER RESILIENCY IN THE SYSTEM LIFE CYCLE

The following section describes general considerations for applying cyber resiliency concepts and framework constructs to system life cycle stages and processes. Considerations include addressing the similarities and differences in security and cyber resiliency terminology and how the application of cyber resiliency goals, objectives, techniques, implementation approaches, and design principles can impact systems at key stages in the life cycle. Figure 3 lists the system life cycle processes and illustrates their application across all stages of the system life cycle. It must be emphasized, however, that cyber resiliency engineering does not assume any specific life cycle or system development process and that cyber resiliency analysis can be performed at any point in, and iteratively throughout, the life cycle.[28]

---

[28] See Section 3.2.

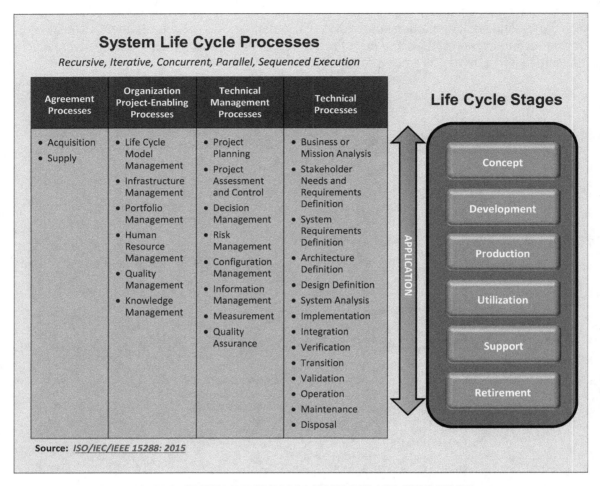

**FIGURE 3: SYSTEM LIFE CYCLE PROCESSES AND LIFE CYCLE STAGES**

Cyber resiliency constructs are interpreted and cyber resiliency engineering practices are applied in different ways, depending on the system life cycle stages. During the *Concept* stage, cyber resiliency goals and objectives are tailored in terms of the concept of use for the system-of-interest. Tailoring actions are used to elicit stakeholder priorities for the cyber resiliency goals and objectives. The organization's risk management strategy is used to help determine which strategic design principles are most relevant. The strategic design principles and corresponding structural design principles are aligned with design principles from other specialty engineering disciplines. Notional or candidate system architectures are analyzed with respect to how well the prioritized cyber resiliency goals and objectives can be achieved and how well the relevant strategic cyber resiliency design principles can be applied. The tailoring of objectives can also be used to identify or define potential metrics or measures of effectiveness for proposed cyber resiliency solutions. Once again, the risk management strategy which constrains risk response or risk treatment (e.g., commitment to specific technologies, requirements for interoperability with or dependence on other systems) is used to help determine which techniques and approaches can or cannot be used in cyber resiliency solutions. In addition, during the *Concept* stage, cyber resiliency concerns for enabling systems for production, integration, validation, and supply chain management are identified and strategies for addressing those concerns are defined.

During the *Development* stage, the relevant structural cyber resiliency design principles (i.e., those principles which can be applied to the selected system architecture and which support the strategic cyber resiliency design principles) are identified and prioritized based on how well the design principles enable the prioritized cyber resiliency objectives to be achieved. The cyber resiliency techniques and approaches indicated by the structural design principles are analyzed with respect to whether and where they can be used in the selected system architecture given the constraints identified earlier. Cyber resiliency solutions are defined and analyzed with respect to potential effectiveness and compatibility with other aspects of trustworthiness. Analysis of potential effectiveness considers the relative effectiveness of the solution against potential threat events or scenarios [SP 800-30] and the measures of effectiveness for cyber resiliency objectives. Analysis of compatibility with other aspects of trustworthiness considers potential synergies or conflicts associated with technologies, design principles, or practices specific to other specialty engineering disciplines, particularly security, reliability, survivability, and safety. In addition, specific measures for assessing whether or not the cyber resiliency contributing or prerequisite requirements have been satisfied within the solution space are defined. This may include, for example, a determination of the baseline reliability of the technology components needed to deliver cyber resilient capabilities within a system element.

In addition, during the *Development* stage, the implementation of cyber resiliency solutions is analyzed and evaluated. The verification strategy for cyber resiliency solutions typically includes adversarial testing or demonstration of mission or business function measures of performance in a stressed environment which includes adversarial activities. The operational processes and procedures for using technical solutions are defined, refined, and validated with respect to the ability to meet mission and business objectives despite adversity involving systems containing cyber resources. The cyber resiliency perspective calls for testing and other forms of validation or verification to include adversarial threats among (and in combination with) other stresses on the system. During this life cycle stage, resources (e.g., diverse implementations of critical system elements, alternative processing facilities) required to implement specific courses of action are also developed.

During the *Production* stage, the verification strategy is applied to instances or versions of the system-of-interest and to associated spare parts or components. The verification strategy for the cyber resiliency requirements as applied to such instances and to such system elements includes adversarial testing or demonstration in a stressed environment. In addition, during the *Production* stage, cyber resiliency concerns for enabling systems for production, integration, validation, and supply chain management continue to be identified and addressed.

During the *Utilization* stage, the effectiveness of cyber resiliency solutions in the operational environment is monitored. Effectiveness may decrease due to changes in the operational environment (e.g., new mission or business processes, increased user population, deployment in new locations, addition or removal of other systems or system elements with which the system-of-interest interacts), the threat environment (e.g., new threat actors, new vulnerabilities in commonly used technologies), or the technical environment (e.g., the introduction of new technologies into other systems with which the system-of-interest interacts). Cyber resiliency solutions may need to be adapted to address such changes (e.g., by defining new courses of action, by changing mission or business processes and procedures, by reconfiguring system elements). New stakeholders may arise from changes in the operational environment, and their concerns may change the relative priorities of cyber resiliency objectives. Changes in the threat or technical environment may make some techniques or approaches less feasible, while changes in the technical or operational environment may make others more viable.

During the _Support_ stage, maintenance and upgrade of the system or system elements can include integration of new cyber resiliency solutions into the system-of-interest. This stage also provides opportunities to revisit the prioritization and tailoring of cyber resiliency objectives. Upgrades to or modifications of system capabilities can include significant architectural changes to address accumulated changes to the operational, threat, and technical environments. System modifications and upgrades can also introduce additional vulnerabilities, particularly with architectural changes.

During the _Retirement_ stage, system elements or the entire system-of-interest are removed from operations. The retirement process can affect other systems with which the system-of-interest interacts and can decrease the cyber resiliency of those systems and of the supported mission or business processes. Retirement strategies can include, for example, phased removal of system elements, turnkey removal of all system elements, phased replacement of system elements, and turnkey replacement of the entire system-of-interest. Cyber resiliency objectives and priorities are identified for the systems, missions, and business functions in the operational environment to inform analysis of the potential or expected effects of different retirement strategies on the ability to achieve those objectives. Like the support stage, the retirement stage can introduce significant vulnerabilities, particularly during disposal and unintended residue remaining from decommissioned assets.

Table 4 illustrates changes in emphasis for the different cyber resiliency constructs, particularly with respect to cyber resiliency objectives (**bolded**).

**TABLE 4: CYBER RESILIENCY IN LIFE CYCLE STAGES**

| LIFE CYCLE STAGES | ROLE OF CYBER RESILIENCY CONSTRUCTS |
|---|---|
| Concept | • Prioritize and tailor objectives.<br>• Prioritize design principles and align with other disciplines.<br>• Limit the set of techniques and approaches to use in solutions. |
| Development | • Use techniques and approaches to define alternative solutions.<br>• Apply design principles to refine and analyze alternative solutions.<br>• Develop capabilities to achieve the Prevent/Avoid, Continue, Constrain, Reconstitute, and Understand objectives. |
| Production | • Implement and evaluate the effectiveness of cyber resiliency solutions.<br>• Provide resources (or ensure that resources will be provided) to achieve the Prepare objective. |
| Utilization | • Monitor the effectiveness of cyber resiliency solutions using capabilities to achieve Understand and Prepare objectives.<br>• Reprioritize and tailor objectives as needed, and adapt mission, business, and/or security processes to address environmental changes (Transform objective). |
| Support | • Revisit the prioritization and tailoring of objectives; use the results of monitoring to identify new or modified requirements.<br>• Revisit constraints on techniques and approaches.<br>• Modify or upgrade capabilities consistent with changes as noted (Re-Architect objective). |

**TABLE 4: CYBER RESILIENCY IN LIFE CYCLE STAGES**

| LIFE CYCLE STAGES | ROLE OF CYBER RESILIENCY CONSTRUCTS |
|---|---|
| Retirement | • Prioritize and tailor objectives for the environment of operation.<br>• Ensure that disposal processes enable those objectives to be achieved, modifying or upgrading capabilities of other systems as necessary (<u>Re-Architect</u> objective). |
|  |  |

## 2.3 RISK MANAGEMENT AND CYBER RESILIENCY

Organizations manage the mission, business function, and operational risks related to a dependence on systems that include cyber resources as part of a larger portfolio of risks,[29] including financial and reputational risks; programmatic or project-related risks associated with developing a system (e.g., cost, schedule, performance); security risks associated with the organization's mission or business activities, information the organization processes/handles, or requirements arising from legislation, regulations, policies, or standards; and cybersecurity risks. A proposed cyber resiliency solution, while intended primarily to reduce mission/business risk or operational risk, can reduce other types of risk (e.g., security risk, supply chain risk, reputational risk, cybersecurity risk, performance risk). However, it can also increase other types of risk (e.g., financial, cost, or schedule risk). As part of a multidisciplinary systems engineering effort, systems security engineers and risk management professionals are responsible for articulating the potential risk impacts of alternative solutions, to determine whether those impacts fall within organizational risk tolerance, whether adoption of a proposed solution is consistent with the organization's risk management strategy, and to inform the organization's risk executive (function) of risk trade-offs.[30]

---

[29] These risks are typically addressed by organizations as part of an Enterprise Risk Management (ERM) program.

[30] See Section 3.2.1 and Appendix D.4.

CHAPTER THREE

# CYBER RESILIENCY IN PRACTICE

APPLYING CYBER RESILIENCY CONCEPTS, CONSTRUCTS, PRACTICES

This chapter identifies considerations for determining which cyber resiliency constructs are most relevant to a system-of-interest and describes a tailorable process for applying cyber resiliency concepts, constructs, and practices to a system.

## 3.1 SELECTING AND PRIORITIZING CYBER RESILIENCY CONSTRUCTS

The variety of concerns, technologies, and practices related to cyber resiliency results in an extensive framework for cyber resiliency engineering. For example, the engineering framework identifies fourteen cyber resiliency techniques and nearly fifty cyber resiliency implementation approaches. It is also complex, with relationships among the constructs of goals, objectives, design principles, techniques, and approaches as discussed in Appendix E. Cyber resiliency design principles, techniques, and approaches build on, complement, or function in synergy with mechanisms intended to ensure other quality properties (e.g., security, safety, and system resilience). The variety of circumstances and types of systems for which cyber resiliency can be applied means that no single cyber resiliency technique, approach, or set of approaches is universally optimal or universally applicable. Systems security engineering seeks to manage risk rather than to provide a universal solution. The choice of a risk-appropriate set of cyber resiliency techniques and approaches depends on various trade space considerations and risk factors that are assessed during the systems engineering processes. Employing all cyber resiliency techniques and approaches is not needed to achieve the cyber resiliency objectives prioritized by stakeholders. In fact, is not possible to employ all techniques and approaches simultaneously. The following subsections describe factors to consider in selecting a set of cyber resiliency techniques and implementation approaches that best fits the system-of-interest.

### 3.1.1 ACHIEVEMENT OF GOALS AND OBJECTIVES

Cyber resiliency techniques and associated implementation approaches are employed to achieve mission or business objectives. The relative priorities of cyber resiliency goals and objectives are determined by the mission or business objectives. The selection of specific cyber resiliency techniques and approaches is therefore driven in part by the relative priorities of the objectives they support.[31]

### 3.1.2 CYBER RISK MANAGEMENT STRATEGY

An organization's cyber risk management strategy (i.e., its strategy for managing risks stemming from dependencies on systems which include cyber resources) is part of its risk management strategy and includes its risk-framing for cyber risks.[32] The organization's risk frame identifies

---

[31] See Appendix E, Table E-13.

[32] A risk management strategy consists of four major elements: risk framing, risk assessment, risk response, and risk monitoring [SP 800-39]. Risk response is also referred to as risk treatment [SP 800-160 v1] [ISO 73]. Organizational risk tolerance is determined as part of the risk framing component [SP 800-39] and defined in the risk management strategy.

which risks or risk factors (i.e., which potential impacts or consequences) are unacceptable. For cyber resiliency, the risk frame assumes an advanced adversary with a persistent presence in organizational systems. The risk response portion of the risk management strategy can include priorities or preferences for the types of effects on adversary activities[33] to seek in cyber resiliency solutions.

An organization's risk management strategy is constrained by such factors as legal, regulatory, and contractual requirements as reflected in organizational policies and procedures; financial resources; legacy investments; and organizational culture. These constraints can be reflected in the selection and tailoring of cyber resiliency techniques, approaches, and design principles. For example, organizational policies and culture can strongly influence whether and how the cyber resiliency technique of Deception is used. The risk management strategy can define an order of precedence for responding to identified risks analogous to the safety order of precedence such as "harden, sensor, isolate, obfuscate." Together with the strategic design principles selected and specifically tailored to a given program, mission, business function, or system, the order of precedence can guide the selection and application of structural design principles at different locations in an architecture.[34]

### 3.1.3  TYPE OF SYSTEM

The set of cyber resiliency techniques and approaches which are most relevant to and useful in a system depends on the type of system. The following present some general examples of system types and examples of techniques and approaches that might be appropriate for those types of systems. Additional (more specific) examples are provided in Appendix I (Use Cases). In addition to the techniques and approaches listed in the examples below, there may be other techniques and approaches that could be useful for a particular type of system. The specific aspects of the system in question will impact the selection as well.

- **Enterprise IT Systems, Shared Services, and Common Infrastructures**

  Enterprise IT (EIT) systems are typically general-purpose systems, very often with significant processing, storage, and bandwidth capabilities, capable of delivering information resources which can meet the business or other mission needs of an enterprise or a large stakeholder community. As such, all of the cyber resiliency techniques and associated approaches may potentially be viable although their selection would depend on the other considerations noted in this section.

- **Large-Scale Processing Environments**

  Large scale processing environments (LSPEs) handle large numbers of events (e.g., process transactions) with high confidence in service delivery. The scale of such systems makes them highly sensitive to disruptions in or degradation of service. Therefore, the selective use of the Offloading and Restriction implementations approaches can make the scale of such systems more manageable. This in turn will support the application of Analytic Monitoring and the Mission Dependency and Status Visualization approach to Contextual Awareness in a manner that does not significantly affect performance. LPSEs often implement Dynamic Positioning functionality that can be repurposed to help improve cyber resiliency via the

---

[33] See Appendix H.

[34] See Appendix E.

Functional Relocation of Cyber Resources, Fragmentation, and Distributed Functionality approaches.

- **System-of-Systems**

  Many cyber resiliency techniques are likely to be applicable to a system-of-systems, but some techniques and approaches can offer greater benefit than others. For example, Contextual Awareness implemented via Mission Dependency and Status Visualization can be applied to predict the potential mission impacts of cyber effects of adversary activities on constituent systems or system elements. The Calibrated Defense-in-Depth and Consistency Analysis approaches to the technique of Coordinated Protection can help ensure that the disparate protections of the constituent systems operate consistently and in a coordinated manner to prevent or delay the advance of an adversary across those systems. For a system-of-systems involving constituent systems which were not designed to work together and which were developed with different missions and risk frames, Realignment could also be beneficial. In particular, the Offloading and Restriction approaches could be used to ensure that the core system elements are appropriately aligned to the overall system-of-system mission.

- **Critical Infrastructure Systems**

  Critical infrastructure systems are often specialized, high-confidence, dedicated, purpose-built systems that have highly deterministic properties. As such, these systems often have limitations regarding storage and processing capabilities; strict timing constraints; and severe if not catastrophic consequences of failure. As such, they often have limitations regarding storage and processing capabilities, strict timing constraints, and severe, if not catastrophic, consequences of failure. Thus, the availability and integrity of the functionality of the systems is very important as the corruption or lack of availability of some of the key system elements could result in significant harm. For these reasons, techniques adapted from cyber resiliency, such as Redundancy (particularly the Protected Backup and Restore and Surplus Capacity approaches) coupled with aspects of Diversity (e.g., Architectural Diversity, Supply Chain Diversity), could prevent attacks from having mission or business consequences and also maximize the chance of continuation of the critical or essential mission or business operations. Segmentation can isolate highly critical system elements that protect it from an adversary's activities. Approaches such as Trust-Based Privilege Management and Attribute-Based Usage Restriction could constrain the potential damage that an adversary could inflict on a system.

- **Cyber-Physical Systems**

  As with critical infrastructure systems, cyber-physical systems (CPS) often have significant limitations regarding storage capacity, processing capabilities, and bandwidth. In addition, many of these systems often have a high degree of autonomy with very limited human interaction. Some cyber-physical systems often operate with no active network connection, although they may connect to a network under specific circumstances (e.g., scheduled maintenance). Non-Persistent Services support the periodic refreshing of software and firmware from a trusted source (e.g., an off-line redundant component), in effect flushing out any malware. However, that approach applies only if the organization can allow for the periodic downtime that the refresh would entail. Similarly, the Integrity Checks approach to Substantiated Integrity, implemented via cryptographic checksums on critical software, could help enable embedded systems to detect corrupted software components.

- **Internet of Things**

  An Internet of Things (IoT) system consists of system elements with network connectivity, which communicate with an Internet-accessible software application. That software application, which is part of the IoT system, orchestrates the behavior of or aggregates the data provided by constituent system elements. As in a cyber-physical system, the system elements have limitations in the areas of power consumption, processing, storage capacity, and bandwidth, which in turn may limit the potential for such processing-intensive cyber resiliency approaches as Obfuscation or Adaptive Management at the device level. Because many "things" (e.g., light bulbs, door locks) are small and relatively simple, they often lack the capacity for basic protection. However, the Integrity Checks approach to Substantiated Integrity could still be viable, applied in conjunction with reliability mechanisms. An IoT system assumes Internet connectivity, although the set of "things" are usually capable of functioning independently if not connected. Because many IoT systems do not assume technical expertise on the part of users, cyber resiliency techniques and approaches that involve human interaction (e.g., Disinformation, Misdirection) may not be appropriate. In addition, the design of IoT systems accommodates flexibility and repurposing of the capabilities of constituent "things." Thus, an application that orchestrated the behavior of one set of "things" may be upgraded to orchestrate additional sets, the members of which were not designed with that application in mind. Such changes to the IoT systems of which that application or the additional sets originally belong can benefit from the application of Realignment. At the level of an IoT system (rather than at the level of individual system elements), Segmentation and Consistency Analysis can be applied.

### 3.1.4 CYBER RESILIENCY CONFLICTS AND SYNERGIES

Cyber resiliency techniques can interact in several ways. One technique can depend on another so that the first cannot be implemented without the second; for example, Adaptive Response depends on Analytic Monitoring or Contextual Awareness since a response requires a stimulus. One technique can support another making the second more effective; for example, Diversity and Redundancy are mutually supportive. One technique can use another so that more design options are available than if the techniques were applied independently; for example, Analytic Monitoring can use Diversity in a design which includes a diverse set of monitoring tools.

However, one technique can also conflict with or complicate the use of another. For example, Diversity and Segmentation can each make Analytic Monitoring and Contextual Awareness more difficult; a design which incorporates Diversity requires monitoring tools which can handle the diverse set of system elements, while implementation of Segmentation can limit the visibility of such tools. In selecting techniques in accordance with the risk management strategy and design principles, synergies and conflicts between various techniques are taken into consideration. The text below offers three illustrative examples of the interplay, focusing on techniques which increase an adversary's work factor.

As a first example, Dynamic Positioning and Non-Persistence enable operational agility by making it more difficult for an adversary to target critical resources. These techniques support the Continue, Constrain, and Reconstitute objectives and are part of applying the Support agility and architect for adaptability strategic design principle and the Change or disrupt the attack surface structural design principle. At the same time, these techniques (and the associated

NIST SP 800-160, VOLUME 2

implementation approaches) also make it more difficult for an organization to maintain situational awareness of its security posture. That is, Dynamic Positioning and Non-Persistence complicate the use of Contextual Awareness and aspects of Analytic Monitoring, and thus can conflict with the Maintain situational awareness structural design principle.

As a second example, Redundancy and Diversity together are very effective in resisting adversary attacks. These techniques enhance the organization's ability to achieve the Continue and Reconstitute objectives and apply the Plan and manage diversity and Maintain redundancy structural design principles. However, the implementation of both Redundancy and Diversity will increase the organization's attack surface.

As a final example, Deception can lead the adversary to waste effort and reveal tactics, techniques, and procedures (TTP), but it can also complicate the use of aspects of Analytic Monitoring and Contextual Awareness. In general, while Redundancy, Diversity, Deception, Dynamic Positioning, and Unpredictability will likely greatly increase the adversary work factor, they come at a cost to some other cyber resiliency objectives, techniques, and design principles.

No technique or set of techniques is optimal with respect to all decision factors. There are always ramifications for employing any given technique. The determination of the appropriate selection of techniques is a trade decision that systems engineers make. A more complete identification of potential interactions (e.g., synergies and conflicts) between cyber resiliency techniques is presented in Appendix D.

## 3.1.5  OTHER DISCIPLINES AND EXISTING INVESTMENTS

Many of the techniques and implementation approaches supporting cyber resiliency are well-established. Some technologies or processes are drawn from other disciplines (e.g., Continuity of Operations [COOP], cybersecurity) but are used or executed in a different manner to support cyber resiliency. These include Adaptive Response, Analytic Monitoring, Coordinated Protection, Privilege Restriction, Redundancy, and Segmentation. Others are drawn from disciplines that deal with non-adversarial threats (e.g., safety, reliability, survivability). These include Contextual Awareness, Diversity, Non-Persistence, Realignment, and Substantiated Integrity. Still others are cyber adaptations of non-cyber concepts drawn from disciplines that deal with adversarial threats (e.g., medicine, military, sports). These include Deception, Dynamic Positioning, and Unpredictability. Legacy investments made by an organization in these other disciplines can influence which cyber resiliency techniques and approaches are most appropriate to pursue.

### 3.1.5.1  Investments from Cybersecurity, COOP, and Resilience Engineering

Redundancy-supporting approaches, such as backup, surplus capacity, and replication, are well-established in COOP programs. In cyber resiliency, however, there is a recognition that these approaches are not sufficient to protect against the APT. A threat actor might choose to target backup servers as optimum locations to implant malware if those servers are not sufficiently protected. In addition, remote backup servers that employ the same architecture as the primary server are vulnerable to malware that has compromised the primary server. However, if an organization has already invested in backup services (in support of COOP or cybersecurity), those services can be enhanced by requiring an adversary to navigate multiple distinct defenses or authentication challenges (Calibrated Defense-in-Depth approach to Coordinated Protection) or some form of Synthetic Diversity to compensate for known attack vectors.

Contextual Awareness and Analytic Monitoring capabilities are often provided by performance management and cybersecurity functions, including, for example, cyber situational awareness, anomaly detection, and performance monitoring. However, the off-the-shelf implementations of these functions are generally insufficient to detect threats from advanced adversaries whose actions are very stealthy. Enhancing existing investments in both detection and monitoring by integrating data from sensor and monitor readings from disparate sources is a way to take these existing investments and make them an effective cyber resiliency tool. Another way to make existing technology more cyber resilient is to complement the existing monitoring services with information from threat intelligence sources, enabling these tools to be better-tuned to look for known observables (e.g., adversary TTPs).

Some approaches to Segmentation and Coordinated Protection appear in information security or cybersecurity. Predefined Segmentation, as reflected in boundary demilitarized zones (DMZs), is a well-established construct in cybersecurity. One important distinction of cyber resiliency is that the segmentation is applied throughout the system, not just at the system boundary. In addition, the Dynamic Segmentation and Isolation approach allows for changing the placement and/or activation of the protected segments. ForCoordinated Protection, the defense-in-depth approach is often used for security or system resilience. Ensuring that those protections work in a coordinated fashion is one of the distinguishing aspects of cyber resiliency.

### 3.1.5.2 Investments from Non-Adversarial Disciplines

Some cyber resiliency techniques and approaches come from disciplines such as safety. Diversity and certain implementations of Substantiated Integrity, such as Byzantine quorum systems[35] or checksums on critical software, can be traced back to the safety discipline.[36] Therefore, systems that have been designed with safety in mind may already have implemented some of these capabilities. However, the safety capabilities were designed with the assumption that they were countering non-adversarial threat events. To make these capabilities useful against the APT, certain changes are needed. From a safety perspective, it may be sufficient to only employ polynomial hashes on critical software to ensure that the software has not been corrupted over time. However, such hashes are not sufficient when dealing with the APT, which is able to corrupt the software and data and then recalculate the checksum. Instead, what is needed in those instances are cryptographic-based polynomial checksums. Capabilities such as Non-Persistence are very common in cloud and virtualization architectures. Again, this capability was not designed or employed to specifically counter the APT but to facilitate rapid deployment of implementations. From a system design and implementation perspective, it is most likely easier to employ existing virtualization technology and change the criteria of when and why to refresh critical services (e.g., periodically refresh the software and firmware with the goal of flushing out malware) than it is to deploy Non-Persistence in a system that cannot implement the capability.

### 3.1.5.3 Investments from Adversarial Disciplines

Several of the cyber resiliency techniques and approaches are cyber adaptions of non-cyber measures used in adversary-oriented disciplines (e.g., medicine, military, sports). These include

---

[35] The National Aeronautics and Space Administration (NASA) Space Shuttle Program applied this concept in multiple computers which would vote on certain maneuvers.

[36] This is an example of *operational redundancy* where specific failure modes are managed as part of the nominal operation of the system. Redundant Array of Independent Disks (RAID) storage systems and "hyper-converged" computing architectures (i.e., those relying on erasure code for distributed data stores) also fall into this category.

Deception, Unpredictability, and Dynamic Positioning. None of those cyber resiliency techniques or approaches are employed in non-adversarial disciplines; there is no reason in resilience engineering to attempt to mislead a hurricane, nor is there any benefit in safety engineering to include an element of unpredictability. The value of these constructs in non-cyber environments is very well established. Because these adversarial-derived techniques and approaches are not typically found in disciplines such as safety, resilience engineering, or COOP, it is much more challenging to provide them by enhancing existing constructs. Therefore, they may be more challenging to integrate into an existing system.

### 3.1.6 ARCHITECTURAL LOCATIONS

The selection of cyber resiliency techniques or approaches depends, in part, on where (i.e., at what layers, in which components or system elements, at which interfaces between layers or between system elements) in the system architecture cyber resiliency solutions can be applied. The set of layers, like the set of system components or system elements, in an architecture depends on the type of system. For example, an embedded system offers a different set of possible locations than an enterprise architecture that includes applications running in a cloud. The set of possible layers can include, for example, an operational (people-and-processes) layer, a support layer, and a layer to represent the physical environment.

Different cyber resiliency techniques or approaches lend themselves to implementation at different architectural layers.[37] Some approaches can be implemented at multiple layers, in different ways, and with varying degrees of maturity. Other approaches are highly specific to a layer; for example, Asset Mobility is implemented in the operations layer or in the physical environment. For some layers, many approaches may be applicable; for others, relatively few approaches may be available. For example, relatively few approaches can be implemented at the hardware layer. These include Dynamic Reconfiguration, Architectural Diversity, Design Diversity, Replication, Predefined Segmentation, and Integrity Checks.

Similarly, some cyber resiliency approaches lend themselves to specific types of components or system elements. For example, Fragmentation applies to information stores. Some approaches assume that a system element or set of system elements has been included in the architecture specifically to support cyber defense. These include Dynamic Threat Awareness, Forensic and Behavioral Analysis, and Misdirection. Other cyber resiliency approaches assume that a system element has been included in the architecture, explicitly or virtually, to support the mission, security, or business operations; these include Sensor Fusion and Analysis, Consistency Analysis, Orchestration, and all of the approaches to Privilege Restriction.

Finally, some techniques or approaches lend themselves to implementation at interfaces between layers or between system elements. These include, for example, Monitoring and Damage Assessment, Segmentation, and Behavior Validation.

### 3.1.7 EFFECTS ON ADVERSARIES, THREATS, AND RISKS

The selection of cyber resiliency techniques and approaches can be motivated by potential effects on adversary activities or on risk. Two resiliency techniques or approaches listed as both potentially having the same effect may differ in how strongly that effect applies to a given threat

---

[37] See Appendix E, Table E-4.

event, scope (i.e., the set of threat events for which the effect is or can be produced), and affected risk factors. For example, all approaches to Non-Persistence can degrade an adversary's ability to maintain a covert presence via the malicious browser extension TTP; closing the browser session when it is no longer needed, a use of Non-Persistent Services, degrades the adversary's activity more than do the other Non-Persistence approaches. Some techniques or approaches will affect more risk factors (e.g., reduce likelihood of impact or reduce level of impact) than others. The security mechanisms or processes used to implement a cyber resiliency approach will also vary with respect to their scope and strength. For example, a Misdirection approach to the Deception technique, implemented via a deception net, and the Sensor Fusion and Analysis approach to Analytic Monitoring, implemented via holistic suite of intrusion detection systems, will both achieve the detect effect. However, the effectiveness and scope of the two vary widely. For this reason, engineering trade-offs among techniques, approaches, and implementations should consider the actual effects to be expected in the context of the system's architecture, design, and operational environment.

In general, systems security engineering decisions seek to provide as complete a set of effects as possible, and to maximize those effects with the recognition that this optimization problem will not have a single solution. The rationale for selecting cyber resiliency techniques or approaches that have complete coverage of the potential effects relates to the long-term nature of the threat campaigns. Potentially, engagements with the APT may go on for months, if not years, possibly starting while a system is in development or even earlier in the life cycle. Given the nature of the threat, its attacks will likely evolve over time in response to a defender's actions. Having a selection of techniques and approaches—where each technique and approach supports (to different degrees and in different ways) multiple effects on the adversary, and the union of the techniques and approaches allows for all potential effects on an adversary— provides the systems engineers the flexibility of evolving and tailoring the effects to the adversary's changing actions. This is analogous to team sports where the one team will change its game plan in response to player injuries and the changing game plan of the other team. A team with players that can play multiple positions gives it flexibility to respond to changes by the opposition and to potentially replace injured players with others that can play the position of the injured player.

Different cyber resiliency techniques and approaches can have different effects on threat events and on risk. No single technique or approach can create all possible effects on a threat event, and no technique or approach or set of techniques or approaches can eliminate risk. However, by considering the desired effects, systems engineers can select a set of techniques that will collectively achieve those effects.[38]

### 3.1.8 MATURITY AND POTENTIAL ADOPTION

Approaches to applying cyber resiliency techniques vary in maturity and adoption. The decision to use less mature technologies depends on the organization's risk management strategy and its strategy for managing technical risks. Many highly mature and widely adopted technologies and processes that were developed to meet the general needs for performance, dependability, or security can be used or repurposed to address cyber resiliency concerns. These pose little, if any, technical risk. Changes in operational processes, procedures, and configuration changes may be

---

[38] See Appendix H.

needed to make these technologies and processes effective against the APT and thus part of cyber resiliency solutions.

A growing number of technologies are specifically oriented toward cyber resiliency, including moving target defenses and deception toolkits. These technologies are currently focused on enterprise IT environments. As these technologies become more widely adopted, the decision to include the technologies is influenced more by policy than by technical risk considerations. This is particularly the case for applications of the Deception and Unpredictability cyber resiliency techniques.

Cyber resiliency is an active research area. Technologies are being explored to improve the cyber resiliency of cyber-physical systems, high-confidence dedicated-purpose systems, and large-scale processing environments. The integration of solutions involving new technologies and thereby reducing risks due to the APT should be balanced against risks associated with perturbing such systems.

## 3.2  ANALYTIC PRACTICES AND PROCESSES

In the context of systems security engineering, cyber resiliency analysis is intended to determine whether the cyber resiliency properties and behaviors of a system-of-interest, regardless of its system life cycle stage, are sufficient for the organization using that system to meet its mission assurance, business continuity, or other security requirements in a threat environment that includes the APT. Cyber resiliency analysis is performed with the expectation that such analysis will support systems engineering and risk management decisions about the system-of-interest. Depending on the life cycle stage, programmatic considerations, and other factors discussed above, a cyber resiliency analysis could recommend architectural changes, integration of new products or technologies into the system, changes in how existing products or technologies are used, or changes in operating procedures or environmental protections consistent with and designed to implement the organization's risk management strategy.

The following sub-sections describe a general, tailorable process for cyber resiliency analysis consisting of steps and tasks, as summarized in Table 5. A variety of motivations for a cyber resiliency analysis are possible, including ensuring that cyber risks due to the APT are fully considered as part of the RMF process or other risk management process, supporting systems security engineering tasks, and recalibrating assessments of risk and risk responses based on information about new threats (e.g., information about a cyber incident or an APT actor), newly discovered vulnerabilities (e.g., discovery of a common design flaw), and problematic dependencies (e.g., discovery of a supply chain issue). Although described in terms of a broad analytic scope, the process can be tailored to have a narrow scope, for example to analyze the potential cyber resiliency improvement that could be achieved by integrating a specific technology or to identify ways to ensure adequate cyber resiliency against a specific threat scenario.

The analytic processes and practices related to cyber resiliency are intended to be integrated with those for other specialty engineering disciplines, including security, systems engineering, resilience engineering, safety, cybersecurity, and mission assurance.[39] In addition, analytic

---

[39] See Appendix D.3.

processes and practices related to cyber resiliency can leverage system representations offered by model-based systems engineering (MBSE) and analytic methods (including those involving artificial intelligence [AI] and machine learning [ML]) integrated into MBSE.

A variety of artifacts can provide information used in a cyber resiliency analysis depending on its scope, the life cycle stage of the system or systems within the scope of the analysis, the step in the RMF of the in-scope system or systems, the extent to which the organization relying on the system or systems has done contingency planning, and (for systems in the Utilization life cycle stage) reports on security posture and incident response. These artifacts can include engineering project plans, system security plans [SP 800-18], contingency plans [SP 800-34], supply chain risk management plans [SP 800-161], reports on security posture produced as part of the Monitor step of the RMF [SP 800-37], risk analyses [SP 800-30], penetration test results, after-action reports from exercises, incident reports, and recovery plans [NIST CSF].

Cyber resiliency analysis complements both system life cycle and RMF tasks. The life cycle and RMF tasks produce information that can be used in cyber resiliency analysis, and cyber resiliency analysis enables cyber risks to be considered more fully in life cycle and RMF tasks.

### TABLE 5:  TAILORABLE PROCESS FOR CYBER RESILIENCY ANALYSIS

| ANALYSIS STEP | MOTIVATING QUESTION | TASKS |
|---|---|---|
| **Understand the context** | How do stakeholder concerns and priorities translate into cyber resiliency constructs and priorities? | • Identify the programmatic context.<br>• Identify the architectural context.<br>• Identify the operational context.<br>• Identify the threat context.<br>• Interpret and prioritize cyber resiliency constructs. |
| **Establish the initial cyber resiliency baseline** | How well is the system doing—how well does it meet stakeholder needs and address stakeholder concerns—with respect to the aspects of cyber resiliency that matter to stakeholders? | • Identify existing capabilities.<br>• Identify gaps and issues.<br>• Define evaluation criteria and make initial assessment. |
| **Analyze the system** | How do cyber risks affect mission, business, or operational risks? | • Identify critical resources, sources of fragility, and attack surfaces.<br>• Represent the adversary perspective.<br>• Identify and prioritize opportunities for improvement. |
| **Define and analyze specific alternatives** | How can mission or operational resilience be improved by improving cyber resiliency? | • Define potential technical and procedural solutions.<br>• Define potential solutions for supporting systems and processes.<br>• Analyze potential solutions with respect to criteria. |
| **Develop recommendations** | What is the recommended plan of action? | • Identify and analyze alternatives.<br>• Assess alternatives.<br>• Recommend a plan of action. |

### 3.2.1 UNDERSTAND THE CONTEXT

The problem of providing sufficient cyber resiliency properties and behaviors is inherently situated in a programmatic, operational, architectural, and threat context. This step is intended to ensure that the context is sufficiently understood that cyber resiliency constructs can be interpreted in that context, the relative priorities of cyber resiliency objectives can be assessed, and the applicability of cyber resiliency design principles, techniques, and approaches can be determined. The activities in this step can and should be integrated with activities under the Technical Management Processes in [SP 800-160 v1] and the Prepare and Categorize steps of the RMF [SP 800-37].

#### 3.2.1.1 Identify the Programmatic Context

The programmatic context identifies how the system-of-interest is being acquired, developed, modified, or repurposed, including the life cycle stage, life cycle model, or system development approach (e.g., spiral, waterfall, agile, DevOps). Identification of the life cycle stage, life cycle model, and system development approach enables maturity as a consideration in defining cyber resiliency solutions. The programmatic context also identifies the stakeholders for the system-of-interest, the roles and responsibilities related to the system-of-interest, and the entities (organizations, organizational units, or individuals) in those roles.

In particular, the programmatic context identifies the entities responsible for directing, executing, and determining the acceptability of the results of engineering efforts related to the system (e.g., program office, systems engineer, systems integrator, authorizing official, and mission or business function owner). Each of these key stakeholders has a risk management strategy focused on different potential risks (e.g., cost, schedule, and technical or performance risks for a program office or systems engineer; security risks for an authorizing official; mission or business risks for a mission or business function owner). When these entities are part of the same organization, the risk management strategies for their respective areas of responsibility instantiate or are aligned with the organization's cyber risk management strategy.[40]

Technical or performance risks can include risks that quality properties (e.g., security, safety, system resilience, cyber resiliency) are insufficiently provided, as evidenced by the absence or poor execution of behaviors that should demonstrate those properties. The programmatic risk management strategy can reflect the relative priorities other stakeholders—in particular, the mission or business process owner and the authorizing official—assign to different quality properties. In addition, the programmatic risk management strategy can include constraints on less mature technologies, less commonly used products, or less commonly applied operational practices as part of managing technical or performance risks.[41]

In addition, other stakeholders may have their own risk management strategies, or may be represented by an official within these entities (e.g., a system security officer to represent the security concerns of program managers whose proprietary information is handled by the system-of-interest) with a corresponding risk management strategy. An appreciation of the different risk management strategies—how the various stakeholders frame risk, including what threats and potential harms or adverse consequences are of concern to them, what their risk

---

[40] See Section 3.1.2.
[41] See Section 3.1.8.

tolerances are, and what risk-risk trade-offs they are willing to make—will enable the threat model to be defined and cyber resiliency constructs to be interpreted and prioritized in subsequent steps.

Identification of the programmatic context highlights the aspects of the programmatic risk management strategy which constrain possible solutions. One aspect is the relative priority of such quality attributes as safety, security, reliability, maintainability, system resilience, and cyber resiliency. Another is the relative preference for operational changes versus technical changes. Depending on the life cycle stage and the programmatic risk management strategy, changes to operational processes and procedures may be preferred to technical changes to the system.

### 3.2.1.2  *Identify the Architectural Context*

The architectural context identifies the type of system, its architecture or architectural patterns if already defined, and its interfaces with or dependencies on other systems with consideration of whether it is (or is intended to be) part of a larger system-of-systems or a participant in a larger ecosystem. Key technologies, technical standards, or products included (or expected to be included) in the system are identified. Depending on the life cycle stage, identification of the architectural context can also include system locations, sub-systems or components, or layers in the architecture where cyber resiliency solutions could be applied. If this information is not yet available, it will be developed in a subsequent step.[42]

Identification of the type of system begins with identification of its general type (e.g., CPS,[43] application, enterprise service, common infrastructure as part of enterprise IT (EIT) or a large-scale processing environment (LSPE), EIT as a whole, or LSPE as a whole). The type of system determines which cyber resiliency techniques and approaches are most relevant.[44] Each type of system has an associated set of architectural patterns. For example, a CPS device typically includes a sensor, a controller (which is present in cyberspace), an actuator, and a physical layer; EIT typically includes enterprise services (e.g., identity and access management, mirroring and backup, email), common infrastructures (e.g., an internal communications network, a storage area network, a virtualization or cloud infrastructure), a demilitarized zone (DMZ) for interfacing with the Internet, and a collection of enterprise applications.

Identification of other systems with which the system-of-interest interfaces or on which it depends includes consideration of federation, networking, and scope. Federation typically restricts the set of solutions which can be applied and the metrics which can be defined and used since different system owners may be unwilling or unable to use the same technologies or to share certain types or forms of information. Some systems are designed to operate without a network connection, at least transiently and often normally. The cyber resiliency solutions and means of assessing system cyber resiliency or solution effectiveness will be limited by whether the system is operating in detached mode. Depending on the programmatic context, the scope

---

[42] See Section 3.2.3.3.

[43] Multiple levels of aggregation have been defined for CPS: a device, a system, or a system-of-systems [CPSPWG16]. For example, a smart meter is an example of a CPS device; a vehicle is an example of a CPS; the Smart Grid is an example of a system-of-systems CPS.

[44] See Section 3.1.3.

of "other systems" can include those constituting the system's development, test, or maintenance environment.

### 3.2.1.3 *Identify the Operational Context*

The operational context identifies how the system-of-interest is used or will be used (i.e., its usage context, which is closely related to the architectural context), how it will be administered and maintained (i.e., its support context, which is closely related to the programmatic and architectural contexts), how it interacts with or depends on other systems (i.e., its dependency context), and how usage and dependencies change depending on the time or circumstances (i.e., its temporal context).

The *usage context* identifies the primary mission or business functions the system supports, any secondary or supporting missions or business functions, and the criticality and reliability with which the missions or business functions are to be achieved. Thus, the usage context can:

- Describe the system in terms of its intended uses, which include not only its primary mission or business function, but also secondary or likely additional uses. The description includes identification of external interfaces—to networks, to other supporting infrastructures and services, and to end users—in a functional sense, keeping in mind that these interfaces can vary;

- Describe the system's criticality to its missions, stakeholders, end users, or the general public. Criticality is "an attribute assigned to an asset that reflects its relative importance or necessity in achieving or contributing to the achievement of stated goals"[SP 800-160 v1] and relates strongly to the potential impacts of system malfunction, degraded or denied performance, or not performing to the missions it supports, human life or safety, national security, or economic security (e.g., as in the context of critical infrastructure [NIST CSF]).

- Identify whether the system is or contains high value assets (HVAs) (e.g., as defined in [OMB M-19-03], repositories of large volumes of PII or financial assets) or plays a central role (even if non-critical) in a critical infrastructure sector (e.g., financial services, Defense Industrial Base [DIB]) since these characteristics could attract specific types of adversaries.

- If possible, identify measures of effectiveness (MOEs) and measures of performance (MOPs) for mission or business functions. Cyber resiliency effectiveness metrics (which can be defined and used later in the analysis process)[45] can sometimes repurpose mission MOEs/MOPs, can sometimes repurpose data collected to evaluate MOEs/MOPs, and (particularly for cyber resiliency metrics related to Withstand or Recover) can often be related to MOEs/MOPs.

The usage context also provides a general characterization of the system user population, including its size, scope, and assumed user awareness of and ability to respond to cyber threats. The usage context also indicates whether cyber defenders are actively involved in monitoring the system and responding to indications and warnings (I&W) of adverse conditions or behaviors.

The *support context* similarly provides a general characterization of the administrative and maintenance population, describes how system maintenance or updates are performed, and

---

[45] See Section 3.2.2.3 and Section 3.2.4.3.

describes operational restrictions on maintenance activities or updates. For example, updates to embedded control units (ECUs) in a vehicle should be disallowed when driving. These aspects of the operational context determine the extent to which procedural solutions can be applied to the system-of-interest.

The *dependency context* identifies adjacent systems (i.e., systems with which the system-of-interest is connected); describes the types of information received from, supplied to, or exchanged with those systems; and identifies the criticality of the information connection to the system-of-interest and to the mission or business functions it supports. The dependency context also identifies infrastructures on which the system-of-interest depends (e.g., networks, power suppliers, and environmental control systems). These aspects of the operational context are used to bound the scope of the analysis (e.g., whether and for which adjacent or infrastructure systems changes are in scope, whether characteristics and behavior of these systems can be investigated or must be assumed). If the system-of-interest is part of a larger system-of-systems or is a participant in a larger ecosystem, the dependency context also identifies the implications of aggregation or federation for governance, system administration, and information sharing with other organizations or systems.

The *temporal context* identifies whether and how the usage and dependency contexts can change, depending on whether the system is operating under normal, stressed, or maintenance conditions; whether the system is being used for one of its secondary purposes; and how the system's usage and dependencies change over the course of executing mission or business functions.

Information about the support and dependency contexts can be used at this point in the analysis to characterize and subsequently identify the system's attack surfaces.[46] The operational context can be communicated by defining a motivating operational scenario or a small set of operational scenarios.

### 3.2.1.4  Identify the Threat Context

The threat context identifies threat sources, threat events, and threat scenarios of concern for the system-of-interest. In particular, the threat context identifies the characteristics and the behaviors of adversaries whose attacks would necessarily undermine the system's ability to execute or support its missions, as well as the characteristics of relevant non-adversarial threats. Adversaries can include insiders as well as individuals or groups located outside of the system's physical and logical security perimeter. Adversary goals are identified and translated into cyber and mission effects. Adversary behaviors (i.e., threat events, attack scenarios, or TTPs) are also identified.

The threat context can:

- Identify the types of threats considered in programmatic or organizational risk framing. In addition to adversarial threats, these can include non-adversarial threats of human error, faults and failures, and natural disasters. A cyber resiliency analysis can identify scenarios in which adversaries can take advantage of the consequences of non-adversarial threat events.

---

[46] See Section 3.2.3.1.

- Identify the adversary's characteristics, constructing an adversary profile. Characteristics can include, for example, the adversary's ultimate goals and intended cyber effects, the specific timeframe over which the adversary operates, the adversary's persistence (or, alternately, how easily the adversary can be deterred, discouraged, or redirected to a different target), the adversary's concern for stealth, and the adversary's targeting, which relates to the scope or scale of the effects the adversary intends to achieve. Note that multiple adversaries can be profiled.

- Identify the types of threat events or adversarial behaviors of concern. Behaviors are described in terms of adversary TTPs and can be categorized using the categories of the National Security Agency/Central Security Service (NSA/CSS) Technical Cyber Threat Framework (NTCTF, [NSA18]), the Adversarial Tactics, Techniques, and Common Knowledge (ATT&CK) framework [Strom17], or .govCAR [DHS18].

- Identify the representative attack scenarios of concern, describing each scenario with a phrase or a sentence. A set of general attack scenarios (e.g., as identified in [Bodeau18a] [Bodeau16]) can serve as a starting point. The attack scenarios of concern in the cyber resiliency use case should be clearly related to the system's mission. Note that a cyber resiliency analysis can focus on a single attack scenario or can consider a set of scenarios.

A threat model can also include representative threat scenarios related to non-adversarial threat sources. For these, the scope or scale of effects, duration or timeframe, and types of assets affected are identified. If possible, provide a reference to a publicly available description of a similar scenario to serve as an anchoring example.

Depending on its scope and purpose, a cyber resiliency analysis can focus on a single threat scenario. For example, a cyber resiliency analysis can be motivated by a publicized incident with the purpose of the analysis being to determine the extent to which a particular system, mission or business function, or organization could be affected by a similar incident.

### 3.2.1.5  *Interpret and Prioritize Cyber Resiliency Constructs*

To ensure that cyber resiliency concepts and constructs are meaningful in the identified contexts, one or more of the following sub-tasks can be performed:

- Restate and prioritize cyber resiliency objectives[47] and sub-objectives.[48] Identify, restate, and prioritize capabilities or activities which are needed to achieve relevant sub-objectives in light of the identified threat context. These constructs are restated in terms that are meaningful in the architectural and operational contexts and prioritized based on programmatic considerations and stakeholder concerns. Note that responsibility for some capabilities or activities may be allocated to system elements outside the scope of the engineering or risk management decisions the cyber resiliency analysis is intended to support.

- Determine the potential applicability of cyber resiliency design principles. This involves considering organizational and programmatic risk management strategies to determine which strategic design principles may apply. It also involves considering the architecture, operational context, and threat environment to identify the relevance of structural design

---

[47] See Section 3.1.1.

[48] See Appendix E, Table E-1.

principles to this situation. Relevant structural design principles are restated in situation-specific terms (e.g., in terms of the technologies that are part of the system).

- Determine the potential applicability of cyber resiliency techniques and (depending on the level of detail with which the architectural context is defined) implementation approaches. This involves considering the architecture, operational context, and threat context. The relevance of the techniques and approaches to this situation is described and assessed. Relevant techniques and approaches can be restated and described in terms of architectural elements (e.g., allocating an implementation approach to a specific system element or identifying an architectural layer at which a technique can be applied). However, detailed descriptions are generally deferred to a later stage in a cyber resiliency analysis.[49]

The determination that some cyber resiliency constructs are not applicable, based on the considerations discussed in Section 3.1, narrows the focus of subsequent steps in the cyber resiliency analysis, saving work and increasing the usefulness of the results.

### 3.2.2 ESTABLISH THE INITIAL CYBER RESILIENCY BASELINE

In order to determine whether cyber resiliency improvement is needed, the baseline for the system (as it is understood at the stage in the life cycle when the cyber resiliency analysis is performed) must be established.

#### 3.2.2.1 Establish the Initial Cyber Resiliency Baseline

As discussed in Section 3.1.5.1, a system reflects architectural and design decisions and investments in specific technologies and products motivated by other specialty engineering disciplines. Capabilities are identified from such functional areas as COOP and contingency planning; security, cybersecurity, and cyber defense; performance management; reliability, maintainability, and availability (RMA); safety; and survivability. Identification of capabilities can involve decomposition of the system-of-interest into constituent sub-systems, functional areas, and/or architectural locations.[50]

Capabilities can be characterized in terms of the cyber resiliency techniques and approaches they can implement and/or the cyber resiliency design principles they can be used to apply. Capabilities can also be characterized in terms of how easily their configuration or operational use can be adapted to address specific cyber resiliency concerns, how dynamically they can be reconfigured or repurposed, and how compatible they are with other cyber resiliency techniques and approaches (e.g., deception, unpredictability).

#### 3.2.2.2 Identify Gaps and Issues

Depending on the life cycle stage, issues may already be tracked, or it may be possible to identify gaps in required capabilities and issues with the system's design, implementation, or use. Such information can be found in after-action reports from exercises, penetration test reports, incident reports, and reporting related to ongoing assessments and ongoing risk response actions (RMF tasks M-2 and M-3) [SP 800-37]. Security gaps may also have been identified from a coverage analysis with respect to a taxonomy of attack events or TTPs [DHS18].

---

[49] See Section 3.2.3.3.

[50] See Section 3.1.6.

Because senior leadership is often aware of issues and gaps, recommended cyber resiliency solutions will need to be characterized in terms of how and how well the solutions address the issues and gaps, as well as in terms of other benefits the recommended solutions provide (e.g., improved stability, improved performance).

### 3.2.2.3 *Define Evaluation Criteria and Make Initial Assessment*

One or more evaluation criteria are established and used to make an initial assessment. Cyber resiliency can be evaluated in multiple ways, including:

- How well the system achieves (or, assuming it meets its requirements, will achieve) cyber resiliency objectives and sub-objectives (considering the priority weighting established earlier),[51] can provide capabilities, or perform activities supporting achievement of cyber resiliency objectives. An initial assessment can be expressed as high-level qualitative assessments (e.g., on a scale from Very Low to Very High) for the cyber resiliency objectives and subsequently refined based on analysis of the system. An initial assessment can also take the form of a cyber resiliency coverage map, indicating whether and how well the relevant cyber resiliency constructs that were determined to be relevant have been applied.[52] Alternately (if the information is available) or subsequently (based on the analysis described in Section 3.2.3.1 and Section 3.2.3.3),[53] this assessment can be expressed as a cyber resiliency score.

- How well the system's capabilities cover (i.e., have at least one effect on) adversary activities as identified by the threat context.[54] This can be expressed as a threat heat map [DHS18] or a simple threat coverage score. For an initial assessment, coverage can be in terms of attack stages (e.g., Administration, Preparation, Engagement, Presence, Effect, Ongoing Processes [NSA18]) or adversary objectives.[55] Alternately or subsequently, a more nuanced threat coverage score based on the organization's risk management strategy can be computed using the relative priorities of the general types of effects (e.g., increase adversary cost, decrease adversary benefits, increase adversary risk) and of the specific effects (e.g., redirect, preclude, impede, detect, limit, expose) if the risk management strategy establishes such priorities.

- The level of cyber risk in terms of risk to missions or business functions, or other forms of risk (e.g., security, safety). An assessment of this form is possible if the organization has established a risk model, or at least a consequence model, for such forms of risk. An initial assessment will typically rely on an existing security risk assessment [SP 800-30].

- The level of operational resilience (i.e., mission or business function resilience) in terms of functional performance measures under stress. An assessment of this form is possible if the organization has established such performance measures. An initial assessment will typically rely on an existing performance assessment, which describes operational resilience in the face of prior incidents and will be subject to uncertainty since prior incidents may be poor predictors of future ones.

---

[51] See Section 3.2.1.5.

[52] See Section 3.2.1.5.

[53] See Section 3.2.4.3.

[54] See Appendix H.

[55] See Appendix H.2.

Additional evaluation criteria can consider how well the system meets its security requirements or achieves its security objectives and how well the system satisfies its mission or business function requirements. While such evaluations are independent of cyber resiliency analysis, they can form part of the baseline against which potential solutions can be evaluated.

Stakeholder concerns and priorities are used to determine which (or which combination) of these will be used to evaluate alternative solutions. Approaches to assessment (e.g., scoring systems, qualitative assessment scales, metrics and measures of effectiveness) and candidate metrics can be identified for use in subsequent steps. In addition, evaluation criteria can involve assessments of potential costs in terms of financial investment over subsequent life cycle stages (e.g., acquiring, integrating, operating, and maintaining a cyber resiliency solution), opportunity costs (e.g., constraints on future engineering decisions or system uses), and increased programmatic risk (e.g., potential cost risk, schedule impacts, performance impacts).

### 3.2.3  ANALYZE THE SYSTEM

In this step, the system is analyzed in its operational context from two perspectives. First, a mission or business function perspective is applied to identify critical resources (i.e., those resources for which damage or destruction would severely impact operations) and sources of system fragility. Second, an adversarial perspective is applied to identify high value primary and secondary targets of APT actors [OMB M-19-03] and develop representative attack scenarios. Based on this analysis and the results of the previous baseline assessment, opportunities for architectural improvement are identified.

#### 3.2.3.1  *Identify Critical Resources, Sources of Fragility, and Attack Surfaces*

A critical resource can be a resource for which damage (e.g., corruption or reduced availability), denial-of-service, or destruction results in the inability to complete a critical task. In addition, if a resource is used in multiple tasks, it can be highly critical overall even if it is not critical to any of those functions individually—if its damage, denial, or destruction results in a delay for a time-critical mission or business function. Critical resources can be identified using a variety of methods specific to contingency planning, resilience engineering, and mission assurance. These include Criticality Analysis [IR 8179], Mission Impact Analysis (MIA), Business Impact Analysis (BIA) [SP 800-34], Crown Jewels Analysis (CJA), and cyber mission impact analysis (CMIA).

For cyber resiliency analysis, identification of critical resources is based on an understanding of functional flows or of mission or business function threads. A resource can be highly critical at one point in a functional flow or a mission thread and of very low criticality at other points. A functional flow analysis or a mission thread analysis can reveal such time dependencies.

Systems can also be analyzed to identify sources of fragility or brittleness. While identification of single points of failure is a result of the analysis methods mentioned above, network analysis or graph analysis (i.e., analysis of which system elements are connected, how and how tightly the system elements are connected, and whether some sets of system elements are more central) can determine whether the system is fragile (i.e., whether it will break if a stress beyond a well-defined set is applied). Similarly, graphical analysis of the distribution of different types of components can help determine how easily a given stress (e.g., exploitation of a zero-day vulnerability) could propagate.

Finally, the attack surfaces to which cyber resiliency solutions can be applied can be identified. Information about the programmatic, architectural, and operational context determines which attack surfaces are within the scope of potential cyber resiliency solutions. For example, if the programmatic context determines support systems to be in scope, those systems are an attack surface in addition to the interfaces and procedures by which updates are made to the system-of-interest; if the system-of-interest is an enterprise service (architectural context), its interfaces to other services on which it depends as well as to applications which use it are also an attack surface; if the system has users (operational context), the user community is an attack surface.[56]

### 3.2.3.2  Represent the Adversary Perspective

As described in Section 3.2.1, cyber resiliency analysis assumes an architectural, operational, and threat context for the system being analyzed. These contextual assumptions provide the starting point for more detailed analysis of how an adversary could adversely affect the system and thereby cause harm to the mission or business functions it supports, the organization, individuals about whom the system handles PII or whose safety depends on the system, or the environment. The attack scenarios of concern that were identified as part of the threat context serve as a starting point.[57] Depending on the scope of the analysis,[58] these attack scenarios can be complemented by scenarios driven by adversary goals, scenarios targeting critical assets or high value assets,[59] or scenarios that take advantage of sources of fragility.

The adversary perspective—what harm can be done, how easily, and at what cost to the attacker—can be represented in different ways, depending on the stage of the system life cycle and the corresponding level and amount of information about the system architecture, design, implementation, and operations. At a minimum, an attack scenario can identify stages in the attack (e.g., administer, engage, persist, cause effect, and maintain ongoing presence [NSA18]), the adversary objectives or categories of TTPs at each stage (e.g., reconnaissance, exploitation, lateral movement, denial), and the system elements compromised in each stage. Depending on the system life cycle stage, it may be possible to identify individual TTPs (e.g., pass the hash) or examples of specific malware.[60]

Attack scenarios can be represented as part of a model-based engineering effort; using attack tree or attack graph analysis; in terms of fault tree analysis or failure modes, effects, and criticality analysis (FMECA); or based on identification of loss scenarios from System-Theoretic Process Analysis (STPA). Common elements across the attack scenarios (e.g., recurring adversary TTPs) can be identified as a starting point for identifying potential alternative solutions.

Depending on the scope of the cyber resiliency analysis, attack scenarios can be developed which target supporting systems. Such attack scenarios may be the result of a supply chain risk analysis or a cyber resiliency or cybersecurity analysis of systems or organizations responsible for development, integration, testing, or maintenance.

---

[56] See Appendix E.5.1.3.

[57] See Section 3.2.1.4.

[58] As noted in Section 3.2.1.4, a cyber resiliency analysis can be focused on a single attack scenario.

[59] See OMB M-19-03.

[60] However, specific malware should be treated as a motivating example only. Cyber resiliency engineering assumes that unforeseen malware can be used and seeks to mitigate types of adversary actions.

### 3.2.3.3  *Identify and Prioritize Opportunities for Improvement*

The identification of potential areas of improvement typically relies on the interpretation and prioritization of cyber resiliency constructs performed earlier.[61] Potential cyber resiliency techniques or implementation approaches can be identified in system-specific terms, mapped to system elements or architectural layers, and stated as desired improvements to system elements or to the system as a whole. Desired improvements are prioritized based on how and how well they are expected to reduce risks as identified by stakeholders.[62]

In more detail, this task in the analysis process can include the following sub-tasks:

- Identify potentially applicable techniques or approaches. If the set of potentially applicable techniques and approaches has already been identified,[63] it can be narrowed by identifying the set of techniques and approaches related to prioritized objectives using Appendix E, Table E-13 or to potentially applicable structural design principles using Table E-15. (If only the applicable strategic design principles were identified, Table E-14 can be used to identify relevant objectives and Table E-10 can be used to identify relevant structural design principles.) Otherwise, the set of techniques and approaches related to prioritized objectives or structural design principles can be refined by taking the architectural and programmatic context into consideration. The potentially applicable techniques or approaches are described in system-specific terms.

- Identify locations where cyber resiliency solutions could be applied.[64] The set of locations (i.e., sub-systems or components, layers in the architecture, or interfaces between sub-systems or between layers) where cyber resiliency solutions could be applied is determined by the system architecture as constrained by context.[65] For example, the programmatic context may prioritize cyber resiliency solutions that change how existing technologies are used over changes to the system architecture (e.g., replacing specific system elements); the architectural context may restrict possible locations to specific interfaces (e.g., if the system-of-interest is an enterprise service, solutions may be applied to its interfaces with sub-systems or applications which use it or with supporting services, particularly security services); the operational context may constrain the extent to which new user procedures can be made part of the system (e.g., depending on the size of, expected cyber expertise of, or organizational control over the user population).

- Identify desired improvements to system elements or to the system-of-interest as a whole. Statements of desired improvements described in terms specific to the architectural and operational context can be more meaningful to stakeholders than general statements about improved use of a cyber resiliency technique or a more effective application of a cyber resiliency design principle. Potential improvements can be described in terms of improved protection for critical resources, reduced fragility, or the ability to address threats more effectively.

---

[61] See Section 3.2.1.5.
[62] See Section 3.2.1.1.
[63] See Section 3.2.1.5.
[64] See Section 3.1.6.
[65] See Section 3.2.1.

- Prioritize desired improvements using the identified evaluation criteria (e.g., improve the ability of a given system element to continue functioning by enabling that element to be dynamically isolated, decrease adversary benefits by reducing the concentration of highly-sensitive information in a single asset, or reduce mission risks by providing extra resources for high-criticality tasks).

### 3.2.4  DEFINE AND ANALYZE SPECIFIC ALTERNATIVES

In this step, specific ways to make desired improvements—architectural changes, ways to implement cyber resiliency techniques in the context of the existing architecture, ways to use existing system capabilities more effectively to improve resilience—are identified and analyzed in terms of potential effectiveness. These specific alternatives form a solution set, which will be used in the final step to construct potential courses of action.

#### 3.2.4.1  Define Potential Technical and Procedural Solutions

Potential applications of cyber resiliency techniques and implementation approaches to the system-of-interest in its environment of operations in order to provide one or more desired improvements are identified.[66] These applications—potential solutions to the problem of improving mission or operational resilience by improving cyber resiliency—can be purely technical, purely procedural, or combinations of the two.

Potential solutions can incorporate or build on investments from other disciplines.[67] The set of technologies and products that are available at some level of maturity[68] for incorporation into the system depends on the type of the system.[69] The degree to which relatively immature technologies can be considered depends on the programmatic risk management strategy.[70]

The level of detail with which a potential solution is described depends on how specifically the context was described in the first step.[71] In particular, if the architectural and operational contexts were described in general terms, potential solutions will necessarily be described at a high-level. On the other hand, if the cyber resiliency analysis is being performed for an existing system, a potential solution can be described in terms of specific technologies or products to be integrated into the system, where in the system those technologies will be used, how they will interface with other system elements, configuration settings or ranges of settings for products, and processes or procedures to make effective use of existing or newly acquired technologies.

The description of a potential solution can include identification of the gaps it is expected to address,[72] the threats (e.g., attack scenarios, adversary objectives or categories of TTPs, or adversary actions) it is intended to address,[73] or reduced exposure of critical resources, sources

---

[66] See Section 3.2.3.3.

[67] See Section 3.1.5.

[68] See Section 3.1.8.

[69] See Section 3.1.3.

[70] See Section 2.3 and Section 3.2.1.1.

[71] See Section 3.2.1.

[72] See Section 3.2.2.2.

[73] See Section 3.2.3.2.

of fragility, or attack surfaces to threats.[74] These different elements of a potential solution's description can be used to evaluate the solution.[75]

### 3.2.4.2  Define Potential Solutions for Supporting Systems and Processes

If the programmatic and operational contexts support improvements to supporting systems and processes, potential applications of cyber resiliency techniques and approaches to these are also identified. Such applications can include modifications to contracting to ensure that controlled unclassified information (CUI) or other sensitive information is protected effectively [SP 800-171], improvements to supply chain risk management (SCRM) as determined by SCRM analysis [SP 800-161], and restrictions on or re-architecting of system development, testing, or maintenance environments to improve the cyber resiliency of those environments.

### 3.2.4.3  Analyze Potential Solutions with Respect to Criteria

Potential solutions can be analyzed with respect to one or more criteria.[76] Evaluation can employ qualitative or semi-quantitative assessments (using subject matter expert [SME] judgments) or quantitative metrics (evaluated in a model-based environment, laboratory, cyber range, or test environment; metrics to support analysis of alternatives are typically not evaluated in an operational environment). Potential solutions can be analyzed to determine, for example:

- How much the solution could improve the ability of the system to achieve its (priority-weighted) cyber resiliency objectives or sub-objectives. This can be expressed as a change in a cyber resiliency score or as a coverage map for the relevant cyber resiliency constructs. Alternately or in support of scoring, performance metrics for activities or capabilities related to cyber resiliency sub-objectives can be evaluated.

- How well the system, with the solution applied, addresses adversary activities or attack scenarios as identified by the threat context. As noted in Section 3.2.2.3, this can take the form of a threat heat map or a threat coverage score using a taxonomy of adversary activities (e.g., [NSA18]). It can also take the form of an adversary return on investment (ROI) score or a more nuanced threat coverage score.[77] Alternately or in support of scoring, performance metrics for specific types of effects on adversary actions can be defined and evaluated before and after the solution is applied (e.g., length of time it takes an adversary to move laterally across a system or an enclave).

- How much the solution could improve the system's coverage of adversary TTPs using capabilities defined in [NIST CSF]. This can be expressed as a change in a score or using a threat heat map [DHS18].

- How much the solution could decrease the level of cyber risk or a specific component of risk (e.g., level of consequence). As discussed in Appendix H,[78] effects on adversary activities have associated effects on risk.

---

[74] See Section 3.2.3.1.
[75] See Section 3.2.4.3.
[76] See Section 3.2.2.3.
[77] See Appendix H.
[78] See Table H-1.

- How much the solution could improve the level of operational resilience in terms of functional performance measures under stress. As discussed in Appendix E.5.1, some strategic design principles for cyber resiliency are closely related to design principles for Resilience Engineering. Thus, a solution that applies one or more of those design principles can be expected to improve resilience against non-adversarial as well as adversarial threats.

- Whether and how much the solution could improve the system's ability to meet its security requirements. Evaluation with respect to this criterion can involve qualitative assessments by Subject Matter Experts (SME), an explanatory description, a list of previously unmet requirements which the solution can help meet, or specific security performance metrics which can be evaluated before and after the solution is applied.

- Whether and how much the solution could improve the system's ability to meet its mission or business function performance requirements. Similar to a security requirements criterion, evaluation with respect to this criterion can involve an explanatory description, qualitative assessments by SMEs, a list of previously unmet requirements which the solution can help meet, or specific functional performance metrics which can be evaluated before and after the solution is applied.

In addition, the potential costs of a solution can be identified or assessed.

The product of this step is a list of alternative solutions, each characterized (e.g., via a coverage map, via a description) or assessed with respect to the identified criteria.

### 3.2.5  DEVELOP RECOMMENDATIONS

Unless the scope of the cyber resiliency analysis is narrow, the number and variety of potential solutions may be large. Sets of potential solutions which could be implemented at the same time can be constructed and analyzed to ensure compatibility, identify possible synergies, and determine whether specific solutions should be applied sequentially rather than simultaneously. In addition, programmatic and operational risks associated with alternative solutions can be identified. The result of this step is a recommended plan of action.

#### 3.2.5.1  Identify and Analyze Alternatives

One or more alternatives—sets of potential solutions which could be implemented at the same time or sequentially (e.g., in successive spirals)—can be identified using either total cost or a requirement for a consistent level of maturity[79] (e.g., requiring all technical solutions in the set to be available as commercial products by a specific milestone) to bound each set. Where possible, a set of potential solutions should be defined to take advantage of synergies (as discussed in Section 3.1.4 and identified in Appendix E, Table E-3); at a minimum, each set should be analyzed to ensure that there are no internal conflicts. If the solutions in a set are to be implemented sequentially, functional dependencies among those solutions should be identified. In addition, functional dependencies on other system elements (particularly those involving investments due to other disciplines)[80] should be identified since changes in system elements can be made for a variety of reasons.

---

[79] See Section 3.1.8.

[80] See Section 3.1.5.

### 3.2.5.2  Assess Alternatives

Each alternative can be assessed or characterized in terms of the evaluation criteria.[81] To support assessments, the adversarial analysis[82] can be revisited for each alternative. Note that, due to synergies or other interactions between cyber resiliency techniques, changes in scores, heat maps, or coverage maps must be determined by analysis rather than by simply combining previously determined values.

In addition, each alternative should be analyzed to determine whether it makes new attack scenarios (or non-adversarial threat scenarios) possible. If it does, those scenarios should be analyzed to determine whether changes should be made to the alternative.

Each alternative can also be described in terms of the issues it resolves, the gaps it fills,[83] or in terms of improved protection for critical resources, reduced fragility, or the ability to address threats more effectively. Finally, each alternative can be assessed or described in terms of its effects on programmatic risk (e.g., total costs, changes to schedule risk, changes to technical or performance risk) or other risks of concern to stakeholders. If an alternative diverges from the risk management strategies of one or more stakeholders, this divergence should be noted so that, if the alternative is in fact recommended, a compensating risk management approach can be made part of the recommendation.

### 3.2.5.3  Recommend a Plan of Action

A recommended plan of action resulting from a cyber resiliency analysis can take the form of a set of selected alternatives to be implemented in successive phases. For each phase, the costs, benefits, and risk management approaches can be identified, accompanied by identification of circumstances which could indicate the need to revisit the recommendations. However, as noted in Section 3.1, a cyber resiliency analysis can be narrowly focused. If this is the case, the recommendations resulting from the analysis will take a form directed by the focus of the analysis.

---

[81] See Section 3.2.4.3.

[82] See Section 3.2.3.2.

[83] See Section 3.2.2.2.

APPENDIX A

# REFERENCES

LAWS, POLICIES, DIRECTIVES, REGULATIONS, STANDARDS, AND GUIDELINES

**LAWS AND EXECUTIVE ORDERS**

Freedom of Information Act (FOIA), 5 U.S.C. § 552, As Amended By Public

Executive Order 13800 (2017), Strengthening the Cybersecurity of Federal Networks and Critical Infrastructure. (The White House, Washington, DC), DCPD-201700327, May 11, 2017.
https://www.govinfo.gov/app/details/DCPD-201700327/

**REGULATIONS, DIRECTIVES, INSTRUCTIONS, PLANS, AND POLICIES**

Committee on National Security Systems (2014) Security Categorization and Control Selection for National Security Systems. (National Security Agency, Fort George G. Meade, MD), CNSS Instruction 1253. Available at
https://www.cnss.gov/CNSS/openDoc.cfm?HSjOTWr2HMkv0zk2nLvB8A==

Committee on National Security Systems (2015) Committee on National Security Systems (CNSS) Glossary. (National Security Agency, Fort George G. Meade, MD), CNSS Instruction 4009. Available at
https://www.cnss.gov/CNSS/openDoc.cfm?pR8Egv4JDxhquaRPbbdq8A==

Department of Defense (DoD) Directive 8140.01, *Cyberspace Workforce Management*, August 2015. Available at
https://www.esd.whs.mil/Portals/54/Documents/DD/issuances/dodd/814001_2015_dodd.pdf

[HSPD23]   National Security Presidential Directive/NSPD-54 Homeland Security Presidential Directive/HSPD-23, Cybersecurity Policy, January 2008.

[OMB M-19-03]   Office of Management and Budget (2018) Management of High Value Assets. (The White House, Washington, DC), OMB Memorandum M-19-03, December 2018. Available at
https://www.whitehouse.gov/wp-content/uploads/2018/12/M-19-03.pdf

Presidential Policy Directive (PPD) 21, *Critical Infrastructure Security and Resilience,* February 2013. Available at https://www.dhs.gov/sites/default/files/publications/PPD-21-Critical-Infrastructure-and-Resilience-508.pdf

**STANDARDS, GUIDELINES, AND REPORTS**

International Organization for Standardization/International

International Organization for Standardization/International

National Institute of Standards and Technology (2004) Standards for Security Categorization of Federal Information and Information Systems. (U.S. Department of Commerce, Washington, DC), Federal Information Processing Standards Publication (FIPS) 199. https://doi.org/10.6028/NIST.FIPS.199

[SP 800-18]  Swanson MA, Hash J, Bowen P (2006) Guide for Developing Security Plans for Federal Information Systems. (National Institute of Standards and Technology, Gaithersburg, MD), NIST Special Publication (SP) 800-18, Rev.

Joint Task Force Transformation Initiative (2012) Guide for Conducting Risk

Swanson MA, Bowen P, Phillips AW, Gallup D, Lynes D (2010) Contingency Planning Guide for Federal Information Systems. (National Institute of Standards and Technology, Gaithersburg, MD), NIST Special Publication (SP) 800-34, Rev. 1, Includes updates as of November 11, 2010. https://doi.org/10.6028/NIST.SP.800-34r1

Joint Task Force (2018) Risk Management Framework for Information

Joint Task Force Transformation Initiative (2011) Managing Information Security Risk: Organization, Mission, and Information System View. (National Institute of Standards and Technology, Gaithersburg, MD), NIST Special Publication (SP) 800-39.
https://doi.org/10.6028/NIST.SP.800-39

[SP 800-53]    Joint Task Force Transformation Initiative (2019) Security and Privacy Controls for Information Systems and Organizations. (National Institute of Standards and Technology, Gaithersburg, MD), NIST Special Publication (SP) 800-53, Rev. 5.

Stouffer KA, Lightman S, Pillitteri VY, Abrams M, Hahn A (2015) Guide to

Singhal A, Winograd T, Scarfone KA (2007) Guide to Secure Web Services.

Chandramouli R (2016) Secure Virtual Network Configuration for Virtual

Ross RS, Oren JC, McEvilley M (2016) Systems Security Engineering:

Boyens JM, Paulsen C, Moorthy R, Bartol N (2015) Supply Chain Risk

Ross RS, Dempsey KL, Viscuso P, Riddle M, Guissanie G (2016) Protecting Controlled Unclassified Information in Nonfederal Systems and Organizations. (National Institute of Standards and Technology, Gaithersburg, MD), NIST Special Publication (SP) 800-171, Rev. 1, Includes updates as of June 7, 2018.
https://doi.org/10.6028/NIST.SP.800-171r1

Voas, J (2016) Networks of 'Things'. (National Institute of Standards and

Rose S, Borchert O, Mitchell S, Connelly S (2019) Zero Trust Architecture.

Burns MJ, Greer C, Griffor ER, Wollman DA (2017) Framework for Cyber-

Brooks S, Garcia M, Lefkovitz N, Lightman S, Nadeau E (2017) An

Paulsen C, Boyens JM, Bartol N, Winkler K (2018) Criticality Analysis Process

Yaga DJ, Mell PM, Roby N, Scarfone KA (2018) Blockchain Technology

Fagan M, Megas KN, Scarfone KA, Smith M (2019) Core Cybersecurity

Department of Defense (2012) *MIL-STD-882E – Standard Practice: System
Safety* (U.S. Department of Defense, Washington, DC). Available at
https://www.dau.edu/cop/esoh/Pages/Topics/System%20Safety%20Methodology.
aspx

## MISCELLANEOUS PUBLICATIONS AND WEBSITES

[Alexander17]    Alexander O (2017) *ICS ATT&CK* [presentation]. Available at
https://www.acsac.org/2017/workshops/icss/Otis-Alexander-ICS,%20Adversarial%20Tactics,%20Techniques.pdf

Assante MJ, Lee RM (2015) *The Industrial Control System Cyber Kill Chain*. Available at
https://www.sans.org/reading-room/whitepapers/ICS/industrial-control-system-cyber-kill-chain-36297

Avižienis A, Laprie JC, Randell B (2004) Dependability and Its Threats: A Taxonomy. *Building the Information Society, IFIP International Federation for Information Processing*, ed Jacquart R (Springer, Boston, MA), Vol. 156, pp 91-120.
https://doi.org/10.1007/978-1-4020-8157-6_13

Bodeau D, Graubart R (2011) Cyber Resiliency Engineering Framework, Version 1.0.
https://www.mitre.org/sites/default/files/pdf/11_4436.pdf

Bodeau D, Graubart R, Heinbockel W, Laderman E (2015) Cyber Resiliency

Bodeau D, Graubart R (2016) Cyber Prep 2.0: Motivating Organizational

Bodeau D, Graubart R (2017) Cyber Resiliency Design Principles: Selective

Bodeau DJ, McCollum CD, Fox DB (2018) Cyber Threat Modeling: Survey,

Bodeau D, Graubart R, McQuaid R, Woodill J (2018) Cyber Resiliency Metrics, Measures of Effectiveness, and Scoring: Enabling Systems Engineers and Program Managers to Select the Most Useful Assessment Methods. (The MITRE Corporation, Bedford, MA), MITRE Technical Report MTR-180314. Available at
https://www.mitre.org/sites/default/files/publications/pr-18-2579-cyber-resiliency-metrics-measures-of-effectiveness-and-scoring.pdf

Bodeau D, Graubart R, Laderman E (2019) Relationships Between Cyber Resiliency Constructs and Cyber Survivability Attributes. (The MITRE Corporation, Bedford, MA), MITRE Product MP-190668. Available at https://www.mitre.org/sites/default/files/pdf/CR-Cyber-Survivability.pdf

Styczynski J, Beach-Westmoreland N, Stables S (2016) When the Lights

Brtis J (2016) How to Think about Resilience in a DoD Context. (The MITRE

Cyber-Physical Systems Public Working Group (2016) Framework for Cyber-

Marron J, Gopstein A, Bartol N. Feldman V (2019) Cybersecurity Framework

Department of Homeland Security Risk Steering Committee (2010) DHS Risk

Department of Homeland Security (2018) .gov Cybersecurity Architecture Review (.govCAR) Methodology. (U.S. Department of Homeland Security, Washington, DC).

Department of Defense, "Department of Defense Cybersecurity Test and Evaluation Guidebook, Version 2.0," April 2018. Available at https://www.dau.edu/cop/test/DAU%20Sponsored%20Documents/CSTE%20Guide book%202.0_FINAL%20(25APR2018).pdf

Department of Defense (2016) Mission Assurance (U.S. Department of Defense, Washington, DC), DoD Directive (DODD) 3020.40. Available at https://www.esd.whs.mil/Portals/54/Documents/DD/issuances/dodd/302040_dod d_2016.pdf

Dragos, Inc. (2017) CrashOverride: Analysis of the Threat to Electric Grid Operations. Available at https://dragos.com/wp-content/uploads/CrashOverride-01.pdf

Defense Science Board (2013) Resilient Military Systems and the Advanced Cyber Threat. (U.S. Department of Defense, Washington, DC). Available at https://www.acq.osd.mil/dsb/reports/2010s/ResilientMilitarySystemsCyberThreat. pdf

Peter Fairley (2019) Unplugging From Digital Controls to Safeguard Power

Government Accountability Office (2018) Weapon Systems Cybersecurity.

Heckman KE, Stech FJ, Thomas RK, Schmoder B, Tsow AW (2015) Cyber Denial, Deception and Counter Deception: A Framework for Supporting Active Cyber Defense, _Advances in Information Security_ (Springer, Cham, Switzerland), Vol. 63.

Höller A, Rauter T, Iber J, Kreiner C (2015) Towards Dynamic Software Diversity for Resilient Redundant Embedded Systems. _Proceedings of Software Engineering for Resilient Systems: 7th International Workshop, SERENE 2015_ (Springer, Paris, France), pp 16-30. https://doi.org/10.1007/978-3-319-23129-7_2

[Hutchins11]    Hutchins EM, Cloppert MJ, Amin RM (2011) Intelligence-driven computer network defense informed by analysis of adversary campaigns and intrusion kill chains. _Leading Issues in Information Warfare & Security Research_, ed Ryan J (Academic Publishing International, Reading, UK), Vol. 1, pp 78-104.

Institute of Electrical and Electronics Engineers (1990) _IEEE Standard Computer Dictionary: A Compilation of IEEE Standard Computer Glossaries_, (IEEE, New York, NY).

Institute of Electrical and Electronics Engineers, Association for Computing Machinery (2017) _Enterprise IT Body of Knowledge – Glossary. Enterprise IT Body of Knowledge_. Available at http://eitbokwiki.org/Glossary#eit

International Council for Systems Engineering (2011) *Resilient Systems Working Group Charter*. (INCOSE, San Diego, CA).

[INCOSE14]    International Council on Systems Engineering (2015) *System Engineering Handbook—A Guide for System Engineering Life Cycle Processes and Activities*. (John Wiley & Sons, Hoboken, NJ), 4th Ed.

Jackson S, Ferris T (2013) Resilience Principles for Engineered Systems.

Jajodia S, Ghosh AK, Subrahmanian VS, Swarup V, Wang C, Wang XS (eds.) (2013) *Moving Target Defense II: Application of Game Theory and Adversarial Modeling* (Springer-Verlag, New York, NY), Advances in Information Security, Vol. 100, pp 204.

Joint Chiefs of Staff (2017) Cyber Survivability Endorsement Implementation Guide (CSEIG). (U.S. Department of Defense, Washington, DC), v1.01.

Leveson NG (2012) *Engineering a Safer World: Systems Thinking Applied to Safety* (MIT Press, Cambridge, MA), pp 560.

[Madni07]    Madni AM (2007) Designing for Resilience. *ISTI Lecture Notes on Advanced Topics in Systems Engineering* (University of California at Los Angeles (UCLA), Los Angeles, CA).

Madni AM, Jackson S (2009) Towards a Conceptual Framework for

The MITRE Corporation (2019) *Common Attack Pattern Enumeration and*

The MITRE Corporation (2018) *Adversarial Tactics, Techniques & Common Knowledge (ATT&CK)*. Available at
https://attack.mitre.org

Musman S, Agbolosu-Amison S, Crowther K (2019) Metrics Based on the

Neumann P (2004) Principled Assuredly Trustworthy Composable

National Highway Traffic Safety Administration, U.S. Department of

National Infrastructure Advisory Council (NIAC) (2010) A Framework for

National Institute of Standards and Technology (2018) Framework for

National Institute of Standards and Technology (2019) *Computer Security*

National Security Agency (2018) NSA/CSS Technical Cyber Threat

Office of the Director of National Intelligence (2017) *Cyber Threat*

Okhravi H, Rabe MA, Mayberry TJ, Leonard WG, Hobson TR, Bigelow D,

Pitcher S (2019) New DoD Approaches on the Cyber Survivability of
Weapon Systems [presentation]. Available at
https://www.itea.org/wp-content/uploads/2019/03/Pitcher-Steve.pdf

Fraade-Blanar L, Blumenthal MS, Anderson JM, Kalra N, (2018) Measuring


Ricci N, Rhodes DH, Ross AM (2014) Evolvability-Related Options in Military


SAE International (2016) *SAE J3061_201601 – Cybersecurity Guidebook for Cyber-Physical Vehicle Systems* (SAE International, Warrendale, PA).

[SAEJ3101]     SAE International (2012) *SAE J3101 – Requirements for Hardware-Protected Security for Ground Vehicle Applications (Work-in-Progress)* (SAE International, Warrendale, PA).

Stamp JE, Veitch CK, Henry JM, Hart DH, Richardson BT (2015) Microgrid


SANS Industrial Control Systems, Electricity Information Sharing and


SANS Industrial Control Systems, Electricity Information Sharing and Analysis Center (E-ISAC) (2017) ICS Defense Use Case No. 6: Modular ICS Malware. (E-ISAC, Washington, DC). Available at https://ics.sans.org/media/E-ISAC_SANS_Ukraine_DUC_6.pdf

[SEBok]        BKCASE Editorial Board (2019) The Guide to the Systems Engineering Body of Knowledge (SEBoK), v. 2.0, ed Cloutier RJ (The Trustees of the Stevens Institute of Technology, Hoboken, NJ). BKCASE is managed and maintained by the Stevens Institute of Technology Systems Engineering Research Center, the International Council on Systems Engineering, and the Institute of Electrical and Electronics Engineers Computer Society. Available at http://www.sebokwiki.org/wiki/Guide_to_the_Systems_Engineering_Body_of_Knowledge_(SEBoK)

Sheard S (2008) A Framework for System Resilience Discussions. *INCOSE*

Shetty S, Yuchi X, Song M (2016) *Moving Target Defense for Distributed*

Steiger S (2018) Countering Ukrainian Power Grid Events Using Cyber

Sterbenz J, Hutchinson D (2006) ResiliNets: Multilevel Resilient and Survivable Networking Initiative. Available at https://www.ittc.ku.edu/resilinets/

Sterbenz JPG, Hutchison D, Çetinkaya EK, Jabbar A, Rohrer JP, Schöller M, Smith P (2010) Resilience and survivability in communication networks: Strategies, principles, and survey of disciplines. *Computer Networks* 54:1245-1265. Available at http://www.ittc.ku.edu/resilinets/papers/Sterbenz-Hutchison-Cetinkaya-Jabbar-Rohrer-Scholler-Smith-2010.pdf

Sterbenz JP, Hutchison D, Çetinkaya EK, Jabbar A, Rohrer JP, Schöller M,

Strom BE, Battaglia JA, Kemmerer MS, Kupersanin W, Miller DP, Wampler C,

Swearingen M, Brunasso S, Weiss J, and Huber D (2013) What You Need to Know (and Don't) About the AURORA Vulnerability, Power Magazine. Available at https://www.powermag.com/what-you-need-to-know-and-dont-about-the-aurora-vulnerability

Zimmerman C (2014) Ten Strategies of a World-Class Cybersecurity Operations Center. (The MITRE Corporation, Bedford, MA). Available at http://www.mitre.org/sites/default/files/publications/pr-13-1028-mitre-10-strategies-cyber-ops-center.pdf

Ware W (1970) Security Controls for Computer Systems: Report of the Defense Science Board Task Force on Computer Security. (The Rand Corporation, Santa Monica, CA). Available at https://csrc.nist.gov/csrc/media/publications/conference-paper/1998/10/08/proceedings-of-the-21st-nissc-1998/documents/early-cs-papers/ware70.pdf

## APPENDIX B

# GLOSSARY

COMMON TERMS AND DEFINITIONS

Appendix B provides definitions for terminology used in NIST Special Publication 800-160, Volume 2. Sources for terms used in this publication are cited as applicable. Where no citation is noted, the source of the definition is Special Publication 800-160, Volume 2.

| | |
|---|---|
| **adaptability** | The property of an architecture, design, and implementation which can accommodate changes to the threat model, mission or business functions, systems, and technologies without major programmatic impacts. |
| | See *advanced persistent threat*. |
| | *Note 1:* The phrase "advanced cyber threat" implies either that an adversary executes a cyber-attack or that an adversary subverts the supply chain in order to compromise cyber resources. |
| **advanced persistent threat** [SP 800-39] | An adversary that possesses sophisticated levels of expertise and significant resources which allow it to create opportunities to achieve its objectives by using multiple attack vectors including, for example, cyber, physical, and deception. These objectives typically include establishing and extending footholds within the IT infrastructure of the targeted organizations for purposes of exfiltrating information, undermining or impeding critical aspects of a mission, program, or organization, or positioning itself to carry out these objectives in the future. The advanced persistent threat pursues its objectives repeatedly over an extended period; adapts to defenders' efforts to resist it; and is determined to maintain the level of interaction needed to execute its objectives. |
| | *Note 1:* While some sources define APT (or advanced cyber threat) as an adversary at Tier V or Tier VI in the threat model in [DSB13]—in particular, to be a state actor—the definition used here includes criminal actors. |
| | *Note 2:* For brevity, "the APT" refers to any adversary with the characteristics described above or to the set of all such adversaries; "an APT actor" refers to a representative member of that set. |
| | *Note 3:* The APT may establish its foothold by subverting the supply chain in order to compromise cyber resources. Thus, the APT may be able to achieve its objectives without executing a cyber-attack against the organization's systems (e.g., by inserting a logic bomb or time). |
| | *Note 4:* The term "APT" does not include the insider threat. However, if an APT actor establishes and extends its foothold by masquerading as a legitimate system user and taking advantage of that user's authorized access privileges, it may be indistinguishable from an insider threat. |

| | |
|---|---|
| **adversity** | Adverse conditions, stresses, attacks, or compromises. |
| | *Note 1:* The definition of adversity is consistent with the use of the term in [SP 800-160 v1] as disruptions, hazards, and threats. |
| | *Note 2:* Adversity in the context of the definition of cyber resiliency specifically includes, but is not limited to, cyber-attacks. |
| **agility** | The property of a system or an infrastructure which can be reconfigured, in which resources can be reallocated, and in which components can be reused or repurposed, so that cyber defenders can define, select, and tailor cyber courses of action for a broad range of disruptions or malicious cyber activities. |
| **approach** | See *cyber resiliency implementation approach*. |
| **asset**<br>[SP 800-160 v1] | An item of value to stakeholders. An asset may be tangible (e.g., a physical item such as hardware, firmware, computing platform, network device, or other technology component) or intangible (e.g., humans, data, information, software, capability, function, service, trademark, copyright, patent, intellectual property, image, or reputation). The value of an asset is determined by stakeholders in consideration of loss concerns across the entire system life cycle. Such concerns include but are not limited to business or mission concerns. |
| **attack surface**<br>[GAO18] (adapted, based on SP 800-53) | The set of points on the boundary of a system, a system element, or an environment where an attacker can try to enter, cause an effect on, or extract data from. |
| | *Note*: An attack surface can be *reduced* by removing points on the boundary (reducing the *extent* of the attack surface, e.g., by reducing the amount of code running) or reducing the *exposure* of some points to an attacker (e.g., by placing inessential functions on a different system element than essential functions, by layering defenses, by reducing the period of exposure); *changed* by changing the set of points on the boundary (e.g., by moving some points), by changing the exposure of some points to an attacker (e.g., by adding logic to check data or commands), or by changing the properties of some points (e.g., by applying principles of least privilege and least functionality); or *disrupted* by making changes unpredictably or by reducing its extent or exposure for limited time periods (e.g., by temporarily isolating components). |
| **blockchain**<br>[IR 8202] | A distributed digital ledger of cryptographically signed transactions that are grouped into blocks. Each block is cryptographically linked to the previous one (making it tamper evident) after validation and undergoing a consensus decision. As new blocks are added, older blocks become more difficult to modify (creating tamper resistance). New blocks are replicated across copies of the ledger within the network, and any conflicts are resolved automatically using established rules. |
| **control**<br>[ISACA] | The means of managing risk, including policies, procedures, guidelines, practices, or organizational structures, which can be of an administrative, technical, management, or legal nature. |

| | |
|---|---|
| **criticality**<br>[SP 800-160 v1] | An attribute assigned to an asset that reflects its relative importance or necessity in achieving or contributing to the achievement of stated goals. |
| **cyber incident**<br>[CNSSI 4009] | Actions taken through the use of an information system or network that result in an actual or potentially adverse effect on an information system, network, and/or the information residing therein. |
| **cyber resiliency** | The ability to anticipate, withstand, recover from, and adapt to adverse conditions, stresses, attacks, or compromises on systems that use or are enabled by cyber resources. |
| **cyber resiliency concept** | A concept related to the problem domain and/or solution set for cyber resiliency. Cyber resiliency concepts are represented in cyber resiliency risk models as well as by cyber resiliency constructs. |
| **cyber resiliency construct** | Element of the cyber resiliency engineering framework (i.e., a goal, objective, technique, implementation approach, or design principle). Additional constructs (e.g., sub-objectives or methods, capabilities or activities) may be used in some modeling and analytic practices. |
| **cyber resiliency control** | A control as defined in [SP 800-53] which requires the use of one or more cyber resiliency techniques or approaches, or which is intended to achieve one or more cyber resiliency objectives. |
| **cyber resiliency design principle** | A guideline for how to select and apply cyber resiliency techniques, approaches, and solutions when making architectural or design decisions. |
| **cyber resiliency engineering practice** | A method, process, modeling technique, or analytical technique used to identify and analyze cyber resiliency solutions. |
| **cyber resiliency implementation approach** | A subset of the technologies and processes of a cyber resiliency technique, defined by how the capabilities are implemented or how the intended consequences are achieved. |
| **cyber resiliency objective** | A statement of what must be performed (e.g., what a system must achieve in its operational environment and throughout its life cycle) to meet stakeholder needs for mission assurance and resilient security. |
| **cyber resiliency risk model** | A risk model which explicitly represents the threats and classes of harm considered by those concerned with cyber resiliency. (This accommodates other stakeholders, in addition to systems security engineers.)<br><br>*Note:* A cyber resiliency risk model emphasizes (but is not limited to) the APT as a threat source, and emphasizes the effects on missions and organizations of malicious cyber activities, as well as harm to systems that include cyber resources. |

| | |
|---|---|
| **cyber resiliency solution** | A combination of technologies, architectural decisions, systems engineering processes, and operational processes, procedures, or practices which solves a problem in the cyber resiliency domain. A cyber resiliency solution provides enough cyber resiliency to meet stakeholder needs and to reduce risks to mission or business capabilities in the presence of advanced persistent threats. |
| **cyber resiliency sub-objective** | |
| **cyber resource** | An information resource which creates, stores, processes, manages, transmits, or disposes of information in electronic form and which can be accessed via a network or using networking methods. |
| | *Note:* A cyber resource is an element of a system that exists in or intermittently includes a presence in cyberspace. |
| **cyber risk** | The risk of depending on cyber resources, i.e., the risk of depending on a system or system elements which exist in or intermittently have a presence in cyberspace. |
| | *Note:* Cyber risk overlaps with information security risk [SP 800-30, CNSSI 4009], and includes risks due to cyber incidents, cybersecurity events, and cyberspace attacks. |
| **cybersecurity** [NIST CSF] | The process of protecting information by preventing, detecting, and responding to attacks. |
| [CNSSI 4009] | Prevention of damage to, protection of, and restoration of computers, electronic communications systems, electronic communications services, wire communication, and electronic communication, including information contained therein, to ensure its availability, integrity, authentication, confidentiality, and nonrepudiation. |
| **cybersecurity event** [NIST CSF] | A cybersecurity change that may have an impact on organizational operations (including mission, capabilities, or reputation). |
| **cyberspace** [CNSSI 4009, HSPD23] | The interdependent network of information technology infrastructures, and includes the Internet, telecommunications networks, computer systems, and embedded processors and controllers in critical industries. |

| | |
|---|---|
| **cyberspace attack**<br>[CNSSI 4009] | Cyberspace actions that create various direct denial effects (i.e. degradation, disruption, or destruction) and manipulation that leads to denial that is hidden or that manifests in the physical domains. |
| **damage** | Harm caused to something in such a way as to reduce or destroy its value, usefulness, or normal function.<br><br>*Note 1:* From the perspective of cyber resiliency, damage can be to the organization (e.g., loss of reputation, increased existential risk); to missions or business functions (e.g., decrease in the ability to complete the current mission and to accomplish future missions); to security (e.g., decrease in the ability to achieve the security objectives of confidentiality, integrity, and availability; decrease in the ability to prevent, detect, and respond to cyber incidents); to the system (e.g., decrease in the ability to meet system requirements, unauthorized use of system resources); or to specific system elements (e.g., physical destruction; corruption, modification, or fabrication of information).<br><br>*Note 2*: Damage includes, and in some circumstances can be identified with, asset loss as discussed in [SP 800-160 v1]. |
| **enabling system**<br>[ISO 15288] | A system that provides support to the life cycle activities associated with the system-of-interest. Enabling systems are not necessarily delivered with the system-of-interest and do not necessarily exist in the operational environment of the system-of-interest. |
| **enterprise information technology**<br>[IEEE17] | The application of computers and telecommunications equipment to store, retrieve, transmit, and manipulate data, in the context of a business or other enterprise. |
| **fault tolerant**<br>[SP 800-82] | Of a system, having the built-in capability to provide continued, correct execution of its assigned function in the presence of a hardware and/or software fault. |
| **federation**<br>[SP 800-95] | A collection of realms (domains) that have established trust among themselves. The level of trust may vary, but typically includes authentication and may include authorization. |
| **information resources**<br>[OMB A-130] | Information and related resources, such as personnel, equipment, funds, and information technology. |

| | |
|---|---|
| **information security**<br>[OMB A-130] | The protection of information and information systems from unauthorized access, use, disclosure, disruption, modification, or destruction in order to provide confidentiality, integrity, and availability. |
| **information system**<br>[OMB A-130] | A discrete set of information resources organized for the collection, processing, maintenance, use, sharing, dissemination, or disposition of information.<br><br>*Note:* Information systems also include specialized systems such as industrial/process controls systems, telephone switching and private branch exchange (PBX) systems, and environmental control systems. |
| **information technology**<br>[OMB A-130] | Any services, equipment, or interconnected system(s) or subsystem(s) of equipment, that are used in the automatic acquisition, storage, analysis, evaluation, manipulation, management, movement, control, display, switching, interchange, transmission, or reception of data or information by the agency. For purposes of this definition, such services or equipment if used by the agency directly or is used by a contractor under a contract with the agency that requires its use; or to a significant extent, its use in the performance of a service or the furnishing of a product. Information technology includes computers, ancillary equipment (including imaging peripherals, input, output, and storage devices necessary for security and surveillance), peripheral equipment designed to be controlled by the central processing unit of a computer, software, firmware and similar procedures, services (including cloud computing and help-desk services or other professional services which support any point of the life cycle of the equipment or service), and related resources. Information technology does not include any equipment that is acquired by a contractor incidental to a contract which does not require its use. |
| **mission assurance**<br>[DOD16, adapted] | A process to protect or ensure the continued function and resilience of capabilities and assets, including personnel, equipment, facilities, networks, information and information systems, infrastructure, and supply chains, critical to the execution of organizational mission-essential functions in any operating environment or condition.<br><br>*Note:* This definition differs from the DoD definition by replacing "DoD" with "organizational." |
| **non-adversarial threat** | A threat associated with accident or human error, structural failure, or environmental causes.<br><br>*Note:* See Appendix D of [SP 800-30]. |

| **other system**<br>[ISO 15288] | A system that the system-of-interest interacts with in the operational environment. These systems may provide services to the system-of-interest (i.e., the system-of-interest is dependent on the other systems) or be the beneficiaries of services provided by the system-of-interest (i.e., other systems are dependent on the system-of-interest). |
|---|---|
| **protection**<br>[SP 800-160 v1] | In the context of systems security engineering, a control objective that applies across all types of asset types and the corresponding consequences of loss. A system protection capability is a system control objective and a system design problem. The solution to the problem is optimized through a balanced proactive strategy and a reactive strategy that is not limited to *prevention*. The strategy also encompasses avoiding asset loss and consequences; detecting asset loss and consequences; minimizing (i.e., limiting, containing, restricting) asset loss and consequences; responding to asset loss and consequences; recovering from asset loss and consequences; and forecasting or predicting asset loss and consequences. |
| **quality property**<br>[SP 800-160 v1] | An emergent property of a system that includes, for example: safety, security, maintainability, resilience, reliability, availability, agility, and survivability. This property is also referred to as a *systemic property* across many engineering domains. |
| **reliability**<br>[IEEE90] | The ability of a system or component to function under stated conditions for a specified period of time. |
| **resilience**<br>[OMB A-130] | The ability to prepare for and adapt to changing conditions and withstand and recover rapidly from disruption. Resilience includes the ability to withstand and recover from deliberate attacks, accidents, or naturally occurring threats or incidents. |
| [INCOSE14] | The ability to maintain required capability in the face of adversity. |
| **resilient otherwise**<br>[SP 800-160 v1] | Security considerations applied to enable system operation despite disruption while not maintaining a secure mode, state, or transition; or only being able to provide for partial security within a given system mode, state, or transition.<br><br>See *securely resilient*. |
| **risk**<br>[CNSSI 4009, OMB A-130] | A measure of the extent to which an entity is threatened by a potential circumstance or event, and typically a function of the adverse impacts that would arise if the circumstance or event occurs; and the likelihood of occurrence. |

| **risk analysis**<br>[ISO 73] | Process to comprehend the nature of risk and to determine the level of risk. |
|---|---|
| **risk assessment**<br>[SP 800-39, adapted] | The process of identifying risks to organizational operations (including mission, functions, image, reputation), organizational assets, individuals, other organizations, and the Nation, resulting from the operation of an information system. Part of risk management, incorporates threat and vulnerability analyses, and considers mitigations provided by security controls planned or in place. |
| [ISO 73] | Overall process of risk identification, risk analysis, and risk evaluation. |
| **risk-adaptive access control**<br>[SP 800-95] | Access privileges are granted based on a combination of a user's identity, mission need, and the level of security risk that exists between the system being accessed and a user. RAdAC will use security metrics, such as the strength of the authentication method, the level of assurance of the session connection between the system and a user, and the physical location of a user, to make its risk determination. |
| **risk factor**<br>[SP 800-30] | A characteristic used in a risk model as an input to determining the level of risk in a risk assessment. |
| **risk framing**<br>[SP 800-39] | Risk framing is the set of assumptions, constraints, risk tolerances, and priorities/trade-offs that shape an organization's approach for managing risk. |
| **risk management strategy**<br>[SP 800-39] | Strategy that addresses how organizations intend to assess risk, respond to risk, and monitor risk—making explicit and transparent the risk perceptions that organizations routinely use in making both investment and operational decisions. |
| **risk model**<br>[SP 800-30] | A key component of a risk assessment methodology (in addition to assessment approach and analysis approach) that defines key terms and assessable risk factors. |
| **risk response**<br>[SP 800-39] | Accepting, avoiding, mitigating, sharing, or transferring risk to organizational operations (i.e., mission, functions, image, or reputation), organizational assets, individuals, other organizations, or the Nation. |
| **safety**<br>[SP 800-82, MIL-STD-882E] | Freedom from conditions that can cause death, injury, occupational illness, damage to or loss of equipment or property, or damage to the environment. |
| **securely resilient**<br>[SP 800-160 v1] | The ability of a system to preserve a secure state despite disruption, to include the system transitions between normal and degraded modes. Securely resilient is a primary objective of systems security engineering. |
| **security**<br>[SP 800-160 v1] | Freedom from those conditions that can cause loss of assets with unacceptable consequences. |

[ISO 15288]

| | |
|---|---|
| **security control**<br>[SP 800-160 v1] | A mechanism designed to address needs as specified by a set of security requirements. |
| **security controls**<br>[OMB A-130] | The safeguards or countermeasures prescribed for an information system or an organization to protect the confidentiality, integrity, and availability of the system and its information. |
| **security criteria** | Criteria related to a supplier's ability to conform to security-relevant laws, directives, regulations, policies, or business processes; a supplier's ability to deliver the requested product or service in satisfaction of the stated security requirements and in conformance with secure business practices; the ability of a mechanism, system element, or system to meet its security requirements; whether movement from one life cycle stage or process to another (e.g., to accept a baseline into configuration management, to accept delivery of a product or service) is acceptable in terms of security policy; how a delivered product or service is handled, distributed, and accepted; how to perform security verification and validation; or how to store system elements securely in disposal. |
| | *Note:* Security criteria related to a supplier's ability may require specific human resources, capabilities, methods, technologies, techniques, or tools to deliver an acceptable product or service with the desired level of assurance and trustworthiness. Security criteria related to a system's ability to meet security requirements may be expressed in quantitative terms (i.e., metrics and threshold values), in qualitative terms (including threshold boundaries), or in terms of identified forms of evidence. |
| **security function**<br>[SP 800-160 v1] | The capability provided by the system or a system element. The capability may be expressed generally as a concept or specified precisely in requirements. |
| **security relevance**<br>[SP 800-160 v1] | The term used to describe those functions or mechanisms that are relied upon, directly or indirectly, to enforce a security policy that governs confidentiality, integrity, and availability protections. |

| | |
|---|---|
| **security requirement**<br>[SP 800-160 v1] | A requirement that specifies the functional, assurance, and strength characteristics for a mechanism, system, or system element. |
| **survivability**<br>[Richards09] | The ability of a system to minimize the impact of a finite-duration disturbance on value delivery (i.e., stakeholder benefit at cost), achieved through the reduction of the likelihood or magnitude of a disturbance; the satisfaction of a minimally acceptable level of value delivery during and after a disturbance; and/or a timely recovery. |
| **system**<br>[ISO 15288, SP 800-160 v1] | Combination of interacting elements organized to achieve one or more stated purposes.<br><br>*Note 1:* There are many types of systems. Examples include: general and special-purpose information systems; command, control, and communication systems; crypto modules; central processing unit and graphics processor boards; industrial/process control systems; flight control systems; weapons, targeting, and fire control systems; medical devices and treatment systems; financial, banking, and merchandising transaction systems; and social networking systems.<br><br>*Note 2:* The interacting elements in the definition of system include hardware, software, data, humans, processes, facilities, materials, and naturally occurring physical entities.<br><br>*Note 3:* System-of-systems is included in the definition of system. |
| **system component**<br>[SP 800-53] | Discrete identifiable information technology assets that represent a building block of a system and include hardware, software, firmware, and virtual machines. |
| **system element**<br>[ISO 15288, SP 800-160 v1] | Member of a set of elements that constitute a system.<br><br>*Note 1:* A system element can be a discrete component, product, service, subsystem, system, infrastructure, or enterprise.<br><br>*Note 2:* Each element of the system is implemented to fulfill specified requirements.<br><br>*Note 3:* The recursive nature of the term allows the term *system* to apply equally when referring to a discrete component or to a large, complex, geographically distributed system-of-systems.<br><br>*Note 4:* System elements are implemented by: hardware, software, and firmware that perform operations on data / information; physical structures, devices, and components in the environment of operation; and the people, processes, and procedures for operating, sustaining, and supporting the system elements. |

| | |
|---|---|
| **system-of-interest**<br>[SP 800-160 v1] | A system whose life cycle is under consideration in the context of [ISO/IEC/IEEE 15288:2015].<br><br>*Note:* A system-of-interest can be viewed as the system that is the focus of the systems engineering effort. The system-of-interest contains system elements, system element interconnections, and the environment in which they are placed. |
| **system-of-systems**<br>[SP 800-160 v1, INCOSE14] | System-of-interest whose system elements are themselves systems; typically, these entail large-scale interdisciplinary problems with multiple heterogeneous distributed systems.<br><br>*Note:* In the system-of-systems environment, constituent systems may not have a single owner, may not be under a single authority, or may not operate within a single set of priorities. |
| **technique** | See *cyber resiliency technique*. |
| **threat event**<br>[SP 800-30] | An event or situation that has the potential for causing undesirable consequences or impact. |
| **threat scenario**<br>[SP 800-30] | A set of discrete threat events, associated with a specific threat source or multiple threat sources, partially ordered in time. |
| **threat source**<br>[CNSSI 4009] | Any circumstance or event with the potential to adversely impact organizational operations (including mission, functions, image, or reputation), organizational assets, individuals, other organizations, or the Nation through an information system via unauthorized access, destruction, disclosure, or modification of information, and/or denial of service. |
| **trustworthiness**<br>[SP 800-160 v1] | Worthy of being trusted to fulfill whatever critical requirements may be needed for a particular component, subsystem, system, network, application, mission, business function, enterprise, or other entity. |

## APPENDIX C

# ACRONYMS

COMMON ABBREVIATIONS

| | |
|---|---|
| **ABAC** | Attribute-Based Access Control |
| **AI** | Artificial Intelligence |
| **API** | Application Programming Interface |
| **APT** | Advanced Persistent Threat |
| **ARP** | Address Resolution Protocol |
| **ASIC** | Application-Specific Integrated Circuit |
| **ATT&CK** | Adversarial Tactics, Techniques & Common Knowledge |
| **BIA** | Business Impact Analysis |
| **BMS** | Building Management Systems (BMS) |
| **C3** | Command, Control, and Communications |
| **CAN** | Controller Area Network |
| **CAPEC** | Common Attack Pattern Enumeration and Classification |
| **CCoA** | Cyber Courses of Action |
| **CDM** | Continuous Diagnostics and Mitigation |
| **CERT** | Computer Emergency Response Team |
| **CIS** | Critical Infrastructure System |
| **CJA** | Crown Jewels Analysis |
| **CLI** | Command Line Interface |
| **CMIA** | Cyber Mission Impact Analysis |
| **CNSS** | Committee on National Security Systems |
| **CNSSI** | Committee on National Security Systems Instruction |
| **COOP** | Continuity of Operations |
| **COTS** | Commercial Off-The-Shelf |
| **CPS** | Cyber-Physical System or Systems |
| **CRR** | Cyber Resilience Review |
| **CSA** | Cyber Survivability Attributes |
| **CSRC** | Computer Security Resource Center |
| **DHS** | Department of Homeland Security |
| **DIB** | Defense Industrial Base |

| **DMZ** | Demilitarized Zone |
| **DNS** | Domain Name System |
| **DoD** | Department of Defense |
| **DSB** | Defense Science Board |
| **DSP** | Digital Signal Processor |
| **ECU** | Embedded Control Unit |
| **E-ISAC** | Electricity ISAC |
| **EIT** | Enterprise Information Technology |
| **EMS** | Energy Management System |
| **FDNA** | Functional Dependency Network Analysis |
| **FPGA** | Field-Programmable Gate Array |
| **FMECA** | Failure Modes, Effects, and Criticality Analysis |
| **FIPS** | Federal Information Processing Standard(s) |
| **FISMA** | Federal Information Security Modernization Act |
| **FOIA** | Freedom of Information Act |
| **FOSS** | Free and Open Source Software |
| **GPS** | Global Positioning System |
| **HACS** | Highly Adaptive Cybersecurity Services |
| **HDL** | Hardware Description Language |
| **HMI** | Human-Machine Interface |
| **HVA** | High Value Asset |
| **HVAC** | Heating, Ventilation, and Air Conditioning |
| **I&W** | Indications and Warnings |
| **IdAM** | Identity and Access Management |
| **IACD** | Integrated Adaptive Cyber Defense |
| **ICS** | Industrial Control System |
| **ICT** | Information and Communications Technology |
| **IDS** | Intrusion Detection System |
| **IEC** | International Electrotechnical Commission |
| **IEEE** | Institute of Electrical and Electronics Engineers |
| **INCOSE** | International Council on Systems Engineering |
| **IoT** | Internet of Things |
| **ISO** | International Organization for Standardization |

| | |
|---|---|
| **IT** | Information Technology |
| **ITL** | Information Technology Laboratory |
| **LSPE** | Large-Scale Processing Environment |
| **MCU** | Master Control Unit |
| **MFA** | Multi-Factor Authentication |
| **MIA** | Mission Impact Analysis |
| **MIL-STD** | Military Standard |
| **M&S** | Modeling and Simulation |
| **MBSE** | Model-Based Systems Engineering |
| **ML** | Machine Learning |
| **MOE** | Measures of Effectiveness |
| **MOP** | Measures of Performance |
| **MTD** | Moving Target Defense |
| **NASA** | National Aeronautics and Space Administration |
| **NIAC** | National Infrastructure Advisory Council |
| **NIST** | National Institute of Standards and Technology |
| **NTCTF** | NSA/CSS Technical Cyber Threat Framework |
| **OEM** | Original Equipment Manufacturer |
| **OMB** | Office of Management and Budget |
| **OPSEC** | Operations Security |
| **OT** | Operational Technology |
| **PBX** | Private Branch Exchange |
| **PII** | Personally Identifiable Information |
| **PLC** | Programmable Logic Controller |
| **PPD** | Presidential Policy Directive |
| **RAdAC** | Risk-Adaptive Access Control |
| **RAID** | Redundant Array of Independent Disks |
| **RBAC** | Role-Based Access Control |
| **RMA** | Reliability, Maintainability, Availability |
| **RMF** | Risk Management Framework |
| **RMM** | Resilience Management Model |
| **ROI** | Return on Investment |
| **RTU** | Remote Terminal Unit |

| | |
|---|---|
| **RSWG** | (INCOSE) Resilient Systems Working Group |
| **SAE** | Society of Automotive Engineers |
| **SCADA** | Supervisory Control and Data Acquisition |
| **SCRM** | Supply Chain Risk Management |
| **SDN** | Software Defined Networking |
| **SEI** | Software Engineering Institute |
| **SME** | Subject Matter Expert |
| **SOC** | Security Operations Center |
| **SOW** | Statement of Work |
| **SP** | Special Publication |
| **SSE** | Systems Security Engineering |
| **STAMP** | Systems-Theoretic Accident Model and Processes |
| **STPA** | System-Theoretic Process Analysis |
| **TTP** | Tactics, Techniques, and Procedures |
| **UPS** | Uninterruptible Power Supply |
| **VCU** | Vehicle Control Unit |
| **VOA** | Voice of the Adversary |
| **VOIP** | Voice over Internet Protocol |
| **VPN** | Virtual Private Network |

APPENDIX D

# BACKGROUND
CYBER RESILIENCY IN CONTEXT

This appendix provides background and contextual information on cyber resiliency. It describes how the definition of cyber resiliency relates to other forms of resilience; the distinguishing characteristics of cyber resiliency, including the assumptions which underpin this specialty engineering discipline; the relationship between cyber resiliency engineering and other specialty engineering disciplines; and the relationship between cyber resiliency and risk.

## D.1  DEFINING CYBER RESILIENCY

Cyber resiliency[84] is defined as "the ability to anticipate, withstand, recover from, and adapt to adverse conditions, stresses, attacks, or compromises on systems that include cyber resources." This definition can be applied to a variety of entities including:

- A system;
- A mechanism, component, or system element;
- A shared service, common infrastructure, or system-of-systems identified with a mission or business function;
- An organization;[85]
- A critical infrastructure sector or a region;
- A system-of-systems in a critical infrastructure sector or sub-sector; and
- The Nation.

Cyber resiliency is emerging as a key element in any effective strategy for mission assurance, business assurance, or operational resilience. The definition of cyber resiliency is informed by definitions of the terms *resilience* and *resiliency* across various communities of interest, as illustrated in the following examples (*italics* added to highlight common goals):

---

[84] "Resilience" and "resiliency" are alternative spellings with "resilience" being more common. The term "cyber resiliency" is used in the cyber resiliency engineering framework described in this publication to avoid creating the impression that cyber resiliency engineering is a sub-discipline of resilience engineering. See Appendix D.2 for a discussion of the relationship. The term "cyber resilience" is being used by many organizations today to refer to organizational resilience against cyber threats, with a strong emphasis on effective implementation of good cybersecurity practices and COOP. For example, the DHS Cyber Resilience Review (CRR), which is based on the Software Engineering Institute (SEI) CERT Resilience Management Model (RMM), focuses on good practices against conventional adversaries. Discussions of "cyber resilience" focus on improved risk governance (e.g., making cyber risk part of enterprise risk), improved cyber hygiene to include incident response procedures and ongoing monitoring, and threat information sharing. These aspects of governance and operations are all important to an organization's cyber preparedness strategy [Bodeau16]. However, discussions of "cyber resilience" generally omit the architecture and engineering aspect, which is the focus of the cyber resiliency engineering framework and the design principles discussed in this publication.

[85] See [SP 800-39] for a discussion of the system, mission/business function, and organization levels. See [NIST CSF] for a discussion of critical infrastructure levels. See [SP 800-37, SP 800-160 v1] for a discussion of system-of-systems.

- **Resilience for the Nation:** The ability to *adapt* to changing conditions and *withstand* and rapidly *recover* from emergencies [PPD8].

- **Critical Infrastructure Resilience:** The ability to reduce the magnitude or duration of disruptive events. The effectiveness of a resilient infrastructure or enterprise depends upon its ability to *anticipate, absorb, adapt* to, and/or rapidly *recover* from a potentially disruptive event [NIAC10].

- **Resilience for National Security Systems:** The ability to prepare for and adapt to changing conditions and withstand and recover rapidly from disruptions. Resilience includes the ability to withstand and recover from deliberate attacks, accidents, or naturally occurring threats or incidents. [CNSSI 1253, SP 800-37]

- **Community Resilience:** The ability of a community to *prepare* for anticipated hazards, *adapt* to changing conditions, *withstand* and *recover* rapidly from disruptions [SP 1190].

- **Critical Infrastructure Security and Resilience:** The ability to *prepare* for and *adapt* to changing conditions and *withstand* and *recover* rapidly from disruptions. Resilience includes the ability to withstand and recover from deliberate attacks, accidents, or naturally occurring threats or incidents [PPD21].

- **Information System Resilience:** The ability of a system to *continue* to operate under adverse conditions or stress, even if in a degraded or debilitated state, while maintaining essential operational capabilities and *recover* to an effective operational posture in a time frame consistent with mission needs [SP 800-53].

- **Resilience in Cyberspace:** The ability to *adapt* to changing conditions and *prepare* for, *withstand*, and rapidly *recover* from disruption [DHS10].

- **Network Resilience:** The ability of the network to provide and *maintain* an acceptable level of service in the face of various faults and challenges to normal operation [Sterbenz06].

- **Operational Resilience:** The ability of systems to *resist, absorb*, and *recover* from or *adapt* to an adverse occurrence during operation that may cause harm, destruction, or loss of ability to perform mission-related functions [DOD 8140.01].

- **Resilience Engineering:** The ability to build systems that can *anticipate* and circumvent accidents, *survive* disruptions through appropriate learning and *adaptation*, and *recover* from disruptions by restoring the pre-disruption state as closely as possible [Madni09].

Despite the different scope covered by each definition, there are some commonalities across the definitions. Each definition expresses a common theme of addressing those situations or conditions in which disruption, adversity, errors, faults, or failures occur. The definitions express consistent resiliency goals (shown in *italics* above) when encountering specific situations or conditions causing disruption, adversity, and faults. The definition of cyber resiliency adopted for use in this publication is consistent with the definitions cited above.

## D.2  DISTINGUISHING CHARACTERISTICS OF CYBER RESILIENCY

Any discussion of cyber resiliency is distinguished by its focus and *a priori* threat assumptions. These are reflected in cyber resiliency constructs and engineering practices.

- **Focus on the mission or business functions.**

  Discussions of cyber resiliency focus on capabilities supporting organizational missions or business functions in order to maximize the ability of organizations to complete critical or essential missions or business functions despite an adversary presence in their systems and infrastructure threatening mission-critical systems and system components. This is in contrast to focusing on the protection of information or on ensuring capabilities in a non-adversarial environment. It is also in contrast with focusing on ensuring the resilience of system elements or of constituent systems in a system-of-systems. From the perspective of cyber resiliency, system elements or constituent systems that are less critical to mission or business effectiveness can be sacrificed to contain a cyber-attack and maximize mission assurance.

- **Focus on the effects of the Advanced Persistent Threat.**

  The definition of cyber resiliency encompasses all threats to systems containing cyber resources, whether such threats are cyber or non-cyber (e.g., kinetic) in nature. But the focus of cyber resiliency analysis is on the effects the APT can have on the system-of-interest, and thereby on the mission or business function, the organization, or on external stakeholders.

  In addition to immediately detectable effects (e.g., destruction of data, malfunction of a CPS, denial-of-service), the APT can produce effects that are detectable only after extended observation or forensic analysis of the system-of-interest (e.g., escalation of privileges, modification or fabrication of data or services, exfiltration of data). Consideration of cyber resiliency in systems security engineering seeks to mitigate such effects, independent of when or whether they may be detected.

  The resources associated with the APT, its stealthy nature, its persistent focus on the target of interest, and its ability to adapt in the face of defender actions make it a highly dangerous threat. Moreover, the APT can take advantage of or make its behavior appear to result from other forms of adversity, including human error, structural failure, or natural disaster. By focusing on APT activities and their potential effects, systems engineers produce systems which can anticipate, withstand, recover from, and adapt to a broad and diverse suite of adverse conditions and stresses on systems containing cyber resources.

- **Assume the adversary will compromise or breach the system or organization.**

  A fundamental assumption in any discussion of cyber resiliency is that a sophisticated adversary cannot always be kept out of a system or be quickly detected and removed from that system, despite the quality of the system design, the functional effectiveness of the security components, and the trustworthiness of the selected components. This assumption acknowledges that modern systems are large and complex entities and as such, adversaries will always be able to find and exploit weaknesses and flaws in the systems (e.g., unpatched vulnerabilities, misconfigurations), environments of operation (e.g., social engineering, user vulnerability), and supply chains. As a result, a sophisticated adversary can penetrate an organizational system and achieve a presence within the organization's infrastructure.

- **Assume the adversary will maintain a presence in the system or organization.**

  Any discussion of cyber resiliency assumes that the adversary presence may be a persistent and long-term issue and recognizes that the stealthy nature of the APT makes it difficult for an organization to be certain that the threat has been eradicated. It also recognizes that the ability of the APT to adapt implies that previously successful mitigations may no longer be effective. Finally, it recognizes that the persistent nature of the APT means that even if an organization has succeeded in eradicating its presence, it may return. In some situations, the best outcome an organization can achieve is containing the adversary's malicious code or slowing its lateral movement across the system (or transitively across multiple systems) long enough that the organization is able to achieve its primary mission prior to losing its critical or essential mission capability.

---

**ADVERSARY PERSISTENCE AND LONG-TERM PRESENCE**

Numerous reports of cyber incidents and cyber breaches indicate that extended periods of time transpire (in some cases, months or years) between when an adversary initially established a presence in an organizational system by exploiting a vulnerability reached from cyberspace and when that presence was revealed or detected.

The following examples illustrate the types of situations where an adversary can maintain a long-term presence or persistence in a system, even without attacking the system via cyberspace:

- Compromising the *pre-execution environment* of a system through a hardware or software implant (e.g., compromise of the firmware or microcode of a system element, such as a network switch or a router, that activates before initialization in the system's environment of operation). This is extremely difficult to detect and can result in compromise of the entire environment.

- Compromising the *software development tool-chain* (e.g., compilers, linkers, interpreters, continuous integration tools, code repositories). This allows malicious code to be inserted by the adversary without modifying the source code or without the knowledge of the software developers.

- Compromising a *semiconductor product or process* (e.g., malicious alteration to the hardware description language [HDL] of a microprocessor, a field-programmable gate array [FPGA], a digital signal processor [DSP], or an application-specific integrated circuit [ASIC]).

---

## D.3 RELATIONSHIP WITH OTHER SPECIALITY ENGINEERING DISCIPLINES

Cyber resiliency is an aspect of trustworthiness, as are safety, system resilience, survivability, reliability, and security.[86] Cyber resiliency concepts and engineering practices assume a basic foundation of security and reliability; many cyber resiliency techniques use or rely on security, reliability, resilience, and fault-tolerance mechanisms. The concepts and engineering practices described in this publication build on work in the specialty engineering disciplines of resilience engineering and dependable computing, including survivability engineering and fault tolerance.

- **Safety**

   Safety is defined as "freedom from conditions that can cause death, injury, occupational illness, damage to or loss of equipment or property, or damage to the environment" [SP 800-82]. Safety engineering focuses on identifying unacceptable system behaviors,

---

[86] Trustworthiness requirements can include, for example, attributes of reliability, dependability, performance, resilience, safety, security, and survivability under a range of potential adversity in the form of disruptions, hazards, and threats [SP 800-53].

outcomes, and interactions and helping to ensure that the system does not enter an unacceptable state (i.e., a state in which such behaviors, interactions, or outcomes are possible, thus creating or being an instance of a condition that can cause one of the harms identified above). System safety engineering is based on analytic processes rather than design principles or constructs.

[SP 800-160 v1] states that "The system aspects of secure operation may intersect, complement, or be in direct conflict or contradiction with those of safe operation of the system." A similar statement may be made with respect to cyber resilient operations. The set of unacceptable states defined by safety engineering may constitute a constraint on cyber resiliency solutions or may be used in trade-off analyses. As part of achieving a specific cyber resiliency objective, such as Continue or Reconstitute,[87] a system may need to operate transiently in an unsafe (or insecure) state, depending on how stakeholders prioritize and trade off required system properties and behaviors.

- **Security**

  The relationship between cyber resiliency and security depends on which definition of security is considered. [SP 800-37] defines security as, "A condition that results from the establishment and maintenance of protective measures that enable an organization to perform its mission or critical functions despite risks posed by threats to its use of systems. Protective measures may involve a combination of deterrence, avoidance, prevention, detection, recovery, and correction that should form part of the organization's risk management approach." This definition of security overlaps with, but does not subsume, cyber resiliency since "protective measures" as listed in the definition do not fully cover risk management strategies related to cyber resiliency.[88]

  Cyber resiliency engineering may be viewed as a specialty discipline of systems security engineering. [SP 800-160 v1] defines security as the "freedom from those conditions that can cause loss of assets with unacceptable consequences."[89] In that context, security is concerned with the protection of assets and is primarily oriented to the concept of asset loss.[90] It includes but is not limited to cybersecurity.[91] Cyber resiliency engineering is

---

[87] See Section 2.1.2.

[88] See Appendix D.4.

[89] This is a broader construction than appears in [FIPS 199]. In accordance with [FISMA], FIPS 199 defines three security objectives for information and information systems: confidentiality, integrity, and availability. A loss of confidentiality is the unauthorized disclosure of information; a loss of integrity is the unauthorized modification or destruction of information; and a loss of availability is the disruption of access to or use of information or an information system.

[90] The term _protection_, in the context of systems security engineering, has a very broad scope and is primarily a control objective that applies across all asset types and corresponding consequences of loss. Therefore, the system protection capability is a system control objective and a system design problem. The solution to the problem is optimized through a balanced proactive and reactive strategy that is not limited to prevention. The strategy includes avoiding asset loss and consequences, detecting asset loss and consequences, minimizing (i.e., limiting, containing, or restricting) asset loss and consequences, responding to asset loss and consequences, recovering from asset loss and consequences, and forecasting or predicting asset loss and consequences [SP 800-160 v1].

[91] Cybersecurity is defined as "the process of protecting information by preventing, detecting, and responding to attacks" [NIST CSF] or as "prevention of damage to, protection of, and restoration of computers, electronic communications systems, electronic communications services, wire communication, and electronic communication, including information contained therein, to ensure its availability, integrity, authentication, confidentiality, and nonrepudiation" [OMB A-130].

oriented toward capabilities and harms to systems containing cyber resources. This orientation is consistent with the concept of asset loss since a capability is a form of intangible asset. As noted above, cyber resiliency engineering focuses on capabilities supporting missions or business functions and on the effects of adversarial actions on systems.

While [SP 800-160 v1] views security, asset loss, and protection broadly, much of the security literature and many security practitioners focus narrowly on the security objectives of confidentiality, integrity, and availability of information and information systems [FIPS 199].[92] Cyber resiliency engineering considers a broader range of cyber effects (i.e., effects in cyberspace) than the loss of confidentiality, integrity, or availability of information or of system services. Cyber effects of concern to cyber resiliency engineering do include the effects of concern to security, including service degradation and denial or interruption of service, non-disruptive modification or fabrication as well as corruption or destruction of information resources, and unauthorized disclosure of information. In addition, they include the usurpation or unauthorized use of resources, even when such use is non-disruptive to the system-of-interest; reduced confidence in system capabilities, which can alter system usage behavior; and finally, alterations in behaviors affecting external systems, which can result in cascading failures beyond the system-of-interest.

As noted above, cyber resiliency concepts and engineering practices assume a foundation of security. Some cyber resiliency techniques[93] rely on the correct and effective application of security controls. Some cyber resiliency design principles[94] adapt or are strongly aligned with the security design principles described in [SP 800-160 v1].

An emerging security architectural strategy is Zero Trust Architecture (ZTA), which can be characterized as a collection of concepts, ideas, and component relationships (architectures) designed to eliminate the uncertainty in enforcing accurate access decisions in information systems and services [SP 800-207]. While the ZTA focus is narrower than that of cyber resiliency, ensuring accurate access decisions supports multiple cyber resiliency techniques. In addition, some cyber resiliency techniques, approaches, and design principles can integrated into the design and deployment of a ZTA.

- **Resilience Engineering and Survivability**

  The specialty disciplines of resilience engineering and survivability engineering address system resilience whether or not the system-of-interest contains cyber resources. Cyber resiliency concepts and engineering practices assume that some of the system elements are cyber resources.

  Resilience engineering is "the ability to build systems that can anticipate and circumvent accidents, survive disruptions through appropriate learning and adaptation, and recover from disruptions by restoring the pre-disruption state as closely as possible" [Madni07, Madni09]. Survivability engineering is "the subset of systems engineering concerned with minimizing the impact of environmental disturbances on system performance. Survivability may be defined as the ability of a system to minimize the impact of a finite-duration disturbance on value delivery (i.e., stakeholder benefit at cost), achieved through the

---

[92] Note that Appendix G.3.1 of [SP 800-160 v1] adapts these security objectives to be more broadly applicable.

[93] See Section 2.1.3.

[94] See Section 2.1.4.

reduction of the likelihood or magnitude of a disturbance; the satisfaction of a minimally acceptable level of value delivery during and after a disturbance; and/or a timely recovery" [Richards09].

Cyber resiliency engineering draws concepts and design principles from resilience engineering and survivability engineering. However, as discussed further in Appendix D.4, the threat model for cyber resiliency differs from that typically used in these specialty engineering disciplines, which assume detectable disruptions. Concepts and design principles for survivability and resilience are adapted or extended to reflect malicious cyber activities which can remain undetected for extended periods.

- **Cyber Survivability**

  Cyber survivability is a system property (i.e., the system's ability to prevent, mitigate, and recover from cyber events [Pitcher19 and JCS17]). Cyber survivability and cyber resiliency are closely related but not interchangeable. Cyber survivability is defined for specific types of systems (e.g., weapons systems and systems supporting critical infrastructures) and focuses solely on cyber-attacks (rather than including threat events due to other sources). It does not include adapting to changes in the technical or operational environment. Cyber survivability does include adapting to changes in the threat environment. Engineering for cyber survivability focuses on Cyber Survivability Attributes (CSAs), which are system capabilities that support and serve as indicators of cyber survivability. Many CSAs depend on the same cybersecurity measures and other functionality as cyber resiliency techniques and implementation approaches (e.g., identity, credential, and access management; logging and auditing; performance monitoring). CSAs can use cyber resiliency techniques in their implementation to provide the CSA-required functionality or to make that functionality more effective against adversarial threat actions. For more information on the relationship between cyber resiliency and cyber survivability, see [Bodeau19].

- **Reliability**

  Reliability is defined as "the ability of a system or component to function under stated conditions for a specified period of time" [IEEE90]. Reliability engineering shares many analytic techniques with safety engineering but focuses on failures of systems or system components rather than on potential harms. Cyber resiliency engineering assumes that reliability, including consideration of degradation and failure, is addressed in the overall systems engineering process. The threat model, including the stated conditions for reliability, typically does not include deliberate adversarial behavior and necessarily excludes new and unanticipated attack methods developed by advanced adversaries.

- **Fault Tolerance**

  A fault-tolerant system is one with "the built-in capability to provide continued, correct execution of its assigned function in the presence of a hardware and/or software fault" [SP 800-82]. Classes of faults include development faults, physical faults, and interaction faults. Faults can be characterized by phase of creation or occurrence—whether they are internal or external to a system, whether they are natural or human-made, whether they are in hardware, software, persistence, and properties related to human-made faults [Avizienis04]. An advanced adversary can cause, emulate, or take advantage of a fault. Cyber resiliency engineering draws some techniques or implementation approaches[95] from fault tolerance

---

[95] See Section 2.1.3.

and leverages these capabilities while assuming that actions of an advanced adversary may go undetected.

The analytic processes and practices related to cyber resiliency are intended to be integrated with those for other specialty engineering disciplines, including security, systems engineering, resilience engineering, safety, cybersecurity, and mission assurance. Examples of analytic practices from these disciplines include:

- **Security, Information Security, and Cybersecurity:** Operations security (OPSEC) analysis; information security risk analysis [SP 800-30]; coverage analysis with respect to a taxonomy of attack events or TTPs [DHS18], attack tree or attack graph analysis, attack surface analysis, and Red Team or penetration testing analysis;

- **Systems Engineering:** Modeling and simulation (M&S), model-based systems engineering (MBSE), and Functional Dependency Network Analysis (FDNA);

- **Resilience Engineering:** Criticality Analysis [IR 8179], Mission Impact Analysis (MIA), Business Impact Analysis (BIA) [SP 800-34], fault tree analysis, and Failure Modes, Effects, and Criticality Analysis (FMECA);

- **Safety:** Fault tree analysis, FMECA, System-Theoretic Process Analysis (STPA), and Systems-Theoretic Accident Model and Processes (STAMP) [Leveson12]; and

- **Mission Assurance:** Crown Jewels Analysis (CJA), mission thread analysis, cyber mission impact analysis (CMIA), and supply chain risk management (SCRM) analysis [SP 800-161].

These existing analytic practices are extensible (and in practice have been extended) to include cyber resiliency concepts and concerns, particularly the growing concern that an advanced adversary can establish a covert and persistent presence on a specific a system-of-interest, an enabling system, or another system in the environment of operation of the system-of-interest. Additional analytic practices include, for example, structured analysis of the system architecture and design with respect to cyber resiliency design principles, techniques, and approaches and the adaptation of coverage analysis to include effects on adversary activities described in Appendix H.

## D.4  RELATIONSHIP BETWEEN CYBER RESILIENCY AND RISK

Cyber resiliency solutions are intended to reduce the risk to missions or business functions, to organizations, and to individuals of depending on systems containing cyber resources. This cyber risk arises in several ways, including: cyber resources and the systems that incorporate those resources are increasingly complex, so their behavior and properties in the presence of adversity (or even under expected levels of stress) can be hard to predict; software generally includes vulnerabilities and weaknesses, which can make it fragile and subject to exploitation by an adversary; and the presence of resources in cyberspace exposes them to cyber-attack.[96]

---

[96] The risk due to the potential for a cyber-attack (i.e., an attack via cyberspace, targeting an organization's use of cyberspace for the purpose of disrupting, disabling, destroying, or maliciously controlling a computing environment or infrastructure; destroying the integrity of the data; or stealing controlled information [SP 800-39]) is also referred to as cybersecurity risk [NIST CSF].

Cyber resiliency solutions are intended to reduce the risk of depending on systems containing cyber resources by reducing the extent of the harm from threat events,[97] the likelihood of occurrence of threat events, and the likelihood the threat events will cause harm.[98] The risk model for cyber resiliency identifies the types of threat events and the classes of harm of interest to systems security engineers concerned with cyber resiliency. The extent of potential risk mitigation due to a cyber resiliency solution can be analyzed and assessed in the context of that risk model.

The *risk model* for cyber resiliency builds on risk models for security, cybersecurity, resilience engineering, and survivability. However, the cyber resiliency risk model emphasizes the APT and the effects on missions and organizations of malicious cyber activities or of harm to systems that include cyber resources. Thus, the threat model and the consequence model components of the cyber resiliency threat model have distinctive characteristics.

The *threat model* for cyber resiliency encompasses conventional security threat models which consider threat sources, including accident and human error, structural failure of system elements or supporting infrastructures, natural disasters, and deliberate human actions (including those by malicious insiders). Similarly, the threat model for cyber resiliency encompasses typical cybersecurity risk models.[99] However, the cyber resiliency threat model emphasizes the APT as a primary or as a secondary threat source. As a primary threat source, sophisticated adversaries execute cyber campaigns that can involve multiple systems and organizations and extend for periods of months or even years.[100] In addition, these adversaries can use TTPs typical of less sophisticated cyber threat actors. As a secondary threat source, the APT can take advantage of threat events due to infrastructure failure or natural disaster and imitate or leverage human error or loss of component reliability. Therefore, even when cyber resiliency engineering analysis considers a potential disruption with a non-adversarial source, that analysis includes looking for ways the APT could take advantage of the disruption.

The *consequence model* for cyber resiliency encompasses consequences to information and information systems (i.e., a loss of confidentiality, integrity, or availability, as defined in [FIPS 199]). These general consequences can be translated into more specific harms to information

---

[97] The term *threat event* refers to an event or situation that has the potential for causing undesirable consequences or impact. Threat events can be caused by either adversarial or non-adversarial threat sources [SP 800-30].

[98] While many different risk models are potentially valid and useful, three elements are common across most models. These are: the *likelihood of occurrence* (i.e., the likelihood that a threat event or a threat scenario consisting of a set of interdependent events will occur or be initiated by an adversary); the *likelihood of impact* (i.e., the likelihood that a threat event or scenario will result in an impact given vulnerabilities, weaknesses, and predisposing conditions); and the *level of the impact* [SP 800-30].

[99] [EO 13800] states that "Cybersecurity risk management comprises the full range of activities undertaken to protect IT and data from unauthorized access and other cyber threats, to maintain awareness of cyber threats, to detect anomalies and incidents adversely affecting IT and data, and to mitigate the impact of, respond to, and recover from incidents." While the phrase "cyber threat" is used without definition in such sources as [EO 13800, ODNI17, DSB13, NSA18, DHS18], its use (without the qualification of "advanced") generally implies that the cyber threat actor attacks via cyberspace.

[100] Activities and threat events can be obtained from [SP 800-30 or NSA18] with augmentation or additional detail from other sources; the stages or phases of a cyber-attack can be obtained from NIST, from the Office of the Director of National Intelligence (ODNI) *Cyber Threat Framework* [ODNI17], or from the NSA/CSS Technical Cyber Threat Framework (NTCTF) [NSA18].

and systems that include or are enabled by cyber resources: degraded or disrupted functionality or performance; modified, corrupted, or fabricated information; usurped or misused system resources; or exfiltrated or exposed information. However, the consequence model for cyber resiliency also considers the potential consequences to the missions or business functions supported by the system, to the organization, and sometimes to other stakeholders (e.g., individuals whose personal information may be exfiltrated or exposed, members of the public affected by environmental harms resulting from failure of a critical infrastructure system). In general, a cyber resiliency solution identified and implemented for a given scope is intended to reduce risks at the next level; for example, implementing a solution at the system level can mitigate risks to mission or business function.

Consequences to a mission or business function or to an organization can be defined in terms of impacts on performance of required functions or on preserving required properties. The risk model for cyber resiliency, therefore, aligns well with mission risk models [Musman18]. It can also be used in conjunction with risk models which represent quality properties, such as security, survivability, and resilience.[101]

- **Security.** The threat model for cyber resiliency encompasses the security threat model but emphasizes the APT. Depending on how broadly (e.g., all stakeholder trustworthiness concerns) or narrowly (e.g., specific stakeholder concerns for confidentiality, integrity, or availability) security is construed, the cyber resiliency consequence model can coincide with or can include the security consequence model. The consequence model requires systems engineers analyzing risks to view the system-of-interest in terms of how its environment of operation[102] imposes constraints and also how adversity involving cyber resources, and consequently, the system-of-interest affect that environment.

- **Resilience engineering and survivability.** The threat model for resilience engineering and survivability focuses on an event or a set of circumstances which disrupts performance. Survivability considers finite-duration events, while resilience engineering also considers multiple or repeated events and changes in the operational environment. In either case, the threat model implicitly assumes that the event or its immediate consequences can be detected. The threat model for cyber resiliency, by contrast, assumes that an advanced adversary can operate covertly in the system for an extended period before causing a detectable disruption.

The consequence model is also different: adversary-caused harms, such as fabrication of user accounts or exfiltration of sensitive information, may be non-disruptive. Disruption of normal system performance may in fact result from defensive actions taken after such harms are detected (e.g., removing compromised or suspect components from the system). Thus, the consequence model for cyber resiliency encompasses the consequence model for resilience and survivability.

---

[101] *Quality properties* are emergent properties of systems that include, for example: safety, security, maintainability, resilience, reliability, availability, agility, and survivability [SP 800-160 v1]. These properties are also referred to as *systemic properties* across many engineering domains.

[102] See Figure 2 in [SP 800-160 v1].

## APPENDIX E

# CYBER RESILIENCY CONSTRUCTS

ENGINEERING FRAMEWORK CONSTRUCTS AND RELATIONSHIPS

This appendix provides details on the cyber resiliency constructs (i.e., goals, objectives, techniques, implementation approaches, design principles) that are part of the cyber resiliency engineering framework. It also describes relationships among those constructs.

## E.1  CYBER RESILIENCY GOALS

Cyber resiliency, similar to security, is a concern at multiple levels in an organization. The cyber resiliency goals (i.e., anticipate, withstand, recover, and adapt) support the linkage between risk management decisions at the mission/business process and system levels and the organization's risk management strategy [SP 800-39].

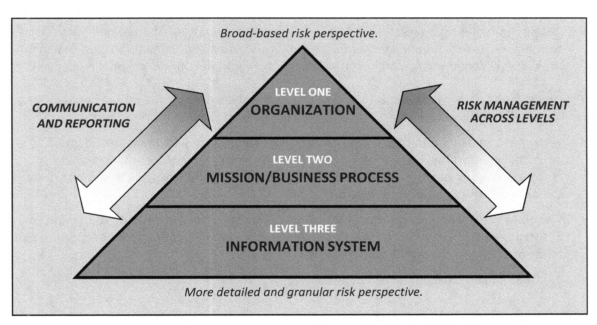

**FIGURE E-1:  ORGANIZATION-WIDE RISK MANAGEMENT APPROACH**

To address cyber resiliency, an organization's risk management strategy needs to include its threat-framing with respect to cyber threats, its strategies for achieving the cyber resiliency goals, and its choice of factors to use when prioritizing and interpreting cyber resiliency objectives at the mission/business level and at the system level. Strategies for achieving cyber resiliency goals include:

- **Anticipate**. Deterrence, avoidance, and prevention are strategies for anticipating potential threats. Other strategies include planning (i.e., identifying available resources and creating plans for using those resources if a threat materializes), preparation (i.e., changing the set of available resources and exercising plans), and morphing (i.e., changing the system on an ongoing basis in order to change the attack surface).

- **Withstand**. Strategies for withstanding the realization of potential threats, even when those threats are not detected, include absorption (i.e., accepting some level of damage to a given set of system elements, taking actions to reduce the impacts to other system elements or to the system as a whole, and repairing damage automatically), deflection (i.e., transferring threat events or their effects to different system elements or to systems other than those that were targeted or initially affected), and discarding (i.e., removing system elements or even a system as a whole based on indications of damage and either replacing those elements or enabling the system or mission/business process to operate without them).

- **Recover**. Strategies for recovery include reversion (i.e., replicating a prior state which is known to be acceptable), reconstitution (i.e., replicating critical and supporting functions to an acceptable level or using existing system resources), and replacement (i.e., replacing damaged, suspect, or selected system elements with new ones or repurposing existing system elements to serve different functions in order to perform critical and supporting functions, possibly in different ways). Detection can support the selection of a recovery strategy. However, a system can apply these strategies independent of detection to change the attack surface.

- **Adapt**. Strategies for adaptation include correction (i.e., removing or applying new controls to compensate for identified vulnerabilities or weaknesses) and redefinition (i.e., changing the system's requirements, architecture, design, configuration, or operational processes).

The organizational risk management strategy includes aspects which can limit the set of cyber resiliency solutions it will consider. These aspects include:[103]

- The organization's risk mitigation philosophy (e.g., compliance with standards of good practice, incorporating state-of-the-art technologies and making trade-offs between standards of good practice and leading-edge protection technologies, pushing the state-of-the-art through cyber defense DevOps).

- The types of external coordination in which the organization will participate (e.g., consumer of threat intelligence, bi-directional threat information-sharing, cooperation or coordination to counter threats, collaboration).

- Whether and how deception can be used.

## E.2 CYBER RESILIENCY OBJECTIVES

Table E-1 provides a description of each cyber resiliency objective and representative examples of sub-objectives. A sub-objective motivates the definition of requirements, and the selection and tailoring of controls. The representative sub-objectives can be used as a starting point for eliciting restatements of objectives and for defining metrics, as illustrated in the table. The representative sub-objectives, suitably restated for the system-of-interest, can be further decomposed into capabilities of (or activities performed by) that system, and threshold and objective values can be stated.[104]

---

[103] See [Bodeau16].

[104] See [Bodeau18b].

**TABLE E-1:  CYBER RESILIENCY SUB-OBJECTIVES**

| OBJECTIVE | REPRESENTATIVE SUB-OBJECTIVES | REPRESENTATIVE EXAMPLES OF METRICS |
|---|---|---|
| **Prevent or Avoid** Preclude the successful execution of an attack or the realization of adverse conditions. | • Apply basic protection measures and controls tailored to the risks of the system-of-interest. <br> • Limit exposure to threat events. <br> • Decrease the adversary's perceived benefits. <br> • Modify configurations based on threat intelligence. | • Time to patch or to apply configuration changes. <br> • Percentage of resources for which configuration changes are made randomly. Percentage of resources for which lifespan limits are applied. <br> • Percentage of sensitive data assets which are encrypted. Adversary dwell time in a deception environment. <br> • Percentage of resources to which more restrictive privileges are applied automatically in response to threat indicators. |
| **Prepare** Maintain a set of realistic courses of action that address predicted or anticipated adversity. | • Create and maintain cyber courses of action. <br> • Maintain the resources needed to execute cyber courses of action. <br> • Validate the realism of cyber courses of action using testing or exercises. | • Number of cyber courses of action (CCoAs) in the cyber playbook. Percentage of identified threat types, categories of threat actions, or TTPs (with reference to an identified threat model) addressed by at least one CCoA in the cyber playbook. <br> • Percentage of cyber resources which are backed up. Time since last exercise of alternative communications paths. Percentage of administrative staff who have been trained in their CCoA responsibilities. <br> • Time since last (random, scheduled) exercise or simulation of one or more CCoAs. |
| **Continue** Maximize the duration and viability of essential mission or business functions during adversity. | • Minimize degradation of service delivery. <br> • Minimize interruptions in service delivery. <br> • Ensure that ongoing functioning is correct. | • Time to perform mission or business function damage assessment. Length of time performance of (specified mission or business function) remained below acceptable levels. <br> • Time from initial disruption to availability (at minimum level of acceptability) of essential functions. <br> • Percentage of essential data assets for which data quality has been validated. Percentage of essential processing services for which correctness of functioning has been validated. |
| **Constrain** Limit damage from adversity. | • Identify potential damage. <br> • Isolate resources to limit future or further damage. <br> • Move resources to limit future or further damage. <br> • Change or remove resources and how they are used to limit future or further damage. | • Percentage of critical components that employ anti-tamper, shielding, and power line filtering. Time from initial indication or warning to completion of scans for potentially damaged resources. <br> • Time from initial indication or warning to completion of component isolation. <br> • Time from initial indication or warning to completion of resource relocation. <br> • Time from initial indication or warning to completion of switch to an alternative. |

| OBJECTIVE | REPRESENTATIVE SUB-OBJECTIVES | REPRESENTATIVE EXAMPLES OF METRICS |
|---|---|---|
| **Reconstitute** Restore as much mission or business functionality as possible after adversity. | • Identify untrustworthy resources and damage.[105]<br>• Restore functionality.<br>• Heighten protections during reconstitution.<br>• Determine the trustworthiness of restored or reconstructed resources. | • Time to identify unavailable resources and represent damage in status visualization.<br>• Time between initiation of recovery procedures and completion of documented milestones in the recovery, contingency, or continuity of operations plan. Percentage of cyber resources for which access control is maintained throughout the recovery process.<br>• Percentage of cyber resources for which additional auditing or monitoring is applied during and after the recovery process. Time to bring online a backup network intrusion detection system. Percentage of reconstituted cyber resources which are placed in a restricted enclave for a period after reconstitution.<br>• Percentage of restored or reconstructed (mission-critical, security-critical, supporting) data assets for which data integrity/quality is checked. |
| **Understand** Maintain useful representations of mission and business dependencies and the status of resources with respect to possible adversity. | • Understand adversaries.<br>• Understand dependencies on and among systems containing cyber resources.<br>• Understand the status of resources with respect to threat events<br>• Understand the effectiveness of security controls and controls supporting cyber resiliency. | • Time between receipt of threat intelligence and determination of its relevance. Adversary dwell time in deception environment.<br>• Time since most recent refresh of mission dependency or functional dependency map. Time since last cyber table-top exercise, Red Team exercise, or execution of controlled automated disruption.<br>• Percentage of system elements for which failure or indication of potential faults can be detected. Percentage of cyber resources monitored.<br>• Number of attempted intrusions stopped at a network perimeter. Average length of time to recover from incidents. |
| **Transform** Modify mission or business functions and supporting processes to handle adversity and address environmental changes more effectively. | • Redefine mission/business process threads for agility.<br>• Redefine mission/business functions to mitigate risks. | • Percentage of mission or business process threads which have been analyzed with respect to common dependencies and potential single points of failure. Percentage of mission or business process threads for which alternative courses of action are documented.<br>• Percentage of essential functions for which no dependencies on resources shared with non-essential functions can be identified. Percentage of problematic data feeds to which risk mitigations have been applied since last analysis. |

---

[105] Damage need not be identified with specific resources. For example, degraded service can be systemic. Resources (e.g., processes) can be untrustworthy even if they appear to be performing correctly.

| OBJECTIVE | REPRESENTATIVE SUB-OBJECTIVES | REPRESENTATIVE EXAMPLES OF METRICS |
|---|---|---|
| **Re-Architect** Modify architectures to handle adversity and address environmental changes more effectively. | • Restructure systems or sub-systems to reduce risks. <br>• Modify systems or sub-systems to reduce risks. | • Size of the (hardware, software, supply chain, user, privileged user) attack surface. Percentage of system components for which provenance can be determined. Percentage of system components which can be selectively isolated. <br>• Percentage of cyber resources for which custom analytics have been developed. Percentage of mission-critical components for which one or more custom-built alternatives are implemented. |

## E.3   CYBER RESILIENCY TECHNIQUES

This section provides definitions for cyber resiliency *techniques*, one of the fundamental cyber resiliency constructs, which also include goals, objectives, approaches, and design principles. The objectives support goals, the techniques support objectives, the approaches support techniques, and the design principles support the realization of the goals and objectives. The relationship among the cyber resiliency constructs to include specific mapping tables for the constructs is provided in Appendix H. Table E-2 lists each cyber resiliency technique and its purpose. Table E-3 identifies potential interactions (e.g., synergies, conflicts) between cyber resiliency techniques.

### TABLE E-2:  CYBER RESILIENCY TECHNIQUES

| TECHNIQUE | PURPOSE |
|---|---|
| **Adaptive Response** Implement agile courses of action to manage risks. | Optimize the ability to respond in a timely and appropriate manner to adverse conditions, stresses, or attacks, or to indicators of these, thus maximizing the ability to maintain mission or business operations, limit consequences, and avoid destabilization. |
| **Analytic Monitoring** Monitor and analyze a wide range of properties and behaviors on an ongoing basis and in a coordinated way. | Maximize the ability to detect potential adverse conditions, reveal the extent of adverse conditions, stresses, or attacks, and identify potential or actual damage. Provide data needed for situational awareness. |
| **Contextual Awareness** Construct and maintain current representations of the posture of missions or business functions considering threat events and courses of action. | Support situational awareness. Enhance understanding of dependencies among cyber and non-cyber resources. Reveal patterns or trends in adversary behavior. |
| **Coordinated Protection** Ensure that protection mechanisms operate in a coordinated and effective manner. | Require an adversary to overcome multiple safeguards (i.e., implement a strategy of defense-in-depth). Increase the difficulty for an adversary to successfully attack critical resources, increasing the cost to the adversary and raising the likelihood of adversary detection. Ensure that the use of any given protection mechanism does not create adverse, unintended consequences by interfering with other protection mechanisms. Validate the realism of cyber courses of action. |

| TECHNIQUE | PURPOSE |
|---|---|
| **Deception**<br>Mislead, confuse, hide critical assets from, or expose covertly tainted assets to the adversary. | Mislead or confuse the adversary or hide critical assets from the adversary, making the adversary uncertain how to proceed, delaying the effect of the attack, increasing the risk of being discovered, causing the adversary to misdirect or waste its resources, and exposing the adversary tradecraft prematurely. |
| **Diversity**<br>Use heterogeneity to minimize common mode failures, particularly threat events exploiting common vulnerabilities. | Limit the possibility of loss of critical functions due to failure of replicated common components. Cause an adversary to expend more effort by developing malware or other TTPs appropriate for multiple targets; increase the probability that the adversary will waste or expose TTPs by applying them to targets for which they are inappropriate; and maximize the probability that some of the defending organization's systems will survive the adversary's attack. |
| **Dynamic Positioning**<br>Distribute and dynamically relocate functionality or system resources. | Increase the ability to rapidly recover from non-adversarial events (e.g., fires, floods). Impede an adversary's ability to locate, eliminate, or corrupt mission or business assets, and cause the adversary to spend more time and effort to find the organization's critical assets, thereby increasing the probability of the adversary revealing its actions and tradecraft prematurely. |
| **Non-Persistence**<br>Generate and retain resources as needed or for a limited time. | Reduce exposure to corruption, modification, or compromise. Provide a means of curtailing an adversary's intrusion and advance and potentially removing malware or damaged resources from the system. |
| **Privilege Restriction**<br>Restrict privileges based on attributes of users and system elements as well as on environmental factors. | Limit the impact and probability that unintended actions by authorized individuals will compromise information or services. Impede an adversary by requiring them to invest more time and effort in obtaining credentials. Curtail the adversary's ability to take full advantage of credentials that they have obtained. |
| **Realignment**<br>Align system resources with current organizational mission or business function needs to reduce risk. | Minimize the connections between mission-critical and noncritical services, thus reducing the likelihood that a failure of noncritical services will impact mission-critical services. Reduce the attack surface of the defending organization by minimizing the probability that non-mission or business functions could be used as an attack vector. Accommodate changing mission or business function needs. |
| **Redundancy**<br>Provide multiple protected instances of critical resources. | Reduce the consequences of loss of information or services. Facilitate recovery from the effects of an adverse cyber event. Limit the time during which critical services are denied or limited. |
| **Segmentation**<br>Define and separate system elements based on criticality and trustworthiness. | Contain adversary activities and non-adversarial stresses (e.g., fires, floods) to the enclave or segment in which they have established a presence. Limit the set of possible targets to which malware can easily be propagated. |
| **Substantiated Integrity**<br>Ascertain whether critical system elements have been corrupted. | Facilitate determination of correct results in case of conflicts between diverse services or inputs. Detect attempts by an adversary to deliver compromised data, software, or hardware, as well as successful modification or fabrication. |
| **Unpredictability**<br>Make changes randomly or unpredictably. | Increase an adversary's uncertainty regarding the system protections which they may encounter, thus making it more difficult for them to ascertain the appropriate course of action. |

**TABLE E-3:  POTENTIAL INTERACTIONS BETWEEN CYBER RESILIENCY TECHNIQUES**

| Technique A / Technique B | Adaptive Response | Analytic Monitoring | Contextual Awareness | Coordinated Protection | Deception | Diversity | Dynamic Positioning | Non-Persistence | Privilege Restriction | Realignment | Redundancy | Segmentation | Substantiated Integrity | Unpredictability |
|---|---|---|---|---|---|---|---|---|---|---|---|---|---|---|
| Adaptive Response | - | D | U | S | | U | U/S | U/S | U/S | | U | U/S | U | U |
| Analytic Monitoring | S | - | S | D | U/C | U | U | | | | | | U/S | |
| Contextual Awareness | S | U | - | | | | | | | S | | | U | |
| Coordinated Protection | U | S | | - | | U | U | U | U/S | U | | U | | |
| Deception | | U/C | C/S | | - | | U | | | | | U | S | U |
| Diversity | S | C/S | C | C/S | | - | S | | U | U | S | | U | S |
| Dynamic Positioning | U/S | C/S | | | S | U | - | U | | | U | | | U/S |
| Non-Persistence | U/S | C | C | | | | S | - | | | | | U | S |
| Privilege Restriction | S | | | U | | | | | - | S | | | U | |
| Realignment | C | | U | C/S | | C/S | | | S | - | C | | | |
| Redundancy | S | | | | | U | S | | | | - | | U | |
| Segmentation | U/S | C | | S | S | | | | | | | - | | U |
| Substantiated Integrity | S | S/U | S | | U | S | | S | S | | S | | - | |
| Unpredictability | C/S | C | | C | S | U | U/S | U | | | | | | - |

**Key:**
- **S** indicates that the technique in the row (Technique A) *supports* the one in the column (Technique B). Technique B is made more effective by Technique A.
- **D** indicates that Technique A *depends on* Technique or Enabler B. Technique A will be ineffective if not used in conjunction with Technique or Enabler B.
- **U** indicates that Technique A can *use* Technique or Enabler B. Technique A can be implemented effectively in the absence of Technique B; however, more options become available if Technique B is also used.
- **C** indicates that Technique A can *conflict with or complicate* Technique B. Some or all implementations of Technique A could undermine the effectiveness of Technique B.

## E.4  CYBER RESILIENCY IMPLEMENTATION APPROACHES

This section identifies representative cyber resiliency *approaches* to implementing cyber resiliency techniques. A cyber resiliency approach is a subset of the technologies and processes included in a cyber resiliency technique, defined by how the capabilities are implemented or how the intended consequences are achieved. Table E-4 lists each cyber resiliency technique, representative approaches that can be used to implement the technique, and representative examples. Where possible, examples are drawn from discussions associated with the controls and control enhancements in [SP 800-53], even when these controls or enhancements do not directly support cyber resiliency as described in Appendix G. However, [SP 800-53] does not address all approaches or all aspects of any individual approach. Therefore, some examples are drawn from system reliability and system resilience practices and technologies, and/or from emerging cyber resiliency technologies. The set of approaches for a specific technique is not exhaustive and represents relatively mature technologies and practices. Thus, technologies emerging from research can be characterized in terms of the techniques they apply, while not being covered by any of the representative approaches.

### TABLE E-4: CYBER RESILIENCY APPROACHES

| TECHNIQUES | APPROACHES | EXAMPLES |
|---|---|---|
| **Adaptive Response** Implement agile courses of action to manage risks. | **Dynamic Reconfiguration** Make changes to individual systems, system elements, components, or sets of cyber resources to change functionality or behavior without interrupting service. | • Dynamically change router rules, access control lists, intrusion detection and prevention system parameters, and filter rules for firewalls and gateways. • Re-assign cyber defense responsibilities to personnel or operating centers. |
| | **Dynamic Resource Allocation** Change the allocation of resources to tasks or functions without terminating critical functions or processes. | • Employ dynamic provisioning. • Reprioritize messages or services. • Implement load-balancing. • Provide emergency shutoff capabilities. • Pre-empt communications. |
| | **Adaptive Management** Change how mechanisms are used based on changes in the operational environment as well as changes in the threat environment. | • Disable access dynamically. • Implement adaptive authentication. • Provide for automatic disabling of the system. • Provide dynamic deployment of new or replacement resources or capabilities. |
| **Analytic Monitoring** Monitor and analyze a wide range of properties and behaviors on an ongoing basis and in a coordinated way. | **Monitoring and Damage Assessment** Monitor and analyze behavior and characteristics of components and resources to look for indicators of adversary activity and to detect and assess damage from adversity. | • Use hardware fault detection. • Employ Continuous Diagnostics and Mitigation (CDM) or other vulnerability scanning tools. • Deploy Intrusion Detection Systems (IDSs) and other monitoring tools. • Use Insider Threat monitoring tools. • Perform telemetry analysis. • Detect malware beaconing. • Monitor open-source information for indicators of disclosure or compromise. |
| | **Sensor Fusion and Analysis** Fuse and analyze monitoring data and analysis results from different information sources or at different times together with externally provided threat intelligence. | • Enable organization-wide situational awareness. • Implement cross-organizational auditing. • Correlate data from different tools. • Fuse data from physical access control systems and information systems. |

| TECHNIQUES | APPROACHES | EXAMPLES |
|---|---|---|
| | **Forensic and Behavioral Analysis** Analyze adversary TTPs, including observed behavior as well as malware and other artifacts left behind by adverse events. | • Deploy an integrated team of forensic and malware analysts, developers, and operations personnel.<br>• Use reverse engineering and other malware analysis tools. |
| **Coordinated Protection** Ensure that protection mechanisms operate in a coordinated and effective manner. | **Calibrated Defense-in-Depth** Provide complementary protective mechanisms at different architectural layers or in different locations, calibrating the strength and number of mechanisms to resource value. | • Design for defense-in-depth.<br>• Employ multiple, distinct authentication challenges over the course of a session to confirm identity.<br>• Combine network and host-based intrusion detection.<br>• Provide increasing levels of protection to access more sensitive or critical resources.<br>• Conduct sensitivity and criticality analyses. |
| | **Consistency Analysis** Determine whether and how protections can be applied in a coordinated, consistent way that minimizes interference, potential cascading failures, or coverage gaps. | • Employ unified Identity and Access Management (IdAM) administration tools.<br>• Analyze mission/business process flows and threads.<br>• Employ privilege analysis tools to support an ongoing review of whether user privileges are assigned consistently.<br>• Interpret attributes consistently.<br>• Coordinate the planning, training, and testing of incident response, contingency planning, etc.<br>• Design for facilitating coordination and mutual support among safeguards. |
| | **Orchestration** Coordinate the ongoing behavior of mechanisms and processes at different layers, in different locations, or implemented for different aspects of trustworthiness to avoid causing cascading failures, interference, or coverage gaps. | • Coordinate incident handling with mission/business process continuity of operations and organizational processes.<br>• Conduct coverage planning and management for sensors.<br>• Use cyber playbooks. |
| | **Self-Challenge** Affect mission/business processes or system elements adversely in a controlled manner to validate the effectiveness of protections and to enable proactive response and improvement. | • Hardware power-on self-test.<br>• Conduct role-based training exercises.<br>• Conduct penetration testing and Red Team exercises.<br>• Test automated incident response.<br>• Employ fault injection.<br>• Conduct tabletop exercises. |
| **Contextual Awareness** Construct and maintain current representations of the posture of missions or business | **Dynamic Resource Awareness** Maintain current information about resources, status of resources, and resource connectivity. | • Maintain real-time integrated situational awareness. |

| TECHNIQUES | APPROACHES | EXAMPLES |
|---|---|---|
| functions considering threat events and courses of action. | **Dynamic Threat Awareness** Maintain current information about threat actors, indicators, and potential, predicted, and observed adverse events. | • Track predicted or impending natural disasters. • Dynamically ingest incident and threat data. • Facilitate integrated situational awareness of threats. |
| | **Mission Dependency and Status Visualization** Maintain current information about the status of missions or business functions, dependencies on resources, and the status of those resources with respect to threats. | • Construct a broad (mission/business function-wide, organization-wide) perspective. |
| **Deception** Mislead, confuse, hide critical assets from, or expose covertly tainted assets to the adversary. | **Obfuscation** Hide, transform, or otherwise obfuscate information from the adversary. | • Encrypt data at rest. • Encrypt transmitted data (e.g., using a Virtual Private Network [VPN]). • Encrypt authenticators. • Conceal or randomize communications patterns. • Conceal the presence of system components on an internal network. • Mask, encrypt, hash, or replace identifiers. • Obfuscate traffic via onion routing. • Apply chaffing to communications traffic. • Add a large amount of valid but useless information to a data store. • Perform encrypted processing. |
| | **Disinformation** Provide deliberately misleading information to adversaries. | • Post questions to a public forum based on false information about the system. • Create false ("canary") credentials and tokens (e.g., honeytokens). |
| | **Misdirection** Maintain deception resources or environments and direct adversary activities there. | • Establish and maintain honeypots, honeynets, or decoy files. • Maintain a full-scale, all-encompassing deception environment. |
| | **Tainting** Embed covert capabilities in resources. | • Use beacon traps. • Employ internal network table cache poisoning (e.g., Domain Name System (DNS), Address Resolution Protocol (ARP)). • Include false entries or steganographic data in files to enable them to be found via open-source analysis. |
| **Diversity** Use heterogeneity to minimize common mode failures, particularly threat events exploiting common vulnerabilities. | **Architectural Diversity** Use multiple sets of technical standards, different technologies, and different architectural patterns. | • Use auditing/logging systems on different OSs to acquire and store audit/logging data. • Apply different audit/logging regimes at different architectural layers. • Deploy diverse operating systems. • Support multiple protocol standards. |

| TECHNIQUES | APPROACHES | EXAMPLES |
|---|---|---|
| | **Design Diversity**<br>Use different designs to meet the same requirements or provide equivalent functionality. | • Employ N-version programming.<br>• Employ mixed-signal design diversity (using both analog and digital signals).<br>• Employ mixed-level design diversity (using both hardware and software implementations). |
| | **Synthetic Diversity**<br>Transform implementations of software to produce a variety of instances. | • Implement address space layout randomization.<br>• Use randomizing compilers. |
| | **Information Diversity**<br>Provide information from different sources or transform information in different ways. | • Apply different analog-to-digital conversion methods to non-digitally-obtained data.<br>• Use multiple data sources. |
| | **Path Diversity**<br>Provide multiple independent paths for command, control, and communications. | • Establish alternate telecommunications services (e.g., ground-based circuits, satellite communications).<br>• Employ alternate communications protocols.<br>• Use out-of-band channels. |
| | **Supply Chain Diversity**<br>Use multiple independent supply chains for critical components. | • Use a diverse set of suppliers. |
| **Dynamic Positioning**<br>Distribute and dynamically relocate functionality or system resources. | **Functional Relocation of Sensors**<br>Relocate sensors or reallocate responsibility for specific sensing tasks to look for indicators of adverse events. | • Relocate (using virtualization) or reconfigure IDSs or IDS sensors. |
| | **Functional Relocation of Cyber Resources**<br>Change the location of cyber resources that provide functionality or information, either by moving the assets or by transferring functional responsibility. | • Change processing locations (e.g., switch to a virtual machine on a different physical component).<br>• Change storage sites (e.g., switch to an alternate data store on a different storage area network). |
| | **Asset Mobility**<br>Securely move physical resources. | • Move a mobile device or system component (e.g., a router) from one room in a facility to another while monitoring its movement.<br>• Move storage media securely from one room or facility to another room or facility.<br>• Move a platform or vehicle to avoid collision or other physical harm, while retaining knowledge of its location. |
| | **Fragmentation**<br>Fragment information and distribute it across multiple components. | • Implement fragmentation and partitioning for distributed databases. |
| | **Distributed Functionality**<br>Decompose a function or application into smaller functions and distribute those functions across multiple components. | • Architect applications so that constituent functions can be located on different system components. |

| TECHNIQUES | APPROACHES | EXAMPLES |
|---|---|---|
| **Non-Persistence**<br>Generate and retain resources as needed or for a limited time. | **Non-Persistent Information**<br>Refresh information periodically, or generate information on demand, and delete it when no longer needed. | • Delete high value mission information after it is processed.<br>• Off-load audit records to off-line storage.<br>• Use one-time passwords or nonces. |
| | **Non-Persistent Services**<br>Refresh services periodically, or generate services on demand and terminate services when no longer needed. | • Employ time-based or inactivity-based session termination.<br>• Re-image components.<br>• Refresh services using virtualization. |
| | **Non-Persistent Connectivity**<br>Establish connections on demand, and terminate connections when no longer needed. | • Implement software-defined networking.<br>• Employ time-based or inactivity-based network disconnection. |
| **Privilege Restriction**<br>Restrict privileges based on attributes of users and system elements as well as on environmental factors. | **Trust-Based Privilege Management**<br>Define, assign, and maintain privileges associated with active entities based on established trust criteria consistent with principles of least privilege. | • Implement least privilege.<br>• Employ time-based account restrictions. |
| | **Attribute-Based Usage Restriction**<br>Define, assign, maintain, and apply usage restrictions on systems containing cyber resources based on the criticality of missions or business functions and other attributes (e.g., data sensitivity). | • Employ Role-Based Access Control (RBAC).<br>• Employ Attribute-Based Access Control (ABAC).<br>• Restrict the use of maintenance tools. |
| | **Dynamic Privileges**<br>Elevate or decrease privileges assigned to a user, process, or service based on transient or contextual factors. | • Implement time-based adjustment to privileges due to status of mission or business tasks.<br>• Employ dynamic account provisioning.<br>• Disable privileges based on a determination that an individual or process is high-risk.<br>• Implement dynamic revocation of access authorizations.<br>• Implement dynamic association of attributes with cyber resources and active entities.<br>• Implement dynamic credential binding. |
| **Realignment**<br>Align system resources with current organizational mission or business function needs to reduce risk. | **Purposing**<br>Ensure systems containing cyber resources are used consistently with mission or business function purposes and approved uses. | • Use whitelisting to prevent installation of such unapproved applications as games or peer-to-peer music sharing.<br>• Use whitelisting to restrict communications to a specified set of addresses.<br>• Ensure that privileged accounts are not used for non-privileged functions. |
| | **Offloading**<br>Offload supportive but non-essential functions to other systems or to an external provider that is better able to support the functions. | • Outsource non-essential services to a managed service provider.<br>• Impose requirements on and perform oversight of external system services. |

| TECHNIQUES | APPROACHES | EXAMPLES |
|---|---|---|
| | **Restriction**<br>Remove or disable unneeded functionality or connectivity, or add mechanisms to reduce the chance of vulnerability or failure. | • Configure the system to provide only essential capabilities.<br>• Minimize non-security functionality. |
| | **Replacement**<br>Replace low-assurance or poorly understood implementations with more trustworthy implementations. | • Remove or replace unsupported system components to reduce risk. |
| | **Specialization**<br>Modify the design of, augment, or configure critical cyber resources uniquely for the mission or business function to improve trustworthiness. | • Re-implement or custom develop critical components.<br>• Develop custom system elements covertly.<br>• Define and apply customized configurations. |
| **Redundancy**<br>Provide multiple protected instances of critical resources. | **Protected Backup and Restore**<br>Back up information and software (including configuration data and virtualized resources) in a way that protects its confidentiality, integrity, and authenticity, and enable restoration in case of disruption or corruption. | • Retain previous baseline configurations.<br>• Maintain and protect system-level backup information (e.g., operating system, application software, system configuration data). |
| | **Surplus Capacity**<br>Maintain extra capacity for information storage, processing, or communications. | • Maintain spare parts (i.e., system components).<br>• Address surplus capacity in service-level agreements with external systems. |
| | **Replication**<br>Duplicate hardware, information, backups, or functionality in multiple locations and keep them synchronized. | • Provide alternate audit capability.<br>• Shadow database.<br>• Maintain one or more alternate storage sites.<br>• Maintain one or more alternate processing sites.<br>• Maintain a redundant secondary system.<br>• Provide alternative security mechanisms.<br>• Implement a redundant name and address resolution service. |
| **Segmentation**<br>Define and separate system elements based on criticality and trustworthiness. | **Predefined Segmentation**<br>Define enclaves, segments, or other types of resource sets based on criticality and trustworthiness so that they can be protected separately and, if necessary, isolated. | • Use virtualization to maintain separate processing domains based on user privileges.<br>• Use cryptographic separation for maintenance.<br>• Partition application from system functionality.<br>• Isolate security functions from non-security functions.<br>• Isolate security tools and capabilities using physical separation.<br>• Isolate components based on mission or business function.<br>• Separate subnets that connect to different security domains. In |

| TECHNIQUES | APPROACHES | EXAMPLES |
|---|---|---|
| | | particular, provide a DMZ for Internet connectivity.<br>• Employ system partitioning.<br>• Employ process isolation.<br>• Implement sandboxes and other confined environments.<br>• Implement memory protection. |
| | **Dynamic Segmentation and Isolation**<br>Change the configuration of enclaves or protected segments, or isolate resources while minimizing operational disruption. | • Implement dynamic isolation of components.<br>• Implement software-defined networking and VPNs to define new enclaves.<br>• Create a virtualized sandbox or detonation chamber for untrusted attachments or URLs. |
| **Substantiated Integrity**<br>Ascertain whether critical system elements have been corrupted. | **Integrity Checks**<br>Apply and validate checks of the integrity or quality of information, components, or services. | • Use tamper-evident seals and anti-tamper coatings.<br>• Use automated tools for data quality checking.<br>• Use blockchain technology.<br>• Use non-modifiable executables.<br>• Use polling techniques to identify potential damage.<br>• Implement cryptographic hashes.<br>• Employ information input validation.<br>• Validate components as part of SCRM.<br>• Employ integrity checking on external systems. |
| | **Provenance Tracking**<br>Identify and track the provenance of data, software, or hardware elements. | • Employ component traceability as part of Supply Chain Risk Management (SCRM).<br>• Employ provenance tracking as part of SCRM.<br>• Implement anti-counterfeit protections.<br>• Implement trusted path.<br>• Implement code signing. |
| | **Behavior Validation**<br>Validate the behavior of a system, service, or device against defined or emergent criteria (e.g., requirements, patterns of prior usage). | • Employ detonation chambers.<br>• Implement function verification.<br>• Verify boot process integrity.<br>• Implement fault injection to observe potential anomalies in error handling. |
| **Unpredictability**<br>Make changes randomly or unpredictably. | **Temporal Unpredictability**<br>Change behavior or state at times that are determined randomly or by complex functions. | • Require re-authentication at random intervals.<br>• Perform routine actions at different times of day. |
| | **Contextual Unpredictability**<br>Change behavior or state in ways that are determined randomly or by complex functions. | • Rotate roles and responsibilities.<br>• Implement random channel-hopping. |

As the examples in Table E-4 illustrate, cyber resiliency techniques and approaches can be applied at a variety of architectural layers or system elements, including elements of the technical system (e.g., hardware, networking, software, and information stores) and system elements that are part of the larger socio-technical system—operations (e.g., people and processes supporting cyber defense, system administration, and mission or business function tasks), support (e.g., programmatic, systems engineering, maintenance and support), and environment of operation (e.g., physical access restrictions and physical location). Table E-5 indicates, for a representative set of architectural layers, approaches which could be applied at those layers. In Table E-5, "other software" includes, but is not limited to, specialized software intended to implement cyber resiliency or cybersecurity capabilities. Note that some approaches (e.g., Calibrated Defense-in-Depth, Consistency Analysis) can involve working across multiple layers or at multiple locations.

**TABLE E-5: ARCHITECTURAL LAYERS AT WHICH CYBER RESILIENCY APPROACHES CAN BE USED**

| TECHNIQUES | APPROACHES | HARDWARE AND FIRMWARE | NETWORKING AND COMMUNICATIONS | OTHER SOFTWARE | OPERATING SYSTEM | CLOUD, VIRTUALIZATION MIDDLEWARE, INFRASTRUCTURE | APPLICATION | INFORMATION STORAGE MANAGEMENT | TECHNICAL SYSTEM AS A WHOLE | OPERATIONS | SUPPORT | ENVIRONMENT OF OPERATION |
|---|---|---|---|---|---|---|---|---|---|---|---|---|
| Adaptive Response | Dynamic Reconfiguration | X | X | | X | X | X | | X | X | | |
| | Dynamic Resource Allocation | | X | | X | X | X | | X | X | | |
| | Adaptive Management | | X | | X | | X | | X | X | | |
| Analytic Monitoring | Monitoring and Damage Assessment | | X | X | | | | | X | X | | |
| | Sensor Fusion and Analysis | | X | X | X | | | | X | X | | |
| | Forensic and Behavioral Analysis | | | X | | | | | X | X | | |
| Coordinated Protection | Calibrated Defense-in-Depth | | | | | | | | X | X | X | |
| | Consistency Analysis | | | X | | | | | X | X | X | |
| | Orchestration | | | | | X | | | X | X | | |
| | Self-Challenge | X | X | X | X | | X | | X | | | |

| TECHNIQUES | APPROACHES | HARDWARE AND FIRMWARE | NETWORKING AND COMMUNICATIONS | OTHER SOFTWARE | OPERATING SYSTEM | CLOUD, VIRTUALIZATION MIDDLEWARE, INFRASTRUCTURE | APPLICATION | INFORMATION STORAGE MANAGEMENT | TECHNICAL SYSTEM AS A WHOLE | OPERATIONS | SUPPORT | ENVIRONMENT OF OPERATION |
|---|---|---|---|---|---|---|---|---|---|---|---|---|
| Contextual Awareness | Dynamic Resource Awareness | | X | X | | | | | X | X | | |
| | Dynamic Threat Awareness | | | X | | | | | X | X | | |
| | Mission Dependency and Status Visualization | | | X | | | | | X | X | | |
| Deception | Obfuscation | X | X | X | X | | X | X | | X | X | |
| | Disinformation | | | | | | X | X | | X | X | |
| | Misdirection | | X | X | | | | | X | X | X | |
| | Tainting | | X | X | | | X | | | | | |
| Diversity | Architectural Diversity | X | X | X | X | X | X | | | | | |
| | Design Diversity | X | X | X | X | X | X | | | | | |
| | Synthetic Diversity | | | | X | X | X | | | | | |
| | Information Diversity | | | | | | | X | | X | | |
| | Path Diversity | | X | | | | | | | X | | |
| | Supply Chain Diversity | X | | | | | | | | | X | |
| Dynamic Positioning | Functional Relocation of Sensors | | X | X | X | X | | | X | X | | |
| | Functional Relocation of Cyber Resources | | X | X | X | X | | | X | X | | |
| | Asset Mobility | | | | | | | | | X | | X |
| | Fragmentation | | | | | | | X | | | | |
| | Distributed Functionality | | | X | | X | X | | X | X | | |
| Non-Persistence | Non-Persistent Information | | | | X | X | X | X | | X | | |
| | Non-Persistent Services | | | | X | X | | | X | | | |

| TECHNIQUES | APPROACHES | SOCIO-TECHNICAL SYSTEM | | | | | | | | | | |
| | | TECHNICAL SYSTEM | | | | | | | | OPERATIONS | SUPPORT | ENVIRONMENT OF OPERATION |
| | | | | SOFTWARE | | | | | | | | |
| | | HARDWARE AND FIRMWARE | NETWORKING AND COMMUNICATIONS | OTHER SOFTWARE | OPERATING SYSTEM | CLOUD, VIRTUALIZATION MIDDLEWARE, INFRASTRUCTURE | APPLICATION | INFORMATION STORAGE MANAGEMENT | TECHNICAL SYSTEM AS A WHOLE | | | |
|---|---|---|---|---|---|---|---|---|---|---|---|---|
| | Non-Persistent Connectivity | | X | | | | | | X | X | | X |
| Privilege Restriction | Trust-Based Privilege Management | | | X | X | | X | | X | | | |
| | Attribute-Based Usage Restriction | X | X | X | X | | X | | X | | | |
| | Dynamic Privileges | | | X | X | | X | | X | | | |
| Realignment | Purposing | | X | X | X | | X | | | X | X | |
| | Offloading | | | X | | | X | | | X | | |
| | Restriction | | X | X | X | | X | | | X | X | |
| | Replacement | X | | X | | | | | | | X | |
| | Specialization | X | | X | | | X | | | | X | |
| Redundancy | Protected Backup and Restore | | | X | X | | X | X | X | X | | |
| | Surplus Capacity | X | X | | | X | X | X | | X | | |
| | Replication | X | X | | | X | X | X | X | X | | |
| Segmentation | Predefined Segmentation | X | X | X | X | X | | | X | X | | X |
| | Dynamic Segmentation and Isolation | X | X | X | X | X | | | | X | | X |
| Substantiated Integrity | Integrity Checks | X | X | X | X | X | X | X | | X | | |
| | Provenance Tracking | X | X | | X | | X | X | | | X | |
| | Behavior Validation | X | X | X | X | X | X | | | X | | |
| | Temporal Unpredictability | | X | X | X | X | X | | | X | | |
| | Contextual Unpredictability | | X | X | X | X | X | | | X | | |

## E.5  CYBER RESILIENCY DESIGN PRINCIPLES

This section provides a description of *strategic* and *structural* cyber resiliency design principles, a key construct in the cyber resiliency engineering framework. It also describes relationships with the design principles from other disciplines, the analytic practices necessary to implement the principles, and how the application of the principles affects risk. In particular, relationships to security design principles as described in Appendix F of [SP 800-160 v1] are identified.[106] As noted in Section 2.1.4, strategic design principles express the organization's risk management strategy, and structural design principles support the strategic design principles.

### E.5.1  *STRATEGIC DESIGN PRINCIPLES*

Strategic cyber resiliency design principles guide and inform engineering analyses and risk analyses throughout the system life cycle and highlight different structural design principles, cyber resiliency techniques, and approaches to applying those techniques. Table E-6 describes five strategic cyber resiliency design principles and identifies the related design principles from other disciplines.[107] [108]

---

[106] Appendix F of [SP 800-160 v1] defines security design principles in three broad categories: Security Architecture and Design, Security Capability and Intrinsic Behaviors, and Life Cycle Security. For a detailed discussion of relationships between security design principles and cyber resiliency techniques as well as cyber resiliency design principles, see [Bodeau17].

[107] Resilience Engineering design principles are described in the Systems Engineering Body of Knowledge [Seok] and [Jackson13]. Resilience Engineering design principles mapped to cyber resiliency design principles in this Appendix are: Absorption (allow the system to withstand threats to a specified level); Human-in-the-Loop (allow the system to employ human elements when there is a need for human cognition); Internode Interaction (allow the nodes of the system to communicate, cooperate, and collaborate with other nodes when this interaction is essential); Modularity (construct the system of relatively independent but interlocking system components or system elements; also called Localized Capacity); Neutral State (allow the system to incorporate time delays that will allow human operators to consider actions to prevent further damage); Complexity Avoidance (incorporate features which enable the system to limit its own complexity to a level not more than necessary); Hidden Interactions Avoidance (incorporate features that assure that potentially harmful interactions between nodes are avoided); Redundancy [functional] (employ an architecture with two or more independent and identical branches); Redundancy [physical] (employ an architecture with two or more different branches; also called Diversity); Loose Coupling (construct the system of elements which depend on each other to the least extent practicable); Defense-in-Depth (provide multiple means to avoid failure; also called Layered Defense); Restructuring (incorporate features that allow the system to restructure itself; also known as Reorganization); and Reparability (incorporate features that allow the system to be brought up to partial or full functionality over a specified period of time and in a specified environment).

[108] Survivability design principles are described in [Richards08]. The Survivability design principles mapped to cyber resiliency design principles in this Appendix are: Prevention (suppress a future or potential future disturbance); Mobility (relocate to avoid detection by an external change agent); Concealment (reduce the visibility of a system from an external change agent); Deterrence (dissuade a rational external agent from committing a disturbance); Preemption (suppress an imminent disturbance); Avoidance (maneuver away from an ongoing disturbance); Hardness (resist deformation); Redundancy (duplicate critical system functions to increase reliability); Margin (allow extra capability to maintain value delivery despite losses); Heterogeneity (vary system elements to mitigate homogeneous disturbances); Distribution (separate critical system elements to mitigate local disturbances); Failure Mode Reduction (eliminate system hazards through intrinsic design: substitute, simplify, decouple, and reduce hazardous materials); Fail-Safe (prevent or delay degradation via physics of incipient failure); Evolution (alter system elements to reduce disturbance effectiveness); Containment (isolate or minimize the propagation of failure); Replacement (substitute system elements to improve value delivery); and Repair (restore the system to improve value delivery).

**TABLE E-6:  STRATEGIC CYBER RESILIENCY DESIGN PRINCIPLES**

| STRATEGIC DESIGN PRINCIPLES | KEY IDEAS | RELATED DESIGN PRINCIPLES FROM OTHER DISCIPLINES |
|---|---|---|
| **Focus on common critical assets.** | Limited organizational and programmatic resources need to be applied where they can provide the greatest benefit. This results in a strategy of focusing first on assets which are both critical and common, then on those which are either critical or common. | **Security:** Inverse Modification Threshold.<br>**Resilience Engineering:** Physical Redundancy, Layered Defense, Loose Coupling.<br>**Survivability:** Failure Mode Reduction, Fail-Safe, Evolution. |
| **Support agility and architect for adaptability.** | Not only does the threat landscape change as adversaries evolve, so do technologies and the ways in which individuals and organizations use them. Both agility and adaptability are integral to the risk management strategy in response to the risk framing assumption that unforeseen changes will occur in the threat, technical, and operational environment through a system's lifespan. | **Security:** Secure Evolvability, Minimized Sharing, Reduced Complexity.<br>**Resilience Engineering:** Reorganization, Human Backup, Inter-Node Interaction.<br>**Survivability:** Mobility, Evolution. |
| **Reduce attack surfaces.** | A large attack surface is difficult to defend, requiring ongoing effort to monitor, analyze, and respond to anomalies. Reducing attack surfaces reduces ongoing protection scope costs and makes the adversary concentrate efforts on a small set of locations, resources, or environments that can be more effectively monitored and defended. | **Security:** Least Common Mechanism, Minimized Sharing, Reduced Complexity, Minimized Security Elements, Least Privilege, Predicate Permission.<br>**Resilience Engineering:** Complexity Avoidance, Drift Correction.<br>**Survivability:** Prevention, Failure Mode Reduction. |
| **Assume compromised resources.** | Systems and system components, ranging from chips to software modules to running services, can be compromised for extended periods without detection. In fact, some compromises may never be detected. Systems must remain capable of meeting performance and quality requirements, nonetheless. | **Security:** Trusted Components, Self-Reliant Trustworthiness, Trusted Communications Channels.<br>*Incompatible with Security:* Hierarchical Protection.<br>**Resilience Engineering:** Human Backup, Localized Capacity, Loose Coupling. |
| **Expect adversaries to evolve.** | Advanced cyber adversaries invest time, effort, and intelligence-gathering to improve existing and develop new TTPs. Adversaries evolve in response to opportunities offered by new technologies or uses of technology, as well as to the knowledge they gain about defender TTPs. In (increasingly short) time, the tools developed by advanced adversaries become available to less sophisticated adversaries. Therefore, systems and missions need to be resilient in the face of unexpected attacks. | **Security:** Trusted Communications Channels.<br>**Resilience Engineering:** Reorganization, Drift Correction.<br>**Survivability:** Evolution. |

Strategic design principles are driven by an organization's risk management strategy and, in particular, by its risk framing. Risk framing includes, for example, assumptions about the threats the organization should be prepared for, the constraints on risk management decision-making (including which risk response alternatives are irrelevant), and organizational priorities and trade-offs.[109] From the standpoint of cyber resiliency, one way to express priorities is in terms of which cyber resiliency objectives are most important. Each strategic design principle supports achievement of one or more cyber resiliency objectives and relates to the design principles, concerns, or analysis processes associated with other specialty engineering disciplines. The relationships between strategic cyber resiliency design principles, risk framing, and analytic practices are indicated in Table E-7. Relationships between design principles and other cyber resiliency constructs are identified in Appendix E.6.

**TABLE E-7: STRATEGIC DESIGN PRINCIPLES DRIVE ANALYSIS AND RELATE TO RISK MANAGEMENT**

| STRATEGIC DESIGN PRINCIPLES AND ANALYTIC PRACTICES | RISK FRAMING ELEMENTS OF RISK MANAGEMENT STRATEGY |
|---|---|
| Focus on common critical assets. <br> *Practices*: Criticality Analysis, Business Impact Analysis (BIA), Mission Impact Analysis (MIA), Mission Thread Analysis | **Threat assumptions:** Conventional adversary; advanced adversary seeking path of least resistance. <br> **Risk response constraints:** Limited programmatic resources. <br> **Risk response priorities:** Anticipate, Withstand, Recover. |
| Support agility and architect for adaptability. <br> *Practices*: Analysis of standards conformance, interoperability analysis, reusability analysis | **Threat assumptions**: Adaptive, agile adversary. <br> **Risk response constraints:** Missions to be supported and mission needs can change rapidly. <br> **Risk response priorities:** Recover, Adapt. |
| Reduce attack surfaces. <br> *Practices*: Supply Chain Risk Management (SCRM) analysis, vulnerability and exposure analysis, Operations Security (OPSEC) analysis, Cyber-attack modeling and simulation | **Threat assumptions:** Conventional adversary; advanced adversary seeking path of least resistance. <br> **Risk response constraints:** Limited operational resources to monitor and actively defend systems. <br> **Risk response priorities:** Anticipate. |
| Assume compromised resources. <br> *Practices*: Cascading failure analysis, Insider Threat analysis, Cyber-attack modeling and simulation | **Threat assumptions:** Advanced adversary. <br> **Risk response constraints:** Ability to assure trustworthiness of system elements is limited. <br> **Risk response priorities:** Anticipate, Withstand. |
| Expect adversaries to evolve. <br> *Practices*: Adversary-driven Cyber Resiliency (ACR) analysis, Red Teaming | **Threat assumptions:** Advanced adversary; adversary can change TTPs and goals unpredictably. <br> **Risk response priorities:** Anticipate, Adapt. |

Sections E.5.1.1 through E.5.1.5 provide detailed descriptions of the five *strategic* cyber resiliency principles.

### E.5.1.1 *Focus on Common Critical Assets*

A focus on critical assets (i.e., resources valued due to their importance to mission or business accomplishment)[110] is central to contingency planning, continuity of operations planning, and operational resilience, as well as to safety analysis. Critical assets can be identified using a variety of mission-oriented analysis techniques, including, for example: Mission Impact Analysis

---

[109] See [SP 800-39].

[110] Critical assets may also be referred to as High Value Assets (HVA) in accordance with [OMB M-19-03].

(MIA), Business Impact Analysis (BIA),[111] Functional Dependency Network Analysis (FDNA), Crown Jewels Analysis (CJA), and Mission Thread Analysis. Failure Modes, Criticality Analysis (FMECA), and Effects can, in some instances, reflect a safety-oriented approach.

Assets that are common to multiple missions or business functions are potential high value targets for adversaries either because those assets are critical or because their compromise increases the adversaries' options for lateral motion[112] or persistence [OMB M-19-03]. Once an asset is identified as critical or common, further analysis involves:

- Identifying how the asset is used in different operational contexts (e.g., normal operations, abnormal operations, crisis or emergency operations, failover). An asset that is common to multiple missions may be critical to one mission in one context but not in a second or critical to a second mission only in the second context.

- Determining which properties or attributes make the asset critical (e.g., correctness, non-observability, availability) or high value (e.g., providing access to a set of critical system elements, providing information which could be used in further malicious cyber activities) and what would constitute an acceptable (e.g., safe, secure) failure mode. Again, properties which are critical to one mission may be non-essential to another, and a failure mode which is acceptable from the standpoint of security may be unacceptable from the standpoint of safety.

- Determining which strategies to use to ensure critical properties, taking into consideration the different usage contexts and potential malicious cyber activities. Strategies for ensuring the correctness and non-observability properties include, for example, disabling noncritical functionality, restoration to default or known-good settings, and selectively isolating or disabling data flows to or from system components. Articulating trade-offs among critical properties and acceptable failure modes is central to effective risk management.

Based on the strategy or strategies that best fit a given type of asset, the most appropriate or relevant structural design principles can be determined.

This strategic design principle makes common infrastructures (e.g., networks), shared services (e.g., identity and access management services), and shared data repositories high priorities for the application of selected cyber resiliency techniques. It recognizes that the resources for risk mitigation are limited and enables systems engineers to focus resources where they will have the greatest potential impact on risk mitigation.

### E.5.1.2  Support Agility and Architect for Adaptability

In Resilience Engineering, *agility* means "the effective response to opportunity and problem, within a mission" [Jackson07] [Sheard08]. In that context, resilience supports agility and counters brittleness. In the context of cyber resiliency, agility is the property of an infrastructure or a system which can be reconfigured, in which components can be reused or repurposed, and in which resources can be reallocated so that cyber defenders can define, select, and tailor cyber courses of action (CCoA) for a broad range of disruptions or malicious cyber activities. This

---

[111] See [SP 800-34].

[112] Lateral motion refers to an adversary's ability to move transitively from one system element to another system element or in a system-of-systems, from one constituent system to another constituent system.

strategy is consistent with the vision that the "infrastructure allows systems and missions to be reshaped nimbly to meet tactical goals or environment changes" [King12]. Agility enables the system and operational processes to incorporate new technologies and/or adapt to changing adversary capabilities.

*Adaptability* is the property of an architecture, a design, and/or an implementation which can accommodate changes to the threat model, mission or business functions, technologies, and systems without major programmatic impacts. A variety of strategies for agility and adaptability have been defined. These include modularity and controlled interfaces to support plug-and-play; externalization of rules and configuration data; and removal or disabling of unused components to reduce complexity. Application of this design principle early in the system life cycle can reduce sustainment costs and modernization efforts.

This design principle means that analyses of alternative architectures and designs need to search for sources of brittleness (e.g., reliance on a single operating system or communications channel; allowing single points of failure; reliance on proprietary interface standards; use of large and hard-to-analyze multi-function modules). Therefore, the analyses need to consider Redundancy, Adaptive Response, and Diversity, and the Coordinated Protection capabilities that enable cyber defenders to make effective use of these techniques. In addition, analyses need to consider where and how to use "cyber maneuver," or moving target defenses, and Deception. Finally, analyses need to consider where and how an architecture, design, or as-deployed system is bound to designated assumptions about the threat, operational, and/or technical environments.

### E.5.1.3 Reduce Attack Surfaces

The term *attack surface* refers to the set of points on the boundary of a system, a system element, or an environment where an attacker can try to enter, cause an effect on, or extract data from that system, system element, or environment. The system's attack surface can be characterized as the accessible areas where weaknesses or deficiencies (including in hardware, software, and firmware system components) provide opportunities for adversaries to exploit vulnerabilities [SP 800-53], or as its exposure to reachable and exploitable vulnerabilities: any hardware, software, connection, data exchange, service, or removable media that might expose the system to potential threat access [DOD15]. Some uses of the term focus on externally exposed vulnerabilities (i.e., the attack surface of a system which connects to a network includes access control points for remote access). However, the assumption that an adversary will penetrate an organization's systems means that internal exposures (i.e., vulnerabilities which can be reached by lateral movement within a system or infrastructure) are also part of the attack surface. Conceptually, the term *attack surface* can also cover aspects of the development, operational, and maintenance environments that an adversary can reach and that could contain vulnerabilities. The supply chain for a system can also present additional attack surfaces. More broadly, an organization can be said to have an attack surface which includes its personnel and external users of organizational systems (if any) and its supply chain both for mission or business operations and for information and communications technology (ICT). To accommodate these broader interpretations of the term, the design principle refers to "attack surfaces."

This design principle is often used in conjunction with the Focus on common critical assets principle. Analysis of internal attack surfaces can reveal unplanned and unexpected paths to critical assets. It makes identification or discovery of attack surfaces a priority in system design analyses,[113] as well as analyses of development, configuration, and maintenance environments (e.g., by considering how using free and open-source software (FOSS) or commercial off-the-shelf (COTS) products which cannot be tailored in those environments expands attack surfaces). It may be infeasible in some architectures (e.g., Internet of Things, bring-your-own-device) or procurement environments (e.g., limited supply chain), for which the Assume compromised resources principle is highly relevant.

As indicated in Table E-8, several alternative strategies for reducing an attack surface can be identified. These strategies are expressed by different controls in [SP 800-53] and apply different cyber resiliency techniques. In Table E-8, the **bolding** in the discussion of the control indicates how the control supports the strategy. These strategies can be reflected by different structural principles. For example, design decisions related to the Maximize transience and Change or disrupt the attack surface structural principles can reduce the duration of exposure; application of the Limit the need for trust principle can reduce exposure. While the controls in Table E-8 focus on attack surfaces within a system, the strategies apply more broadly to the attack surfaces of a mission or an organization. For example, Operations Security (OPSEC) can reduce exposure of the mission or organization to adversary reconnaissance. Supply chain protections can reduce the exposure of key components to tampering.

**TABLE E-8: STRATEGIES FOR REDUCING ATTACK SURFACES[114]**

| STRATEGY | SECURITY CONTROL SUPPORTING STRATEGY | RELATED TECHNIQUES |
|---|---|---|
| Reduce the extent (area) of the attack surface. | Attack surface reduction includes, for example, **employing the concept of layered defenses; applying the principles of least privilege and least functionality; deprecating unsafe functions; applying secure software development practices including, for example, reducing the amount of code executing, reducing entry points available to unauthorized users, and eliminating application programming interfaces (APIs) that are vulnerable to cyber-attacks.** <br> SA-15(5) DEVELOPMENT PROCESS, STANDARDS, AND TOOLS \| ATTACK SURFACE REDUCTION [SP 800-53] | Coordinated Protection <br> Privilege Restriction <br> Realignment |
| Reduce the exposure (aperture or structural accessibility) of the attack surface. | Attack surface reduction includes, for example, **applying the principle of least privilege, employing layered defenses**, applying the principle of least functionality (i.e., restricting ports, protocols, functions, and services), deprecating unsafe functions, and eliminating application programming interfaces (APIs) that are vulnerable to cyber-attacks. <br> SA-15(5) DEVELOPMENT PROCESS, STANDARDS, AND TOOLS \| ATTACK SURFACE REDUCTION [SP 800-53] | Privilege Restriction <br> Coordinated Protection |
| | **Component isolation** reduces the attack surface of organizational information systems. <br> SC-7(20) BOUNDARY PROTECTION \| DYNAMIC ISOLATION AND SEGREGATION [SP 800-53] | Adaptive Response <br> Segmentation |

---

[113] For example, [SP 800-53] control SA-11(7), Developer Security Testing \| Attack Surface Reviews, calls for analysis of design and implementation changes.

[114] The security control supporting strategy includes examples and excerpts from relevant [SP 800-53] controls.

| STRATEGY | SECURITY CONTROL SUPPORTING STRATEGY | RELATED TECHNIQUES |
|---|---|---|
| **Reduce the duration (temporal accessibility) of attack surface exposure.** | Mitigate risk from advanced persistent threats by significantly reducing the targeting capability of adversaries (i.e., **window of opportunity** and available attack surface) to initiate and complete cyber-attacks. SI-14 NON-PERSISTENCE [SP 800-53] | Non-Persistence |

### E.5.1.4  Assume Compromised Resources

A significant number of system architectures treat many, if not all, resources as non-malicious. This assumption is particularly prevalent in cyber-physical systems (CPS) and Internet of Things (IoT) architectures [Folk15]. However, systems and their components, ranging from chips to software modules to running services, can be compromised for extended periods without detection [DSB13]. In fact, some compromises may never be detected. Thus, the assumption that some system resources have been compromised is prudent. While the assumption that some resources cannot be trusted is well-established from the standpoint of security (i.e., the compromised resources cannot be trusted to follow established security policies), the concept of trustworthiness is broader. By compromising a resource, an adversary can affect its reliability, the ability to enforce other policies, or the safety of the larger system or environment of which the resource is a part [SP 1500-201, NIST16], or can use the resource in an attack on other systems.

This design principle implies the need for analysis of how the system architecture reduces the potential consequences of a successful compromise—in particular, the duration and degree of adversary-caused disruption and the speed and extent of malware propagation. An increasing number of modeling and simulation techniques support the analysis of the potential systemic consequences stemming from the compromise of a given resource or set of resources. Such analysis includes identifying different types or forms of systemic consequences (e.g., unreliable or unpredictable behavior of services, unreliable or unpredictable availability of capabilities, or data of indeterminate quality) and subsequently linking these systemic consequences to mission consequences (e.g., mission failure, safety failure) or organizational consequences (e.g., loss of trust or reputation).

### E.5.1.5  Expect Adversaries to Evolve

Advanced cyber adversaries invest time, effort, and intelligence-gathering to improve existing TTPs and develop new TTPs. Adversaries evolve in response to opportunities offered by new technologies or uses of technology, as well as to the knowledge they gain about defender TTPs. In (increasingly short) time, the tools developed by advanced adversaries become available to less sophisticated adversaries. Therefore, systems and missions need to be resilient in the face of unexpected attacks. This design principle supports a risk management strategy which includes but goes beyond the common practice of searching for and seeking ways to remediate known vulnerabilities (or classes of vulnerabilities); a system which has been hardened in the sense of remediating known vulnerabilities will remain exposed to evolving adversaries.

This design principle implies the need for analyses in which the adversary perspective is explicitly represented by intelligent actors who can play the role of an adaptive or evolving adversary. For implemented systems, such analyses are typically part of *red teaming* or *war gaming*. Analyses can use threat intelligence or repositories of attack patterns (e.g., ATT&CK [MITRE18], CAPEC [MITRE07]) to provide concrete examples, but care should be taken not to be constrained by those examples. Voice of the Adversary (VoA) is a design analysis technique in which one or more team members play the role of an adversary to critique alternatives by taking into consideration possible goals, behaviors, and cyber effects assuming varying degrees of system access or penetration. This type of design analysis can use models or taxonomies of adversary behaviors (e.g., the NTCTF [NSA18], cyber-attack life cycle or cyber kill chain models [Hutchins11], CAPEC [MITRE07] or ATT&CK [MITRE18] classes), and languages or taxonomies of cyber effects (e.g., [Temin10]).

This design principle also highlights the value of the Deception and Diversity techniques. Deception can cause adversaries to reveal their TTPs prematurely from the perspective of their cyber campaign plans, enabling defenders to develop countermeasures or defensive TTPs. Diversity can force an adversary to develop a wider range of TTPs to achieve the same objectives.

## E.5.2  STRUCTURAL DESIGN PRINCIPLES

Structural cyber resiliency design principles guide and inform design and implementation decisions throughout the system life cycle. As indicated in Table E-9, many of the structural design principles are consistent with or leverage the design principles for security and/or resilience.[115] The first four design principles are closely related to protection strategies and security design principles and can be applied in mutually supportive ways. The next three design principles are closely related to design principles for resilience engineering and survivability. The next three design principles are driven by the concern for an operational environment (including cyber threats), which changes on an ongoing basis, and are closely related to design principles for evolvability. The final four principles are strongly driven by the need to manage the effects of malicious cyber activities, even when those activities are not observed. Descriptions of how structural design principles are applied, or could be applied, to a system-of-interest can help stakeholders understand how their concerns are being addressed.

**TABLE E-9: STRUCTURAL CYBER RESILIENCY DESIGN PRINCIPLES**

| STRUCTURAL DESIGN PRINCIPLES | KEY IDEAS | RELATED DESIGN PRINCIPLES FROM OTHER DISCIPLINES |
|---|---|---|
| **Limit the need for trust.** | Limiting the number of system elements that need to be trusted (or the length of time an element needs to be trusted) reduces the level of effort needed for assurance, as well as for ongoing protection and monitoring. | **Security:** Least Common Mechanism, Trusted Components, Inverse Modification Threshold, Minimized Security Elements, Least Privilege, Predicate Permission, Self-Reliant Trustworthiness, Trusted Communications Channels. **Resilience Engineering:** Localized Capacity, Loose Coupling. **Survivability:** Prevention. |

---

[115] The relationship between strategic and structural cyber resiliency design principles is presented in Table E-10.

| STRUCTURAL DESIGN PRINCIPLES | KEY IDEAS | RELATED DESIGN PRINCIPLES FROM OTHER DISCIPLINES |
|---|---|---|
| **Control visibility and use.** | Controlling what can be discovered, observed, and used increases the effort needed by an adversary seeking to expand its foothold in or increase its impacts on systems containing cyber resources. | **Security:** Clear Abstraction, Least Common Mechanism, Least Privilege, Predicate Permission. **Resilience Engineering:** Localized Capacity, Loose Coupling. **Survivability:** Concealment, Hardness. |
| **Contain and exclude behaviors.** | Limiting what can be done and where actions can be taken reduces the possibility or extent of the spread of compromises or disruptions across components or services. | **Security:** Trusted Components, Least Privilege, Predicate Permission. **Resilience Engineering:** Localized Capacity, Loose Coupling. **Survivability:** Preemption, Hardness, Distribution. |
| **Layer defenses and partition resources.** | The combination of defense-in-depth and partitioning increases the effort required by an adversary to overcome multiple defenses. | **Security:** Modularity and Layering, Partially Ordered Dependencies, Minimized Sharing, Self-Reliant Trustworthiness, Secure Distributed Composition. **Resilience Engineering:** Layered Defense. **Survivability:** Hardness, Fail-Safe |
| **Plan and manage diversity.** | Diversity is a well-established resilience technique, removing single points of attack or failure. However, architectures and designs should take cost and manageability into consideration to avoid introducing new risks. | **Resilience Engineering:** Absorption, Repairability. **Survivability:** Heterogeneity. |
| **Maintain redundancy.** | Redundancy is key to many resilience strategies but can degrade over time as configurations are updated or connectivity changes. | **Resilience Engineering:** Absorption, Physical Redundancy, Functional Redundancy. **Survivability:** Redundancy, Margin. |
| **Make resources location-versatile.** | A resource bound to a single location (e.g., a service running only on a single hardware component, a database located in a single datacenter) can become a single point of failure and thus a high value target. | **Resilience Engineering:** Localized Capacity, Repairability. **Survivability:** Mobility, Avoidance, Distribution. |
| **Leverage health and status data.** | Health and status data can be useful in supporting situational awareness, indicating potentially suspicious behaviors, and predicting the need for adaptation to changing operational demands. | **Resilience Engineering:** Drift Correction, Inter-Node Interaction. |
| **Maintain situational awareness.** | Situational awareness, including awareness of possible performance trends and the emergence of anomalies, informs decisions about cyber courses of action to ensure mission completion. | **Resilience Engineering:** Drift Correction, Inter-Node Interaction. |

| STRUCTURAL DESIGN PRINCIPLES | KEY IDEAS | RELATED DESIGN PRINCIPLES FROM OTHER DISCIPLINES |
|---|---|---|
| **Manage resources (risk-) adaptively.** | Risk-adaptive management supports agility, providing supplemental risk mitigation throughout critical operations despite disruptions or outages of components. | **Security:** Trusted Components, Hierarchical Trust, Inverse Modification Threshold, Secure Distributed Composition, Trusted Communications Channels; Secure Defaults, Secure Failure and Recovery. **Resilience Engineering:** Reorganization, Repairability, Inter-Node Interaction. **Survivability:** Avoidance. |
| **Maximize transience.** | Use of transient system elements minimizes the duration of exposure to adversary activities, while periodically refreshing to a known (secure) state can expunge malware or corrupted data. | **Resilience Engineering:** Localized Capacity, Loose Coupling. **Survivability:** Avoidance. |
| **Determine ongoing trustworthiness.** | Periodic or ongoing verification and/or validation of the integrity or correctness of data or software can increase the effort needed by an adversary seeking to modify or fabricate data or functionality. Similarly, periodic or ongoing analysis of the behavior of individual users, system components, and services can increase suspicion, triggering responses such as closer monitoring, more restrictive privileges, or quarantine. | **Security:** Self-Reliant Trustworthiness, Continuous Protection, Secure Metadata Management, Self-Analysis, Accountability and Traceability. **Resilience Engineering:** Neutral State. **Survivability:** Fail-Safe. |
| **Change or disrupt the attack surface.** | Disruption of the attack surface can cause the adversary to waste resources, make incorrect assumptions about the system or the defender, or prematurely launch attacks or disclose information. | **Resilience Engineering:** Drift Correction **Survivability:** Mobility, Deterrence, Preemption, Avoidance. |
| **Make the effects of deception and unpredictability user-transparent.** | Deception and unpredictability can be highly effective techniques against an adversary, leading the adversary to reveal its presence or TTPs or to waste effort. However, when improperly applied, these techniques can also confuse users. | **Security:** Efficiently Mediated Access, Performance Security, Human Factored Security, Acceptable Security. **Survivability:** Concealment. |

The selection of structural design principles is driven by strategic design principles, as shown in Table E-10.

**TABLE E-10:  STRATEGIC DESIGN PRINCIPLES DRIVE STRUCTURAL DESIGN PRINCIPLES**

| STRUCTURAL DESIGN PRINCIPLES | STRATEGIC DESIGN PRINCIPLES | | | | |
|---|---|---|---|---|---|
| | Focus on common | Support agility and architect for adaptability | Reduce attack | Assume compromised resources | Expect adversaries |
| Limit the need for trust. | | | X | X | |
| Control visibility and use. | X | | X | X | |
| Contain and exclude behaviors. | X | | | X | X |
| Layer defenses and partition resources. | X | | | X | |
| Plan and manage diversity. | X | X | | X | |
| Maintain redundancy. | X | X | | X | |
| Make resources location-versatile. | X | X | | | X |
| Leverage health and status data. | X | X | | X | X |
| Maintain situational awareness. | X | | | | X |
| Manage resources (risk-) adaptively. | X | X | | | X |
| Maximize transience. | | | X | X | X |
| Determine ongoing trustworthiness. | X | | | X | X |
| Change or disrupt the attack surface. | | | X | X | X |
| Make the effects of deception and unpredictability user-transparent. | | X | X | | |

Structural design principles provide guidance for design decisions intended to reduce risk.[116] This guidance affects the selection and the application of cyber resiliency techniques. Table E-15 describes the relationship between structural design principles and cyber resiliency techniques. Table E-11 describes the application of structural design principles and the intended effects on risk.

**TABLE E-11:  STRUCTURAL DESIGN PRINCIPLES AND EFFECTS ON RISK**

| STRUCTURAL DESIGN PRINCIPLES | INTENDED EFFECTS ON RISK |
|---|---|
| Limit the need for trust. | Reduce likelihood of harm due to malice, error, or failure. |
| Control visibility and use. | Reduce likelihood of occurrence of adversarial events; reduce likelihood of harm due to malice, error, or failure. |
| Contain and exclude behaviors. | Reduce likelihood of occurrence of adversarial events; reduce likelihood of harm due to malice, error, or failure. |
| Layer defenses and partition resources. | Reduce likelihood of harm due to malice, error, or failure; reduce extent of harm. |

---

[116] Harm to a cyber resource can take the form of degradation or disruption of functionality or performance; exfiltration or exposure of information; modification, corruption, or fabrication of information (including software, mission or business information, and configuration data); or usurpation or misuse of system resources. Unless otherwise specified, all forms of harm to systems containing cyber resources are addressed.

| STRUCTURAL DESIGN PRINCIPLES | INTENDED EFFECTS ON RISK |
|---|---|
| Plan and manage diversity. | Reduce likelihood of harm due to malice, error, or failure; reduce extent of disruption. |
| Maintain redundancy. | Reduce likelihood of harm due to malice, error, or failure; reduce extent of disruption or degradation. |
| Make resources location-versatile. | Reduce likelihood of occurrence of adversarial events; reduce extent of disruption or degradation. |
| Leverage health and status data. | Reduce likelihood of harm due to malice, error, or failure by enabling response to changes in system state; reduce extent of harm by enabling detection of and response to indicators of damage. |
| Maintain situational awareness. | Reduce likelihood of harm due to malice, error, or failure by enabling response to indicators; reduce extent of harm by enabling detection of and response to indicators of damage. |
| Manage resources (risk-) adaptively. | Reduce likelihood of harm due to malice, error or failure by enabling response to changes in the operational environment; reduce extent of harm. |
| Maximize transience. | Reduce likelihood of occurrence by reducing the time during which an adverse event could occur; reduce likelihood of harm due to malice, error, or failure by reducing the time during which an event could result in harm. |
| Determine ongoing trustworthiness. | Reduce likelihood of harm due to corrupted, modified, or fabricated information by enabling untrustworthy information to be identified; reduce extent of harm by reducing the propagation of untrustworthy information. |
| Change or disrupt the attack surface. | Reduce likelihood of occurrence by removing the circumstances in which an adversarial event is feasible; reduce likelihood of harm due to adversarial events by making such events ineffective. |
| Make the effects of deception and unpredictability user-transparent. | Reduce the likelihood of occurrence of error; when Deception techniques are applied, reduce the likelihood of occurrence of adversarial events. |

Sections E.5.2.1 through E.5.2.14 provide more detailed descriptions of the 14 structural cyber resiliency principles.

### E.5.2.1  Limit the Need for Trust

Trustworthiness can be defined as an entity worthy of being trusted to fulfill whatever critical requirements may be needed for a component, subsystem, system, network, application, mission, enterprise, or other entity [Neumann04]. Trustworthiness has also been defined as the attribute of [an entity] that provides confidence to others of the qualifications, capabilities, and reliability of that entity to perform specific tasks and to fulfill assigned responsibilities [CNSSI 4009]. Assertions of trustworthiness (e.g., "this software can be relied upon to enforce the following security policies with a high level of confidence") are meaningless without some form of verification, validation, or demonstration (e.g., design analysis, testing). In the absence of some credible form of assurance (which can be costly and can be invalidated by changes in the system or the environment), assertions of trustworthiness constitute assumptions. Reducing the size of the set of trusted entities (whether individuals, software components, or hardware components) by minimizing assumptions about what is or can be trusted reduces the attack surface and lowers assurance costs.

Application of this design principle is most effective early in the system life cycle where the motivation of the Prevent/Avoid objective is clearest. When a system already exists, changes to the operational concept (consistent with the Transform objective) or to the system architecture (applying the Re-Architect objective and the Realignment technique) can increase costs. One approach to applying this design principle (using the Coordinated Protection and Privilege Restriction techniques) is through limitations on inheritance so that privileges or access rights associated with one class of system component are not automatically propagated to classes or instances created from the original one. While limitations on inheritance can increase the burden on developers or administrators initially, they can also reduce the complexity associated with multiple inheritance.

This design principle supports the strategic design principles of Reduce attack surfaces and Assume compromised resources. However, its application increases the difficulty of applying the Support agility and architect for adaptability strategic design principle. This design principle can also be used in conjunction with Determine ongoing trustworthiness; if a system element is assumed or required to have a given level of trustworthiness, some attestation mechanism is needed to verify that it has and continues to retain that trustworthiness level. Minimizing the number of elements with trustworthiness requirements reduces the level of effort involved in determining ongoing trustworthiness. Finally, this design principle can be used in conjunction with Plan and manage diversity; the managed use of multiple sources of system elements, services, or information can enable behavior or data quality to be validated by comparison.

### E.5.2.2  Control Visibility and Use

Controlling visibility counters adversary attempts at reconnaissance from outside or within the system. Thus, the adversary must exert greater effort to identify potential targets, whether for exfiltration, modification, or disruption. Visibility of data can be controlled by such mechanisms as encryption, data hiding, or data obfuscation. Visibility of how some resources are used can also be controlled directly, for example, by adding chaff to network traffic. Visibility into the supply chain, development process, or system design can be limited via operations security (OPSEC), deception [Heckman15], and split or distributed design and manufacturing. Process obfuscation is an area of active research. An increasing number and variety of deception technologies, including for example, deception nets, can be applied at the system level.

Controlling use counters adversary activities and actions in the *Control*, *Execute*, and *Maintain* phases of the cyber-attack life cycle [MITRE18]. To limit visibility or to control use, access to system resources can be controlled from the perspectives of multiple security disciplines, including physical, logical (see the discussion of privileges below), and hybrid (e.g., physical locations in a geographically distributed system or in a complex, embedded system). Restrictions on access and use can be guided by information sensitivity, as in standard security practices. Restrictions can also be based on criticality (i.e., the importance to achieving mission objectives). While some resources can be determined to be mission-critical or mission-essential *a priori*, the criticality of other resources can change dynamically. For example, a resource which is vital to one phase of mission processing can become unimportant after that phase is completed.

Many systems or system components provide the capability to define and manage privileges associated with software, services, processes, hardware, communications channels, and individual users. Assignment of privileges ideally should reflect judgments of operational need (e.g., need-to-know, need-to-use) as well as trustworthiness. Restriction of privileges is well established as a security design principle (i.e., least privilege). Privilege restrictions force adversaries to focus efforts on a restricted set of targets, which can be assured (in the case of software), validated (in the case of data), or monitored (in the case of individuals, processes, communications channels, and services). Non-Persistence and Segmentation can also limit visibility. Thus, this principle can be applied in conjunction with the Contain and exclude behaviors and Maximize transience principles.

### E.5.2.3  Contain and Exclude Behaviors

The behavior of a system or system element, including what resources it uses, which systems or system elements it interacts with, or when it takes a given action, can vary based on many legitimate circumstances. However, analysis of the mission or business functions and the mission/business processes that carry out those missions and functions [SP 800-39] can identify some behaviors which are always unacceptable and others which are acceptable only under specific circumstances. Therefore, excluding behaviors prevents such behaviors from having undesirable consequences. Behaviors can be excluded *a priori* with varying degrees of assurance, from removing functionality to restricting functionality or use, with trade-offs between assurance and flexibility. For example, user activity outside of specific time windows can be precluded. In addition, behaviors can be interrupted based on ongoing monitoring when that monitoring provides a basis for suspicion.

Containing behaviors involves restricting the set of resources or system elements which can be affected by the behavior of a given system element. Such restriction can, but does not have to, involve a temporal aspect. Containment can be achieved *a priori*, via predefined privileges and segmentation. Alternately, or perhaps additionally, Adaptive Response and Dynamic Isolation can be applied. For example, a sandbox or deception environment can be dynamically created in response to suspicious behavior, and subsequent activities can be diverted there.

### E.5.2.4  Layer Defenses and Partition Resources

*Defense-in-depth* is the integration of people, technology, and operations capabilities to establish variable barriers across multiple layers and missions [CNSSI 4009] and is a well-established security strategy. It describes security architectures constructed through the application of multiple mechanisms to create a series of barriers to prevent, delay, or deter an attack by an adversary [SP 800-160 v1]. Multiple mechanisms to achieve the same objective or to provide equivalent functionality can be used at a single layer (e.g., different COTS firewalls to separate zones in a DMZ) or at different layers (e.g., detection of suspicious behavior at the application, operating system, and network layers). To avoid inconsistencies which could result in errors or vulnerabilities, such (multiple) mechanisms should be managed consistently.

Layering of defenses restricts the adversary's movement vertically in a layered security architecture (i.e., a defense at one layer prevents a compromise at an adjacent layer from propagating). Partitioning (i.e., separating sets of resources into effectively separate systems) with controlled interfaces (e.g., cross domain solutions) between them restricts the lateral movement of the adversary. Partitioning can limit the adversary's visibility (see Control visibility and use). It can also serve to Contain and exclude behaviors. Partitioning can be based on administration and policy, as in security domains [SP 800-160 v1], or can be informed by the missions or business functions the system elements in the partition support. Partitions can be implemented physically or logically, at the network layer and within a platform (e.g., via hard or soft partitioning). Partitioning may involve limiting resource-sharing or making fewer resources common. If resources are replicated, the Maintain redundancy principle should be applied.

### E.5.2.5 *Plan and Manage Diversity*

Diversity (usually in conjunction with Redundancy [Sterbenz14]) is a well-established technique for improving system resilience [Sterbenz10, Höller15]. For cyber resiliency, Diversity avoids the risk of system homogeneity, in which compromise of one component can propagate to all other similar components. Diversity offers the benefit of providing alternative ways to deliver required functionality so that if a component is compromised, one or more alternative components which provide the same functionality can be used.

Multiple approaches to diversity can be identified. These include architectural diversity; design diversity; synthetic (or automated) diversity;[117] information diversity; diversity of command, control, and communications (C3) paths (including out-of-band communications); geographic diversity;[118] supply chain diversity [SP 800-160 v1, Bodeau15]; and diversity in operating procedures. In addition, some incidental architectural diversity often results from procurement over time and differing user preferences. Incidental diversity is often more apparent than real (i.e., different products can present significantly different interfaces to administrators or users, while incorporating identical components).

However, diversity can be problematic in several ways. First, it can increase the attack surface of the system. Rather than trying to compromise a single component and propagate across all such components, an adversary can attack any component in the set of alternatives, looking for a path of least resistance to establish a foothold. Second, it can increase demands on developers, system administrators, maintenance staff, and users by forcing them to deal with multiple interfaces to equivalent components. This can result in increased system life cycle costs[119] and also increase the risks that inconsistencies will be introduced, particularly if the configuration alternatives for the equivalent components are organized differently. Third, diversity can be more apparent than real (e.g., different implementations of the same mission functionality all running on the same underlying operating system, applications which reuse selected software components). Thus, analysis of the architectural approach to using diversity is critical. For embedded systems, some approaches to diversity raise a variety of research challenges. And finally, the effectiveness of diversity against adversaries is not an absolute—analysis of diversity strategies is needed to determine the best alternative in the context of adversary TTPs.

Therefore, this design principle calls for the use of Diversity in system architecture and design to take manageability into consideration. It also calls for consideration of diversity in operational processes and practices, including non-cyber alternatives such as out-of-band measures [SP 800-53] for critical capabilities. To reduce cost and other impacts, this design principle is most effective when used in conjunction with the Focus on common critical assets strategic design principle and the Maintain redundancy and Layer and partition defenses structural principles. Measurements related to this design principle can focus on the degree of diversity, the degree of manageability, or both.

---

[117] Synthetic diversity in conjunction with randomization, a form of Unpredictability, is a form of Moving Target Defense (MTD).

[118] Geographic diversity can be used to support the Make resources location-versatile structural design principle.

[119] These costs have historically been acceptable in some safety-critical systems.

### E.5.2.6  Maintain Redundancy

Redundancy is a well-established design principle in Resilience Engineering and Survivability [Sterbenz10]. Approaches to Redundancy include surplus capacity and replication (e.g., cold spares, hot or inline spares) and can be implemented in conjunction with backup and failover procedures. It can enhance the availability of critical capabilities but requires that redundant resources be protected.

Because malware can propagate across homogeneous resources, Redundancy for cyber resiliency should be applied in conjunction with Diversity and should be considered at multiple levels or layers in a layered architecture [Sterbenz14]. However, Redundancy when used in conjunction with Diversity can increase complexity and present scalability challenges.

The extent of Redundancy should be established and maintained through analysis, looking for single points of failure and shared resources. Trends to convergence can, at times, undermine Redundancy. For example, an organization using Voice over Internet Protocol (VOIP) for its phone system cannot assert alternate communications paths for phone, email, and instant messaging.

Because maintaining surplus capacity or spare components increases system life-cycle costs, this design principle is most effective when used in conjunction with the Focus on common critical assets strategic principle—and it is also most effective in conjunction with the Plan and manage diversity and Layer and partition defenses structural principles.

### E.5.2.7  Make Resources Location-Versatile

Location-versatile resources are those resources which do not require a fixed location and can be relocated or reconstituted to maximize performance, avoid disruptions, and better avoid becoming a high value target for an adversary. Different approaches can be used to provide location-versatile resources including virtualization, replication, distribution (of functionality or stored data), physical mobility, and functional relocation. Replication is a well-established approach for high-availability systems using multiple, parallel processes, and high-availability data (sometimes referred to as data resilience) using database sharding[120] (although this can present security challenges).

Replication and distribution can be across geographic locations, hardware platforms, or (in the case of services) virtual machines. While replication can take the form of redundancy, it can also involve providing ways to reconfigure system resources to provide equivalent functionality. Data virtualization (i.e., data management which enables applications to retrieve and use data without specific knowledge of the location or format) supports distribution and reduces the likelihood that local (persistent and unmaintained) data stores will proliferate. Composable services enable alternative reconstitution of mission capabilities, and diverse information sources can be used for alternative reconstitution of mission or business data.

Application of this principle involves the use of Dynamic Positioning, often in conjunction with Redundancy and/or Diversity. This principle supports the Support agility and architect for

---

[120] A database *shard* is a horizontal partition of data in a database. Each individual partition is referred to as a shard or database shard. Each shard is held on a separate database server instance to spread the load.

<u>adaptability</u> strategic principle and can be employed in conjunction with the <u>Maximize transience</u> and <u>Change or disrupt the attack surface</u> structural principles. Some approaches to the reconstitution of mission capabilities can conflict with the <u>Control visibility and use</u> structural principle.

### E.5.2.8  Leverage Health and Status Data

In some architectures, many system components are security-unaware, incapable of enforcing a security policy (e.g., an access control policy), and therefore incapable of monitoring policy compliance (e.g., auditing or alerting on unauthorized access attempts). However, most system components provide health and status data to indicate component availability or unavailability for use. These include, for example, components of CPS (particularly components in space systems) and in the emerging IoT. In addition, system components present health and status data to providers (e.g., application or service on a virtual platform in a cloud to a cloud provider) or service-providing components (e.g., application to operating system, device to network) so that the components can allocate and scale resources effectively. Correlation of monitoring data, including health and status data, from multiple layers or types of components in the architecture can help identify potential problems early so they can be averted or contained.

As architectural convergence between information technology (IT) and operational technology (OT) or the IoT increases [<u>SP 1500-201</u>], application of this structural principle will support the <u>Expect adversaries to evolve</u> strategic principle. Given the increasing number and variety of "smart" components in the IoT, application of this principle may be driven by the <u>Focus on common critical assets</u> principle. In addition, components can erroneously or maliciously report health and status data by design or due to compromise. Thus, application of this principle may be more effective in conjunction with the <u>Determine ongoing trustworthiness</u> principle.

### E.5.2.9  Maintain Situational Awareness

For security and cyber resiliency, situational awareness encompasses awareness of *system elements*, *threats*, and *mission dependencies* on system elements.[121] Awareness of system elements can rely on security status assessment, security monitoring, and performance monitoring and can be achieved in conjunction with the <u>Leverage health and status data</u> design principle. Awareness of threats involves ingesting and using threat intelligence, recognizing that adversaries evolve. Awareness of system elements and threats (via gathered data, correlated data, and processing capabilities) can be centralized or distributed and can be either enterprise-internal or cross-enterprise (e.g., via a managed security service provider).

Awareness of mission dependencies can be determined *a priori*, as part of system design (e.g., using CJA, MIA, or BIA). Alternately or additionally, mission dependencies can be identified during mission operations by tracking and analyzing resource use. This more dynamic approach supports agility, adaptability, and capabilities to <u>Control visibility and use</u> and <u>Contain and exclude behaviors</u>. While cyber situational awareness remains an active area of research,

---

[121] As a foundational capability of a Security Operations Center (SOC), situational awareness provides "regular, repeatable repackaging and redistribution of the SOC's knowledge of constituency assets, networks, threats, incidents, and vulnerabilities to constituents. This capability goes beyond cyber intel distribution, enhancing constituents' understanding of the cybersecurity posture of the constituency and portions thereof, driving effective decision-making at all levels [<u>Zimmerman14</u>]."

analytic capabilities are increasingly being offered, and cyber situational awareness is maturing through tailored applications in specific environments.

### E.5.2.10 *Manage Resources (Risk-) Adaptively*

Risk-adaptive management has been developed in multiple contexts. Cybersecurity mechanisms include risk-adaptive access control (RAdAC) for systems—highly adaptive cybersecurity services (HACS) providing such functionality as penetration testing, incident response, cyber hunting, and risk and vulnerability assessment for programs—and integrated adaptive cyber defense (IACD) for the enterprise and beyond. Strategies for risk-adaptive management include:

- Changing the frequency of planned changes (e.g., resetting encryption keys, switching between operating systems or platforms, or changing the configuration of internal routers);

- Increasing security restrictions (e.g., requiring reauthentication periodically within a single session, two-factor authentication for requests from remote locations, or two-person control on specific actions, increasing privilege requirements based on changing criticality);

- Reallocating resources (e.g., reallocating processing, communications, or storage resources to enable graceful degradation, repurposing resources); and

- Discarding or isolating suspected system elements (e.g., terminating a service or locking out a user account, diverting communications to a deception environment, or quarantining processing).

Strategies for implementing this design principle can be applied in conjunction with strategies for implementing Control visibility and use (dynamically changing privileges), Contain and exclude behaviors (disabling resources and dynamic isolation), Layer defenses and partition resources (dynamic partitioning), Plan and manage diversity (switching from one resource to an equivalent resource), and Make resources location-versatile (reconstituting resources).

To be *risk*-adaptive, the selection and application of a strategy should be based on situational awareness—that is, management decisions are based on indications of changes in adversary characteristics, characteristics of system elements, or patterns of operational use which change the risk posture of the system or the mission or business function it supports. Alternately, strategies can be applied unpredictably to address unknown risks.

### E.5.2.11 *Maximize Transience*

Non-persistence is a cyber resiliency strategy to Reduce attack surfaces in the temporal dimension. Virtualization technologies, which simulate the hardware and/or software on which other software executes [SP 800-125B], enable processes, services, and applications to be transient. At the network layer, technologies for network virtualization, network functions virtualization, software-defined networking, and just-in-time connectivity can support non-persistence. Data virtualization provides a strategy for reducing persistent local data stores. As noted above, this principle is synergistic with Make resources location-versatile. Since transient resources can be virtually isolated, this principle can also be used in conjunction with Contain and exclude behaviors.

Logical transient system elements (e.g., processes, files, connections) need to be expunged (i.e., removed in such a way that no data remains on the shared resources).[122] If an executing process or service has been compromised by malicious software which changes its behavior or corrupts the data it offers to other system elements, expunging it, either by bringing it down or by moving it and deleting the prior instance, also mitigates the compromise. This can be done in response to suspicious behavior or can be deliberately unpredictable.

In addition, system elements can be made attritable and expendable, for example, in the case of unmanned air systems. These physically transient system elements also need mechanisms for ensuring that no data is left behind.

The instantiation of a transient resource depends on being able to Determine ongoing trustworthiness of the resources from which it is constructed. Support for such verification and/or validation can include, for example, gold copies of software and configuration data, policy data for network function virtualization, and data quality validation as part of data virtualization.

### E.5.2.12  Determine Ongoing Trustworthiness

In the *Control* phase of the cyber-attack life cycle [MITRE18], an adversary can modify system components (e.g., modify software, replace legitimate software with malware) and system data (e.g., modify configuration files, fabricate entries in an authorization database, fabricate or delete audit data) or mission or business data (e.g., deleting, changing, or inserting entries in a mission or business database; replacing user-created files with fabricated versions). These modifications enable the adversary to take actions in the *Execute* and *Maintain* phases of the cyber-attack life cycle. Periodic or ongoing validation can detect the effects of adversary activities before those effects become too significant or irremediable.

A variety of Substantiated Integrity mechanisms can be used to identify suspicious changes. Changes can be to properties or to behavior. Some behaviors—for example, the frequency with which a service makes requests, the latency between a request to it and its response, and the size of requests or responses it makes—can be verified or validated by other services. Other behaviors—for example, processor, memory, disk, or network use—can be verified or validated by other system components (e.g., the operating system's task manager). Note that making the behavior capable of being verified or validated can impede the use of unpredictability.

This principle is strongly synergistic with Manage resources (risk-) adaptively. Some changes can trigger the use of Privilege Restriction or Analytic Monitoring mechanisms. Other changes can trigger quarantine via Segmentation. However, such mechanisms can add storage, processing, and transmission overhead. Therefore, this structural principle is most effective in support of the Focus on common critical assets strategic principle.

Ideally, any system element which cannot be determined to be trustworthy—initially via hardware and software assurance processes and subsequently via Substantiated Integrity—should be assumed to be compromised. However, in practice, that assumption is difficult to

---

[122] See [SP 800-53] controls SC-4 (Information in Shared Resources) and MP-6 (Media Sanitization).

apply. This principle is consistent with the weaker assumption that some resources will be compromised and calls for mechanisms to detect and respond to evidence of compromise.

Mechanisms to determine trustworthiness need to be applied in a coordinated manner, across architectural layers, among different types of system elements, and (if applicable) with insider threat controls.

### E.5.2.13  Change or Disrupt the Attack Surface

Disruption of the attack surface can also lead an adversary to reveal its presence. A growing set of moving target defenses are intended to change or disrupt the attack surface of a system. Moving Target Defense (MTD) is an active area of research and development. MTD can be categorized in terms of the _layer_ or level at which the defenses are applied (e.g., software, runtime environment, data, platform, and network). However, MTD can be applied at other layers. For example, when this design principle is used in conjunction with the Make resources location-versatile principle, MTD can also be applied at the physical or geographic levels. MTD is particularly well-suited to cloud architectures [Shetty16] where implementation is at the middleware level.

MTD can also be categorized in terms of strategy: move, morph, or switch. Resources can be moved (e.g., execution of a service can be moved from one platform or virtual machine to another). This approach, which leverages the design principle of Dynamic Positioning, can be used in conjunction with the Make resources location-versatile principle. The terms "cyber maneuver" and MTD are often reserved for morphing—that is, making specific changes to the properties of the data, runtime environment, software, platform, or network [Okhravi13] or by using configuration changes in conjunction with the techniques of Diversity and Unpredictability or randomization [Jajodia11, Jajodia12] rather than including relocation or distribution. Data or software can be morphed using synthetic diversity; the behavior of system elements can be morphed via configuration or resource allocation changes. Morphing can also be part of a Deception strategy. Finally, switching can leverage diversity and distributed resources. Mission applications which rely on a supporting service can switch from one implementation of the service to another. Switching can also be used in conjunction with Deception, as when adversary interactions with the system are switched to a deception environment.

This structural design principle supports the Expect adversaries to evolve strategic principle. It can also support the Reduce attack surfaces strategic principle. Alternately, the principle can support the Assume compromised resources principle. When Unpredictability is part of the way this principle is applied, it should be used in conjunction with the Make the effects of deception and unpredictability user-transparent structural principle.

### E.5.2.14  Make Deception and Unpredictability Effects User-Transparent

Deception and unpredictability are intended to increase the adversaries' uncertainty about the system's structure and behavior, what effects an adversary might be able to achieve, and what actions cyber defenders might take in response to suspected malicious cyber-related activities. [Heckman15] provides a detailed discussion of deception and its role in active cyber defense. Deception includes obfuscation, which increases the effort needed by the adversary and can hide mission activities long enough for the mission to complete without adversary disruption.

Active deception can divert adversary activities, causing the adversary to waste resources and reveal TTPs, intent, and targeting.

Unpredictability can apply to structure, characteristics, or behavior. Unpredictable structure (e.g., dynamically changing partitions or isolating components) undermines the adversary's reconnaissance efforts. Unpredictable characteristics (e.g., configurations, selection of an equivalent element from a diverse set) force the adversary to develop a broader range of TTPs. Unpredictable behavior (e.g., response latency) increases uncertainty about effects and about whether system behavior indicates defender awareness of malicious cyber activities.

Unpredictability and deception can be applied separately, as well as synergistically. These two techniques can be highly effective against advanced adversaries. However, deception and unpredictability, if implemented poorly, can also increase the uncertainty of end-users and administrators about how the system will behave. Such user and administrator confusion can reduce overall resilience, reliability, and security. This uncertainty can, in turn, make detection of unauthorized or suspicious behavior more difficult. This design principle calls for a sound implementation, which makes system behaviors directed at the adversary transparent to end-users and system administrators.

## E.6  RELATIONSHIPS AMONG CYBER RESILIENCY CONSTRUCTS

Sections E.1 through E.5 presented and described the cyber resiliency constructs of goals, objectives, techniques, approaches, and design principles. Table E-12 and Table E-13 illustrate that the mapping between the goals and objectives is many-to-many, as are the mappings between techniques (including the approaches to implementing or applying techniques) and objectives.

**TABLE E-12:  CYBER RESILIENCY OBJECTIVES SUPPORTING CYBER RESILIENCY GOALS**

| Objectives \ Goals | ANTICIPATE | WITHSTAND | RECOVER | ADAPT |
|---|---|---|---|---|
| Prevent/Avoid | X | X | | |
| Prepare | X | X | X | X |
| Continue | | X | X | |
| Constrain | | X | X | |
| Reconstitute | | | X | |
| Understand | X | X | X | X |
| Transform | | | X | X |
| Re-Architect | | | X | X |

**TABLE E-13: TECHNIQUES AND IMPLEMENTATION APPROACHES TO ACHIEVE OBJECTIVES**

| Objectives / Techniques/Approaches | Prevent / Avoid | Prepare | Continue | Constrain | Reconstitute | Understand | Transform | Re-Architect |
|---|---|---|---|---|---|---|---|---|
| **Adaptive Response** | X | X | X | X | X | X | | |
| Dynamic Reconfiguration | X | | X | X | X | X | | |
| Dynamic Resource Allocation | X | | X | X | X | | | |
| Adaptive Management | X | X | X | X | X | X | | |
| **Analytic Monitoring** | | | X | X | X | X | | |
| Monitoring and Damage Assessment | | | X | X | X | X | | |
| Sensor Fusion and Analysis | | | | | | X | | |
| Malware and Forensic Analysis | | | | | | X | | |
| **Contextual Awareness** | | X | X | | X | X | | |
| Dynamic Mapping and Profiling | | X | | | | X | | |
| Dynamic Threat Modeling | | | | | | X | | |
| Mission Dependency and Status Visualization | | X | X | | X | X | | |
| **Coordinated Protection** | X | X | X | | X | X | X | X |
| Calibrated Defense-in-Depth | X | X | | | X | | | |
| Consistency Analysis | X | X | | | X | X | X | X |
| Orchestration | X | X | X | | X | X | X | X |
| Self-Challenge | | X | | | | X | | |
| **Deception** | X | | | | | X | | |
| Obfuscation | X | | | | | | | |
| Disinformation | X | | | | | | | |
| Misdirection | X | | | | | X | | |
| Tainting | | | | | | X | | |
| **Diversity** | X | X | X | X | | | | X |
| Architectural Diversity | | X | X | | | | | X |
| Design Diversity | | X | X | | | | | X |
| Synthetic Diversity | X | X | X | X | | | | |
| Information Diversity | | X | X | | | | | X |
| Path Diversity | | X | X | | | | | X |
| Supply Chain Diversity | | X | X | | | | | X |
| **Dynamic Positioning** | X | | X | X | X | X | | |
| Functional Relocation of Sensors | | | | | X | X | | |
| Functional Relocation of Cyber Resources | X | | X | X | | | | |
| Asset Mobility | X | | X | X | | | | |
| Fragmentation | X | | | | X | | | |
| Distributed Functionality | X | | | | X | | | |
| **Non-Persistence** | X | | | X | | | X | X |
| Non-Persistent Information | X | | | X | | | X | X |
| Non-Persistent Services | X | | | X | | | X | X |
| Non-Persistent Connectivity | X | | | X | | | X | X |
| **Privilege Restriction** | X | | | X | X | | | |
| Trust-Based Privilege Management | X | | | X | | | | |
| Attribute-Based Usage Restriction | X | | | | X | | | |
| Dynamic Privileges | X | | | X | X | | | |
| **Realignment** | X | | | | | | X | X |

| Objectives \ Techniques/Approaches | Prevent / Avoid | Prepare | Continue | Constrain | Reconstitute | Understand | Transform | Re-Architect |
|---|---|---|---|---|---|---|---|---|
| Purposing | X | | | | | | | X |
| Offloading | | | | | | | X | X |
| Restriction | | | | | | | X | X |
| Replacement | | | | | | | X | X |
| Specialization | | | | | | | X | X |
| **Redundancy** | X | X | X | | X | | X | X |
| Protected Backup and Restore | | X | X | | X | | | |
| Surplus Capacity | | X | X | | | | | |
| Replication | X | X | X | | | | X | X |
| **Segmentation** | X | | | X | X | | | X |
| Predefined Segmentation | X | | | X | X | | | X |
| Dynamic Segmentation and Isolation | X | | | X | X | | | |
| **Substantiated Integrity** | | | X | X | X | X | | |
| Integrity Checks | | | X | X | X | X | | |
| Provenance Tracking | | | X | | X | X | | |
| Behavior Validation | | | X | X | X | X | | |
| **Unpredictability** | X | | | X | | | | |
| Temporal Unpredictability | X | | | X | | | | |
| Contextual Unpredictability | X | | | X | | | | |

Appendix E.5 identifies cyber resiliency design principles. Strategic design principles support achieving cyber resiliency objectives as shown in Table E-14, while structural design principles provide guidance on how to apply cyber resiliency techniques as shown in Table E-15. Some techniques are required by a design principle; these techniques are **bolded**. Other techniques (not bolded) are typically used in conjunction with required techniques to apply the design principle more effectively, depending on the type of system to which the principle is applied.

**TABLE E-14: STRATEGIC DESIGN PRINCIPLES AND CYBER RESILIENCY OBJECTIVES**

| Objectives \ Strategic Design Principles | Prevent / Avoid | Prepare | Continue | Constrain | Reconstitute | Understand | Transform | Re-Architect |
|---|---|---|---|---|---|---|---|---|
| **Focus on common critical assets.** | X | | X | | X | X | | X |
| **Support agility and architect for adaptability.** | | X | X | | X | | X | X |
| **Reduce attack surfaces.** | X | | | X | | X | X | X |
| **Assume compromised resources.** | | X | X | X | X | X | X | X |
| **Expect adversaries to evolve.** | | X | | | | X | X | X |

**TABLE E-15:  STRUCTURAL DESIGN PRINCIPLES AND CYBER RESILIENCY TECHNIQUES**

| STRUCTURAL DESIGN PRINCIPLE | RELATED TECHNIQUE |
|---|---|
| Limit the need for trust. | Coordinated Protection, **Privilege Restriction**, **Realignment**, Substantiated Integrity |
| Control visibility and use. | Deception, Non-Persistence, **Privilege Restriction**, **Segmentation** |
| Contain and exclude behaviors. | Analytic Monitoring, Diversity, Non-Persistence, **Privilege Restriction**, **Segmentation**, Substantiated Integrity |
| Layer defenses and partition resources. | Analytic Monitoring, **Coordinated Protection**, Diversity, Dynamic Positioning, Redundancy, **Segmentation** |
| Plan and manage diversity. | Coordinated Protection, **Diversity**, Redundancy |
| Maintain redundancy. | Coordinated Protection, Diversity, Realignment, **Redundancy** |
| Make resources location-versatile. | Adaptive Response, Diversity, **Dynamic Positioning**, Non-Persistence, Redundancy, Unpredictability |
| Leverage health and status data. | **Analytic Monitoring**, **Contextual Awareness**, Substantiated Integrity |
| Maintain situational awareness. | Analytic Monitoring, **Contextual Awareness** |
| Manage resources (risk-) adaptively. | **Adaptive Response**, Coordinated Protection, Deception, Dynamic Positioning, Non-Persistence, Privilege Restriction, Realignment, Redundancy, Segmentation, Unpredictability |
| Maximize transience. | Analytic Monitoring, Dynamic Positioning, **Non-Persistence**, Substantiated Integrity, Unpredictability |
| Determine ongoing trustworthiness. | Coordinated Protection, **Substantiated Integrity** |
| Change or disrupt the attack surface. | Adaptive Response, Deception, Diversity, **Dynamic Positioning**, **Non-Persistence**, Unpredictability |
| Make the effects of deception and unpredictability user-transparent. | Adaptive Response, **Coordinated Protection**, Deception, Unpredictability |

APPENDIX F

# CYBER RESILIENCY IN THE SYSTEM LIFE CYCLE

ADDRESSING CYBER RESILIENCY CONCERNS IN SYSTEMS SECURITY ENGINEERING

This appendix describes how cyber resiliency concerns can be addressed as part of the life cycle processes in systems security engineering. It includes a discussion of cyber resiliency and systems security engineering terminology and how cyber resiliency concepts can be applied in system life cycle processes.

Cyber resiliency is addressed in conjunction with the closely related concerns of system resilience and security. Engineering analysis for cyber resiliency emphasizes the need to meet system requirements and address stakeholder concerns in the face of the APT. Cyber resiliency focuses on capabilities used to ensure accomplishment of mission or business functions, for example, to continue minimum essential operations throughout an attack after the adversary has established a presence in the system as opposed to capabilities to harden the system and to keep the adversary out. The cyber resiliency goals of anticipate, withstand, recover, and adapt are oriented toward missions or business functions, and thus complement such security objectives as confidentiality, integrity, and availability that apply to information and to information systems [SP 800-37]. Similarly, the cyber resiliency objectives complement the cybersecurity functions of identify, protect, detect, respond, and recover that an organization can use to achieve specific cybersecurity outcomes [NIST CSF].

Due to this complementarity, cyber resiliency can be incorporated into existing security activities and tasks described in the systems life cycle processes in [SP 800-160 v1]. No new processes are needed, nor are any new activities or tasks needed for the existing processes. Cyber resiliency offers new considerations for these existing processes, activities, and tasks. However, given that the language in the processes is not cyber resiliency-specific, it may not always be obvious how and where cyber resiliency might be injected into the engineering processes.

## F.1  CYBER RESILIENCY AND SSE TERMINOLOGY

Several phrases are integral to the statement and elaboration of the activities and tasks in systems security engineering processes. These include, for example: security aspects, security objectives, security models, concept of security function, security criteria, security-driven constraints, security requirements, and security-relevance as applied to a variety of terms. To overcome any potential confusion in this publication, the tailoring of statements and any elaborations to address cyber resiliency will frequently replace the term *security* with *security and cyber resiliency*. The interpretation of the key phrases will change accordingly, as indicated in general terms below.

### F.1.1  SECURITY AND CYBER RESILIENCY ASPECTS

The interpretation of the term *security aspect* is context-dependent. In the *Agreement Processes* described in [SP 800-160 v1], the security aspects of an acquisition involve protecting assets and enabling systems and often do not involve cyber resiliency. Therefore, the meaning of security aspect is unchanged for those processes. However, the scope of project management processes may include enabling systems. Depending on how the organization's risk management strategy treats risks to enabling systems and how it treats supply chain risks, *Organizational Project-Enabling Processes* may need to consider security and cyber resiliency aspects rather than simply security aspects.

In the context of *Technical Processes*, security aspects may not include cyber resiliency aspects. For purposes of illustration, two examples are presented. The cyber resiliency aspects of other technical processes are described in the Cyber Resiliency Engineering Purpose or Discussion sections of those processes.

For a *problem* (or opportunity) in the *Business or Mission Analysis* process in [SP 800-160 v1], the cyber resiliency aspects include the relative priorities of cyber resiliency goals to different stakeholders; how cyber resiliency objectives are tailored and prioritized by those stakeholders; and what constraints will limit the applicability of cyber resiliency techniques, approaches, and design principles, and thereby limit how alternative solutions are defined and selected. Similarly, the cyber resiliency aspects of an *opportunity* (e.g., insert a new technology, replace a legacy system element, change a mission or business process to use system elements in a new way) include changes in which cyber resiliency approaches, techniques, or design principles are applied or in how they could be applied, and consequently which cyber resiliency objectives can be achieved and to what extent. The cyber resiliency aspects of a *solution* include which cyber resiliency approaches, techniques, and design principles are applied; how they could be applied (e.g., at what architectural locations, in conjunction with which security capabilities or design principles); and which cyber resiliency objectives are or can be achieved and to what extent.

The security aspects of a verification or a validation strategy as described in the *Verification* and *Validation* processes in [SP 800-160 v1] can include cyber resiliency aspects. Such strategies can include or can be organized around a set of threat scenarios. Cyber resiliency considerations in a verification or a validation strategy include verification or validation of the system's ability to achieve its mission or business objectives in the face of attacks motivated by anticipated adversary goals (as defined in the organization's risk management strategy) and under the assumption that different system elements have been compromised (i.e., have become untrustworthy). The cyber resiliency aspects of the strategy, therefore, need to identify other systems which will be represented in verification or validation procedures, how the systems will be represented (e.g., by using enabling systems for emulation of other systems or for fault injection), and what assumptions about their behavior or trustworthiness properties will be represented. In addition, the cyber resiliency aspects of the strategy need to consider how to represent cascading failures, propagation of malware or incorrect data, ripple effects of threat events, and loss due to unknown reasons.[123]

### F.1.2 SECURITY AND CYBER RESILIENCY CRITERIA

In systems engineering, *criteria* are principles or standards of judgment regarding whether and how well a supplier can conform to laws, directives, regulations, policies, or business processes; whether and how well a supplier can deliver the requested product or service in satisfaction of the stated requirements and in conformance with required business practices; the ability of a specific mechanism, system element, or system to meet its requirements; whether movement

---

[123] This may be represented by some communities as a *threat tree*.

NIST SP 800-160, VOLUME 2

from one life cycle stage or process to another (e.g., to accept a baseline into configuration management, to accept delivery of a product or service) is acceptable; how a delivered product or service is handled, distributed, and accepted; how to perform verification and validation; or how to store system elements in disposal. Criteria related to the ability of a system to meet requirements may be expressed in quantitative terms (i.e., metrics and threshold values), in qualitative terms (including threshold boundaries), or in terms of identified forms of evidence.

*Security criteria* are security-relevant criteria and can include or be complemented by cyber resiliency criteria. *Cyber resiliency criteria* are criteria regarding whether and how well an architecture or design of a system or system element conforms with selected cyber resiliency design principles; whether and to what extent an architecture, design, or implementation incorporates selected cyber resiliency techniques or approaches; whether and to what extent an architecture, design, or implementation can be expected to achieve selected and tailored cyber resiliency objectives; how and the extent to which an architecture, design, or implementation manages risk or affects the activities of a cyber adversary; or how and the extent to which an architecture, design, or implementation enables mission or business objectives to be achieved in the face of adversity, particularly adversity involving the APT. Similar to security criteria, cyber resiliency criteria can be expressed in quantitative or qualitative terms. Cyber resiliency criteria are often defined or expressed as measures of performance (MOPs), measures of effectiveness (MOEs), or other metrics evaluated under adversarial conditions.

### F.1.3  SECURITY AND CYBER RESILIENCY REQUIREMENTS AND CHARACTERISTICS

The definition of *security requirement* in [SP 800-160 v1] is quite broad: a "requirement that specifies the functional, assurance, and strength characteristics for a mechanism, system, or system element." In [SP 800-160 v1], therefore, security requirements include cyber resiliency requirements, just as controls in [SP 800-53] include controls related to security, cybersecurity, privacy, supply chain, and cyber resiliency. However, there are some security requirements that are specifically motivated by cyber resiliency concerns. For brevity, the term *cyber resiliency requirement* is used to mean a security requirement which is traceable to a cyber resiliency objective or design principle or which requires the use of a cyber resiliency technique or approach. Cyber resiliency requirements assume the compromise of system elements by an adversary and are traceable to mission or business needs to achieve the resilience goals of anticipate, withstand, recover, and adapt.

The term *security characteristics* includes the security functions the system performs; the security-relevant capabilities the system provides; the level of assurance in the correctness of those functions and in the consistent enforcement of security policies, even under conditions of stress; and the concept of security function embodied in the system architecture and design. For brevity, the term *cyber resiliency characteristics* means the security characteristics related to the need to achieve the resiliency goals of anticipate, withstand, recover, and adapt, in the face of the compromise of system elements (or the system) by an adversary and adversary activities.

### *F.1.4  CYBER RESILIENCY AND SECURITY FUNCTION, VIEWS, AND MODELS*

Several terms are central to understanding and executing the *Architecture Definition*, *System Analysis*, *Implementation*, *Integration*, and *Verification* processes[124] in [SP 800-160 v1], including the concept of secure function, security viewpoints, security views, and security models. The *concept of secure function* is a basic strategy for system security and includes the protection strategies, methods, and techniques used to apply security design principles and concepts to the system architecture. From a cyber resiliency perspective, the concept of secure function defines a strategy for achieving cyber resiliency objectives, applying cyber resiliency design principles, and using cyber resiliency techniques and approaches consistent with and integrated with the strategy for system security.

A *security viewpoint* (a work product from the systems engineering process) expresses or is driven by the concept of secure function. A security viewpoint identifies the security principles, model types, concepts, correspondence rules, methods, and analysis techniques that are provided by the *security view*.[125] A set of one or more security viewpoints specifies a security view of an architecture (also a work product of the systems engineering process). The security view and viewpoints address concerns for controlling the loss of assets and the associated consequences of asset loss. In principle, cyber resiliency views and viewpoints can be integrated into security views and viewpoints. However, the development of a cyber resiliency view as a separate work product, or alternatively, as a separate section of a security view work product, enables the systems security engineering tasks to focus on whether and how an architecture (and subsequently, a design, an implementation, and an integrated system) achieves the cyber resiliency objectives and also addresses stakeholder concerns related to threat activities and compromised resources. Similarly, a cyber resiliency viewpoint, as a separate work product or as a separate section of a security viewpoint work product, can identify cyber resiliency design principles, concepts, model types, and analysis techniques and can relate these to the corresponding topics in security viewpoints.

A *security model* is a representation of an architecture, design, or system which identifies entities and relationships (e.g., subjects, objects, and a reference monitor; enclaves, boundaries, and information flows; information sources, destinations, and communications paths) in such a way that conformance with security requirements and enforcement of security policies can easily be analyzed. A security model uses or relies on an architecture framework and can be a physical, logical, or information model. A *cyber resiliency model* is behavioral or structural. A *behavioral* cyber resiliency model represents the behavior of a system (at a given architectural layer or range of layers) to facilitate analysis of the cyber effects of adverse events on systems and on system behavior; system behavior with respect to business or mission performance requirements, including security performance under a variety of adverse conditions; and the effects of cyber resiliency solutions or cyber courses of action. Many cyber resiliency models explicitly represent adversarial behavior. A *structural* cyber resiliency model identifies where and how within a system architecture selected cyber resiliency techniques and approaches are implemented or cyber resiliency design principles are applied. Both types of cyber resiliency

---

[124] See Sections 3.4.4 (Architecture Definition), 3.4.6 (System Analysis), 3.4.7 (Implementation), 3.4.8 (Integration), and 3.4.9 (Verification) of [SP 800-160 v1].

[125] [SP 800-160 v1] provides additional information on security views, security viewpoints, and security models.

models support cyber resiliency analysis techniques.[126] Both cyber resiliency models and cyber resiliency analysis techniques explicitly assume that some resources are untrustworthy. While a cyber resiliency model can be an instance of or an integral part of a security model, more often a mapping between the two types of models is needed. Cyber resiliency models do not represent policy requirements, but typically represent adverse events (e.g., adversary behavior, environmental disruption) in a temporal rather than state-transition way.

This document describes the cyber resiliency considerations and contributions to system life cycle processes to produce the cyber resiliency outcomes that are necessary to achieve trustworthy, securely resilient systems. The considerations and contributions are provided as selective and specific modifications to the systems security engineering activities and tasks in [SP 800-160 v1] and are aligned with and developed as cyber resiliency extensions to the system life cycle processes in [ISO 15288].

## F.2  CYBER RESILIENCY IN SYSTEM LIFE CYCLE PROCESSES

The following sections provide examples of cyber resiliency considerations for the system life cycle processes,[127] activities, and tasks in [SP 800-160 v1]. In many cases, no changes are needed. In other cases, a simple replacement of the term "security" with "security and cyber resiliency" suffices, with the understanding that material in Chapter Two and the supporting appendices will be consulted if additional discussion on a specific system life cycle process is needed. Representative examples of such discussion are presented for selected tasks. Those examples illustrate how, although consideration of cyber resiliency is consistent with existing tasks, the underlying assumptions and constructs of cyber resiliency require explicit discussion for some tasks.

As applicable, the *discussion* sections will note where specific cyber resiliency constructs are explicitly cited, where the emphasis of cyber resiliency is different. The discussion is intended to be illustrative and thorough, but not exhaustive. Other activities and tasks for which discussion is not presented in this appendix may be relevant to cyber resiliency. Considerations for cyber resiliency are addressed for the 14 *Technical* processes in [ISO 15288]. Similar considerations arise for the *Agreement*, *Project-Enabling*, and *Technical Management* processes.

### F.2.1  BUSINESS OR MISSION ANALYSIS (BA)

**Cyber Resiliency Engineering Purpose**

When considering cyber resiliency as part of the *Business or Mission Analysis* process, systems security engineering analyzes the organization's business or mission problems or opportunities from the perspective of cyber resiliency goals, objectives, and constraints on the solution space. The problem space is assumed to include activities and attacks by APT actors, which can have asset loss consequences and cause damage to other systems or incur risks at a larger scope or scale than for the system-of-interest. This process identifies and prioritizes cyber resiliency

---

[126] See Section 3.2.

[127] The system life cycle processes can be used for new systems, system upgrades, or systems that are being repurposed; can be employed at any stage of the system life cycle; and can take advantage of any system or software development methodology including, for example, waterfall, spiral, or agile.

objectives, which can be tailored specifically for the organization, stakeholders, or the system-of-interest. In addition, this process identifies constraints or limitations on the solution space. Constraints on the selection of cyber resiliency techniques and approaches may be related to the type of system, may be architectural constraints such as interoperability with a specific product suite or conformance to standards, or may result from the risk management strategy of the organization (e.g., maturity of solutions, policy regarding deception). Constraints on the selection of cyber resiliency design principles may be related to the risk management strategy, the selection of security design principles with which cyber resiliency design principles must be aligned, or design principles from other specialty engineering disciplines.

**Cyber Resiliency Engineering Outcomes**

- Cyber resiliency goals are prioritized.

- Cyber resiliency objectives are tailored and prioritized.

- Assumptions about adversary characteristics are identified.

- Constraints or limitations on the cyber resiliency techniques, approaches, and design principles are identified.

- Risks that assumptions about adversary characteristics or about constraints or limitations are false are captured.

- Measures of success for cyber resiliency objectives are identified.

**Cyber Resiliency Considerations**

**BA-1.2** Review organizational problems and opportunities with respect to desired security **and cyber resiliency** objectives.

**Discussion:** Security and cyber resiliency objectives must be achieved despite adversity, which includes a variety of APT activities and attacks. Cyber resiliency goals and objectives are tailored in organizationally meaningful terms and prioritized to reflect stakeholder concerns.

**BA-2.1** Analyze the problems or opportunities in the context of the security **and cyber resiliency** objectives and measures of success to be achieved.

**Discussion:** Problems include potential consequences to stakeholders, mission or business functions, and other systems, as well as to the system-of-interest and its assets, due to adversary activities and attacks. The (tailored and prioritized) cyber resiliency objectives are used to identify measures of success.

**BA-3.1** Define the security **and cyber resiliency** aspects of the preliminary operational concepts and other concepts in life cycle stages.

**Discussion:** Cyber resiliency considerations inform the integration of cyber courses of action into security operational concepts, particularly for operational scenarios involving APT activities and attacks, in which the system must be securely resilient.

### F.2.2 STAKEHOLDER NEEDS AND REQUIREMENTS DEFINITION (SN)

**Cyber Resiliency Engineering Purpose**

When considering cyber resiliency as part of the *Stakeholder Needs and Requirements Definition* process, systems security engineering elicits stakeholder needs for cyber resiliency and then translates those needs into cyber resiliency requirements. Stakeholder needs can be expressed in terms of methods for achieving cyber resiliency objectives by tailoring and prioritizing the objectives. The relevance of different methods for achieving a particular cyber resiliency objective depends on the constraints on the solution space identified previously and on the preliminary operational concept. Stakeholder needs take asset susceptibility to the APT into consideration. Because of the persistence, capability, and stealth of the APT, this threat should be carefully considered in this process. Finally, the relevant strategic cyber resiliency design principles are identified, consistent with the risk management strategy of the organization.

**Cyber Resiliency Engineering Outcomes**

- Relevant methods for achieving cyber resiliency objectives are identified and tailored in terms meaningful to the stakeholders and the system-of-interest.

- The methods for achieving cyber resiliency objectives are translated into stakeholder requirements.

- Asset susceptibility to adversaries is determined.

- The relevant strategic cyber resiliency design principles are identified.

**Cyber Resiliency Considerations**

**SN-2.1** Define the security context of use across all preliminary life cycle concepts.

**Discussion:** From a cyber resiliency perspective, security context of use includes consideration of users, other stakeholders and individuals, organizations, other systems in the environment of operations, and enabling systems in the supply chain (i.e., collectively, environmental entities) in multiple ways, including: as a threat source (either intentional or unintentional), as attack surfaces extending the attack surface of the system-of-interest, and as potential elements of the cyber resiliency solution space. For example, including a service that facilitates an organization's ability to refresh the system or system elements (perhaps employing a virtualization capability) as part of the solution space would facilitate applying the Maximum transience design principle as well as the Change or disrupt the attack surface design principle. Therefore, the context-of-use description identifies the relationships, including legal, contractual, or technical, which apply to environmental entities.

**SN-2.3** Prioritize assets based on the adverse consequence of asset loss.

**Discussion:** Stakeholder concerns for asset loss generally include loss of sensitive information, availability of services, information quality, and direct consequences of damage to the mission or business functions which depend on those organizational assets. However, from a cyber resiliency perspective, indirect consequences of asset loss are also considered. For example, corrupted information or loss of service reliability can undermine user confidence, lead users to change their usage patterns, and ultimately damage the reputation of the organization. In addition, assets should be identified and prioritized from an adversary's perspective; an asset which initially appears to have low priority to stakeholders can be a high value target to an adversary. Finally, since damage to the system can have cascading adverse effects on other systems and organizations, assets should be identified and prioritized at multiple levels or scopes.

**SN-2.7** Define the stakeholder protection needs and rationale.

**Discussion:** From the standpoint of cyber resiliency, stakeholder protection needs can be expressed as methods or capabilities needed to achieve cyber resiliency objectives. These can subsequently be translated into stakeholder cyber resiliency requirements once the rationale for prioritizing them and making trade-offs among them are captured. For example, some stakeholders may be most concerned with minimizing the propagation of APT-related malware to maximize mission or business accomplishments. In contrast, other stakeholders may be more interested in gaining insight into the nature of the adversary malware to be better positioned to develop mitigations to that malware which can be applied beyond the confines of the system. Stakeholder protection needs can also be defined or described in terms of a risk management strategy and then expressed in terms of strategic cyber resiliency design principles.

**SN-5.4** Resolve stakeholder security requirements issues.

**Discussion:** In addressing stakeholder security issues, there are two considerations regarding cyber resiliency. The first is that cyber resiliency issues need to be explicitly considered. The second is that security requirement issues and cyber resiliency requirement issues may be in conflict. For example, from a cyber security perspective, there may be a security requirement to protect internal communications against unauthorized observation. This security requirement translates into a system requirement to encrypt internal communication traffic to counter the threat of data being sniffed and captured by adversaries. From a cyber resiliency perspective, there may be a requirement that the communication traffic remain unencrypted as those encrypted communication flows are often places that the APT employs to hide exfiltration of data or commands from the adversary to the implanted malware.

### F.2.3 SYSTEM REQUIREMENTS DEFINITION (SR)

#### Cyber Resiliency Engineering Purpose

When considering cyber resiliency as part of the *System Requirements Definition* process, systems security engineering identifies system requirements for cyber resiliency which reflect the identified stakeholder requirements for cyber resiliency. System requirements for cyber resiliency refine and situate stakeholder requirements in the context of cyber resiliency design constraints, which take into consideration the type of system, the existing organizational investments in technologies and processes, the intended effects on adversaries, and the maturity of technologies to be included in the system-of-interest. This analysis helps to determine which cyber resiliency techniques and implementation approaches are applicable. System requirements related to cyber resiliency can be expressed in terms of performance measures.

#### Cyber Resiliency Engineering Outcomes

- Cyber resiliency design constraints are defined.

- Applicable cyber resiliency techniques and approaches are determined.

- Cyber resiliency performance measures are defined.

## Cyber Resiliency Considerations

**SR-2.2**  Define system security **and cyber resiliency** requirements, security **and cyber resiliency** constraints on system requirements, and rationale.

**Discussion:** From a cyber resiliency perspective, susceptibility to disruption, hazard, and threat should be considered not only with respect to direct consequences, but also to deferred and indirect consequences. Direct consequences disrupt, destroy, disable, or otherwise impact the ability of the system to support the mission or business functions. Deferred consequences include an adversary's establishment of a persistent foothold in the system, enabling the adversary to discover assets and functional dependencies and to plan future attacks. Indirect consequences include consequences at a different scale than the system (e.g., use of the system as a launch pad for attacks on other systems, initiation of cascading failure across a critical infrastructure sector).

**SR-3.1**  Analyze the complete set of system requirements in consideration of security **and cyber resiliency** concerns.

**Discussion:** For cyber resiliency, the assumption that an adversary can achieve a persistent foothold in the systems should be explicitly noted.

**SR-4.2**  Maintain traceability of system security requirements and security- **and cyber resiliency-**driven constraints.

**Discussion:** From a cyber resiliency perspective, the system trustworthiness objectives and loss tolerance should include the cyber resiliency objectives that were identified by the stakeholders. In addition, loss tolerance should consider resiliency-unique considerations such as tolerance for training to achieve critical mission and business objectives despite an adversary's malware remaining in the system.

### F.2.4  ARCHITECTURE DEFINITION (AR)

## Cyber Resiliency Engineering Purpose

When considering cyber resiliency as part of the *Architecture Definition* process, systems security engineering generates cyber resiliency views of the system architecture alternatives to guide and inform the selection of one or more alternatives. These cyber resiliency views may be integrated into security views or may be presented separately. In addition, systems security engineering ascertains that cyber resiliency analytic processes have been applied across all representative architecture views to identify functional and assurance dependencies as well as potential consequences of exploitation of vulnerabilities and susceptibilities identified from security engineering analysis. Cyber resiliency analyses of architectural views, particularly of security views, inform multiple types of risk assessments (including programmatic; system security; mission, business, or operational; and organizational), risk treatment, and engineering decision making and trades. This process is fully synchronized with the *System Requirements Definition* and *Design Definition* processes and iterates with the *Business and Mission Analysis* and *Stakeholder Needs and Requirements Definition* processes in order to achieve a negotiated understanding of the relative priorities of the stated cyber resiliency goals, objectives, methods, capabilities, design principles, and the constraints on selecting and applying cyber resiliency techniques and approaches. This process also employs the *System Analysis* process to conduct cyber resiliency analyses of the system and architectural alternatives.

### Cyber Resiliency Engineering Outcomes

- Cyber resiliency concerns of stakeholders are addressed by the architecture.

- The relevant strategic cyber resiliency design principles are embodied in the architecture.

- The perspective that the adversary may achieve a persistent foothold in the system and an architecture should be designed to address that concern is reflected in the concept of secure function for the system.

- Cyber resiliency structural design principles, techniques, and approaches are allocated to architectural elements consistent with strategic design principles.

- Security viewpoints, views, and models of the system architecture incorporate cyber resiliency and threat-informed constructs.

### Cyber Resiliency Considerations

**AR-2.1** Define the concept of secure function for the system at the architecture level.

**Discussion:** From a cyber resiliency perspective, the concept of secure function defines a strategy for achieving cyber resiliency objectives, applying cyber resiliency design principles, and using cyber resiliency techniques and approaches consistent with and integrated with the strategy for system security. The concept of secure function encompasses various security design principles which are closely related to cyber resiliency design principles, including, for example: separation, isolation, encapsulation, non-bypassability, layering, hierarchical trust, modularity, hierarchical protection, and secure distributed composition. To incorporate a cyber resiliency perspective, relevant strategic cyber resiliency design principles (Section 2.1.4 and Appendix E.5.1) are used to guide analysis of architectural alternatives and to select relevant structural cyber resiliency design principles (Appendix E.5.2).

**AR-2.2** Select, adapt, or develop the security viewpoints and model kinds based on stakeholder security **and cyber resiliency** concerns.

**Discussion:** A security view which explicitly takes a cyber resiliency perspective includes the results of analyzing the architecture with respect to relevant strategic cyber resiliency design principles, identifies relevant structural cyber resiliency design principles, and enables the architecture and, subsequently, the design to be analyzed with respect to where and how well those principles are applied. From the standpoint of cyber resiliency, a security viewpoint should include a representation of critical mission or business process flows, as well as of control flows that include critical security functionality. The kinds of models should include cyber resiliency models.

**AR-2.3** Identify the security architecture frameworks to be used in developing the security **and cyber resiliency** models and security **and cyber resiliency** views of the system architecture.

**Discussion:** Security architecture frameworks which can be used in developing cyber resiliency models and views are extensible or mappable to frameworks used in cyber resiliency modeling. The frameworks used in cyber resiliency modeling include the conceptual cyber resiliency engineering framework introduced in Section 2.1 and frameworks that reflect an adversarial perspective. Examples of such frameworks include taxonomies of threat events as in [SP 800-30], the ATT&CK Framework [MITRE18], other cyber-attack life cycle or cyber kill chain modeling frameworks, and frameworks for describing effects on threat events (as discussed in Appendix H).

**AR-3.6** Harmonize the security **and cyber resiliency** models and **the** security **and cyber resiliency** views with each other and with the concept of secure function.

**Discussion:** Harmonization of security and cyber resiliency models focuses on ensuring consistency of the modeled emergent behavior of the system. In addition, harmonization can map functional capabilities represented by different models. For example, a cybersecurity model that focuses on how "identify, protect, detect, respond, and recover"[NIST CSF] are achieved can be aligned with a cyber resiliency model that represents how the cyber resiliency objectives are achieved.

**AR-4.5** Define the security **and cyber resiliency** design principles for the system design and evolution that reflect the concept of secure function.

**Discussion:** The cyber resiliency design principles (Appendix E.5) are considered in this task with emphasis on those cyber resiliency design principles which are included explicitly to address the APT (e.g., Expect adversaries to evolve; Change or disrupt the attack surface).

## F.2.5  DESIGN DEFINITION (DE)

**Cyber Resiliency Engineering Purpose**

When considering cyber resiliency as part of the *Design Definition* process, systems security engineering considers cyber resiliency design characteristics, as well as and in close relationship with security design characteristics. Cyber resiliency design characteristics include where and how the relevant cyber resiliency design principles are applied, how that application relates to the application of the relevant security design principles, and where and how the potentially applicable techniques, subject to design constraints as determined as part of the *System Requirements Definition* process, are or could be applied.

**Cyber Resiliency Engineering Outcomes**

- Relevant structural cyber resiliency design principles are identified and interpreted in the context of the architecture and design.

- Technologies to support the application of cyber resiliency design principles are identified.

**Cyber Resiliency Considerations**

**DE-1.1**  Apply the concept of secure function for the system at the design level.

**Discussion:** The concept of secure function encompasses security design principles and concepts. Examples include: separation, isolation, encapsulation, least privilege, modularity, non-bypassability, layering, hierarchical trust, hierarchical protection, and secure distributed composition. From a cyber resiliency perspective, the various structural cyber resiliency design principles described in Appendix E.5.2 and determined to be relevant based on the constraints identified as part of the *Systems Requirements Definition* process are considered as well. Synergies and interactions among cyber resiliency design principles and between cyber resiliency design principles and security design principles are identified and analyzed.

**DE-1.2**  Determine the security technologies required for each system element composing the system.

**Discussion:** Examples of security technologies include: cryptography; secure operating systems, virtual machines, and hypervisors; identity and strong authentication; domain perimeter, domain separation, and cross-domain technologies; security instrumentation and monitoring; physical and electronic tamper protection; and protection against reverse engineering. From a cyber resiliency perspective, such techniques as Deception (e.g., honeynets), Architectural Diversity, Design Diversity, Non-Persistent Information, Dynamic Positioning (e.g., relocation of assets, fragmenting information), Non-Persistent Services, and Unpredictability are considered, subject to the constraints identified as part of the *Systems Requirements Definition* process. These techniques and approaches are intended to address adversarial threat events in general and the APT in particular.

**DE-1.4**  Define the principles for secure evolution of the system design.

**Discussion:** From a cyber resiliency perspective, the principles for secure evolution of the system design reflect the cyber resiliency goal of Adapt and the cyber resiliency objective of Re-Architect, subject to the relative priorities expressed by stakeholders. The stated goal and objective are intended to ensure that the system can adapt in the face of as yet unseen adversarial threats. The principles for secure evolution of the system design can include concepts for use of systems or services in the environment of operations as new capabilities are offered by such systems or services. For example, using a service that facilitates an ability to refresh the system or system elements (e.g., including a virtualization capability) would facilitate the Maximize transience design principle as well as the Change or disrupt the attack surface design principle.

**DE-1.6**  Identify, plan for, and obtain access to enabling systems or services to support the security aspects of the design definition process.

**Discussion:** From a cyber resiliency perspective, enabling systems or services extends the attack surface of the system-of-interest.

**DE-2.2**  Transform security architectural characteristics into security design characteristics.

**Discussion:** An important security objective of system design is to avoid vulnerability where possible and to minimize, manage, and mitigate vulnerability otherwise. From a cyber resiliency perspective, that is a necessary but not necessarily sufficient objective. Systems are complex entities and, as such, it is not possible to eliminate all vulnerabilities. Therefore, adversaries will be given many opportunities to exploit unmitigated known and unknown vulnerabilities. From a cyber resiliency perspective, the design should facilitate redirecting the adversary, precluding adversary activities, impeding the adversary, limiting the adversary, and exposing the adversary.

### F.2.6  SYSTEM ANALYSIS (SA)

**Cyber Resiliency Engineering Purpose**

As part of the *System Analysis* process, systems security engineering addresses cyber resiliency aspects of analysis. This includes representation of the assumption that the adversary may be able to achieve a persistent foothold in the system. It can also include identification of the extent to which classes of threat events or examples of specific threat events are used in analysis, the extent to which effects of alternative design decisions or cyber resiliency solutions on threat events are analyzed, and which forms of cyber resiliency behavioral modeling (if any) are used.[128] Functional dependencies of cyber resiliency capabilities on underlying security capabilities are identified to determine the potential consequences of misuse or failure of security functionality.

**Cyber Resiliency Engineering Outcomes**

- Cyber resiliency analysis objectives are articulated, including their relationship to security analysis objectives.

- Cyber resiliency assumptions, especially those regarding the nature and capability of the adversary and the classes of threat events to be considered, are articulated.

- The dependency of cyber resiliency functionality on underlying security functionality is identified so that the consequences of misuse or failure of security functionality can be analyzed.

**Cyber Resiliency Considerations**

**SA-1.3**  Define the objectives, scope, level of fidelity, and level of assurance of the security **and cyber resiliency** aspects of system analysis.

**Discussion:** From a cyber resiliency perspective, the objectives of system analysis can include, for example, identification of the extent to which relevant cyber resiliency design principles have been applied, the level of confidence that a given design principle has been applied effectively, the classes of threat events which are addressed by the system, and how and how well the system addresses a given class of threat events. The scope of system analysis can be restricted to the system-of-interest or specific elements of the system-of-interest; it can also be extended to include enabling systems and other systems in the environment of operations. From a cyber resiliency perspective, enabling systems and other systems in the environment of operations extends the attack surface of the system-of-interest. In addition, the consequences of threat events on the system-of-interest can result in consequences to other systems in the environment of operations (e.g., attack propagation or a cascading failure). The minimum acceptable level of fidelity for metrics or measures of effectiveness related to achieving cyber resiliency objectives or meeting cyber resiliency requirements is defined.

**SA-1.5**  Define the security **and cyber resiliency** aspects of the system analysis strategy.

**Discussion:** The importance of dependency analysis is noted in [SP 800-160 v1]. From a cyber resiliency perspective, the dependency analysis should also examine the dependency of cyber resiliency objectives and functions on their corresponding security objectives and functions.

**SA-2.1**  Identify and validate the assumptions associated with the security **and cyber resiliency** aspects of system analysis.

**Discussion:** From a cyber resiliency perspective, one of the critical assumptions is that the adversary will be able to circumvent boundary protection measures, achieve a persistent foothold in the system, evolve, and continually attempt to achieve its goals. The nature of the

---

[128] See Section 3.2.

APT is such that the ability to validate such assumptions will be challenging, and it may not be possible to remove uncertainty about the assumptions.

## F.2.7 IMPLEMENTATION (IP)

**Cyber Resiliency Engineering Purpose**

When considering cyber resiliency as part of the *Implementation* process, systems security engineering focuses on the security aspects of system elements and of the implementation strategy so that cyber resiliency is not a direct consideration. However, the implementation strategy must ensure that the properties and protection capabilities of system elements are provided in such a way as to meet cyber resiliency needs and achieve cyber resiliency objectives.

**Cyber Resiliency Engineering Outcomes**

- The security aspects of implementation that constrain the ability to achieve cyber resiliency objectives or to meet cyber resiliency needs are identified.

**Cyber Resiliency Considerations**

IP-1.2    Identify constraints from the security aspects of the implementation strategy and technology on the system requirements, architecture, design, or implementation techniques.

**Discussion:** The security aspects of the implementation strategy oriented toward the specific choice of implementation technology or the manner in which the system element is to be realized may impose constraints on the selection of cyber resiliency techniques, approaches, or solutions, and, ultimately, on the ability to achieve the cyber resiliency objectives or meet cyber resiliency needs. The identification of these constraints is crucial to guiding and informing engineering trade-offs.

## F.2.8 INTEGRATION (IN)

**Cyber Resiliency Engineering Purpose**

No change from Systems Security Engineering Purpose.

**Cyber Resiliency Engineering Outcomes**

No change from Systems Security Engineering Outcomes.

**Cyber Resiliency Considerations**

If stakeholders do not interpret "security" in the definition or discussion of activities or tasks (e.g., security aspects, security criteria, security requirements, security characteristics) as encompassing cyber resiliency, the term should be replaced by "security and cyber resiliency."

## F.2.9 VERIFICATION (VE)

**Cyber Resiliency Engineering Purpose**

When considering cyber resiliency as part of the *Verification* process, systems security engineering produces evidence that the system satisfies its cyber resiliency-relevant system requirements and has its required cyber resiliency characteristics in light of the assumed threat environment.[129]

**Cyber Resiliency Engineering Outcomes**

- The cyber resiliency aspects of the verification strategy are developed.

- Any enabling systems or services needed to achieve the cyber resiliency aspects of the verification strategy are available.

**Cyber Resiliency Considerations**

**VE-2.1** Define the security **and cyber resiliency** aspects of the verification procedures, each supporting one or a set of security- **and cyber resiliency**-focused verification actions.

**Discussion:** Verification procedures related to cyber resiliency focus on cyber resiliency capabilities in the context of mission or business process objectives and under the assumption of adversary compromise of system elements. The procedures identify the tailored cyber resiliency objectives and the cyber resiliency criteria for acceptance. The procedures identify how potential adversary activities and their effects will be represented.

**VE-2.2** Perform security **and cyber resiliency** verification procedures.

**Discussion:** Cyber resiliency verification, like security verification, can be performed at multiple points in the system life cycle. Modeling and simulation, or model-based systems engineering, methods to evaluate correctness can be used before a system element is implemented, based on design artifacts. Cyber resiliency verification does not typically search for vulnerabilities but can include examining interactions between system elements which could result in cascading failures, propagation of malware or incorrect data, or the ripple effects of threat events. The result of performing cyber resiliency verification procedures which represent the compromise of specific system elements can include the discovery of previously unrecognized functional dependencies.

### F.2.10 TRANSITION (TR)

**Cyber Resiliency Engineering Purpose**

No change from Systems Security Engineering Purpose.

**Cyber Resiliency Engineering Outcomes**

- Aspects of the transition strategy that include the cyber resiliency goals and objectives are developed.

- Threat and APT-informed training for all stakeholders, including users, is developed.

- Threat-informed frameworks and self-challenge tools are developed and employed in preparation for validation of the cyber resiliency of the system.

---

[129] See Appendix F.1.

**Cyber Resiliency Considerations**

**TR-1.1**  Develop the security aspects of the transition strategy.

**Discussion:** The security aspects of transition regarding confidentiality, integrity, availability, and accountability are discussed in [SP 800-160 v1]. The use of Substantiated Integrity to preserve the system security characteristics to maintain the target level of assurance and trustworthiness throughout all transition activities should be included in the transition strategy. From a cyber resiliency perspective, the security aspects of transition should also consider how the transition will preserve the cyber resiliency characteristics needed to achieve the cyber resiliency goals (e.g., ability to Withstand) and objectives (e.g., ability to Constrain) as tailored and prioritized.[130]

**TR-1.4**  Identify and arrange the training necessary for secure system utilization, sustainment, and support.

**Discussion:** Transition is a perfect opportunity for an adversary to attempt to compromise a system as it is not fully functioning and thus unable to protect itself. Therefore, the training necessary for transition should also include training about the APT, what to look for in terms of suspicious activity (indicating corrupted behavior), and other threat-related training.

**TR-2.4**  Demonstrate proper achievement of the security aspects of system installation.

**Discussion:** From a cyber resiliency perspective, security aspects of the system installation should also consider cyber resiliency goals, objectives, techniques, and implementation approaches that may be affected during system installation.

**TR-2.9**  Review the security aspects of the system for operational readiness.

**Discussion:** To help validate the readiness of the system, the organization may consider complementing penetration testing and vulnerability testing with the use of tools that perform a self-challenge (e.g., Simian Army) and use APT-informed threat frameworks (e.g., [MITRE18]) that highlight possible attack paths of an adversary.

## F.2.11  VALIDATION (VA)

**Cyber Resiliency Engineering Purpose**

When considering cyber resiliency as part of the *Validation* process, systems security engineering produces evidence that the system fulfills its business or mission objectives by satisfying its cyber resiliency-relevant stakeholder requirements and demonstrating its required cyber resiliency characteristics in its assumed threat environment.[131]

**Cyber Resiliency Engineering Outcomes**

- The cyber resiliency aspects of the validation strategy are developed.

- Any enabling systems or services needed to achieve the cyber resiliency aspects of the validation strategy are available.

---

[130] See Appendix F.2.1.

[131] See Appendix F.1.

**Cyber Resiliency Considerations**

**VA-1.1** Identify the security **and cyber resiliency** aspects of the validation scope and corresponding security- **and cyber resiliency**-focused validation actions.

**Discussion:** The scope of cyber resiliency validation actions can be broader than the scope of the system element or system for which requirements for cyber resiliency-related behaviors and properties have been stated. The scope of validation includes interactions with external systems on which the system depends or with which the system interfaces. The scope of validation also includes interactions with representations of the APT. The scope of validation determines how interactions will be represented in validation actions (e.g., as assumed behaviors, modeled or simulated, via emulation, or via hands-on injection of inputs from external systems or from a Red Team).

**VA-1.2** Identify the constraints that can potentially limit the feasibility of the security **and cyber resiliency**-focused validation actions.

**Discussion:** Constraints that can potentially affect cyber resiliency-focused validation actions include the rules of engagement for a Red Team, penetration test team, or participants in hybrid tabletop and hands-on exercises. These constraints reflect the limitations placed on application of the Self-Challenge approach.

**VA-2.1** Define the security **and cyber resiliency** aspects of the validation procedures, each supporting one or a set of security- **and cyber resiliency**-focused validation actions.

**Discussion:** Validation procedures related to cyber resiliency focus on specific cyber resiliency capabilities in the context of mission or business process objectives and under the assumption of adversary compromise of system elements or of other systems. The procedures identify the tailored cyber resiliency objectives, describe how cyber courses of action will be selected and represented in the validation procedures, and identify cyber resiliency criteria for acceptance. A validation procedure focused on cyber resiliency is targeted toward the behavior and properties of the system as a whole or toward critical mission or business functions.

**VA-2.2** Perform security **and cyber resiliency** validation procedures in the defined environment.

**Discussion:** Cyber resiliency validation, like security validation, can be performed at multiple points in the system life cycle. Validation procedures can be executed in a laboratory, testbed, or cyber range, as well as in an operational environment. Cyber resiliency validation can include examining interactions between system elements or between the system-of-interest and other systems, which could result in cascading failures, propagation of malware or incorrect data, or ripple effects of threat events.

## F.2.12  OPERATION (OP)

**Cyber Resiliency Engineering Purpose**

When considering cyber resiliency for the *Operation* process, systems security engineering ensures that the operation strategy includes cyber resiliency aspects. The cyber resiliency aspects of the operation strategy focus on ensuring that business or mission objectives are achieved and can make explicit how trade-offs between the execution of business or mission tasks, security, safety, and other aspects of trustworthiness are made in the operational environment under different circumstances.

**Cyber Resiliency Engineering Outcomes**

- The cyber resiliency aspects of the operation strategy are developed.

**Cyber Resiliency Considerations**

**OP-1.1** Develop the security **and cyber resiliency** aspects of the operation strategy.

**Discussion:** The cyber resiliency aspects of the operation strategy ensure that business or mission objectives can be achieved by using the cyber resiliency capabilities of the system in conjunction with capabilities of other systems with which the system-of-interest interacts or on which it depends and that the system's security services are resilient. The cyber resiliency aspects of service availability include consideration of how service priorities change in response to identified business or mission operations or environmental factors. The cyber resiliency aspects of the operation strategy are closely related to contingency and continuity-of-operations planning at the business or mission process level and the organizational level. Information provided by implementing the Analytic Monitoring and Contextual Awareness techniques support gaining insight into performance levels and are central to monitoring changes in hazards and threats. From a cyber resiliency perspective, the operation strategy describes how the Prevent/Avoid, Prepare, Continue, and Constrain cyber resiliency objectives are achieved in the intended operational environment, and under circumstances which, while not intended, may arise (e.g., changes in mission or business processes or priorities).

## F.2.13  MAINTENANCE (MA)

**Cyber Resiliency Engineering Purpose**

No change from Systems Security Engineering Purpose.

**Cyber Resiliency Engineering Outcomes**

No change from Systems Security Engineering Outcomes.

**Cyber Resiliency Considerations**

**MA-1.1** Define the security aspects of the maintenance strategy.

**Discussion:** The security aspects related to replacement can use Architectural Diversity, Design Diversity, and Supply Chain Diversity. The security aspects of the logistics strategy and counterfeit and modification prevention can use Supply Chain Diversity, Integrity Checks, and Provenance Tracking.

## F.2.14  DISPOSAL (DS)

**Cyber Resiliency Engineering Purpose**

When considering cyber resiliency as part of the *Disposal* process, systems security engineering analyzes whether and how removing system elements or the entire system-of-interest can result in decreased cyber resiliency. Removal of a system element can reduce the extent to which some cyber resiliency techniques are used (e.g., Diversity, Redundancy, Segmentation) and can also reduce the effectiveness of some cyber resiliency techniques (e.g., Analytic Monitoring, Contextual Awareness). The disposal strategy should address the resulting risks. The relevance of cyber resiliency design principles to the remaining systems is determined, and the disposal strategy ensures that relevant design principles continue to be applied.

**Cyber Resiliency Engineering Outcomes**

- The risk to or the reduction in cyber resiliency of other systems, missions, business functions, or the organization due to removing system elements or withdrawing the system-of-interest from operations, if any, is understood and accepted by stakeholders.

**Cyber Resiliency Considerations**

**DS-1.1**  Develop the security **and cyber resiliency** aspects of the disposal strategy.

**Discussion:** The disposal strategy for the system identifies and provides steps to manage the potential consequences of the permanent termination of system functions and delivery on the ability of other systems (or of the mission or business function which partially relied on the system) to achieve or maintain stated cyber resiliency objectives. Similarly, the system disposal strategy addresses the potential consequences of transforming the system and its environment into an acceptable state on the ability of other systems to achieve or maintain cyber resiliency objectives. The period of transition between the system operating normally and the system having been completely withdrawn from operations is of particular concern since an adversary can take advantage of uncertainty about behaviors to operate undetectably. Consideration should also be given to hazards or threats resulting from residue left behind from the disposal of the system or system element. For example, materials related to the operational context of a predecessor system may still be relevant to a successor system or system element and therefore may have value to an adversary.

## APPENDIX G

# CONTROLS SUPPORTING CYBER RESILIENCY
NIST SPECIAL PUBLICATION 800-53 SECURITY CONTROLS RELATED TO CYBER RESILIENCY

This appendix identifies controls[132] in [SP 800-53][133] which directly support cyber resiliency. The methodology for determining whether a control directly supports cyber resiliency is outlined below. One of the challenges is that many controls can be considered to provide cybersecurity as well as cyber resiliency. In addition, many security practices that might in principle be considered good cybersecurity practices are not widely employed. Therefore, in these cases, if the control satisfies the other screening questions, the control is included in the listing. For each control in [SP 800-53], the following questions were used to identify controls supporting cyber resiliency.

- Is the control *primarily* focused on helping the system achieve a level of confidentiality, integrity, or availability[134] in situations where threats, excluding APT, are considered? If so, the control supports conventional information security. The control may provide functional, architectural, governance, or procedural capabilities that establish a necessary foundation for cyber resiliency. However, the control does not support cyber resiliency as a primary consideration.

- Is the control *primarily* focused on ensuring continuity of operations against threats of natural disasters, infrastructure failures, or cascading failures in which software or human errors are implicated? If so, the control supports *organizational* or *operational resilience* in the face of conventional threats. The control may provide functional, architectural, governance, or procedural capabilities that establish a necessary foundation for cyber resiliency. However, it does not support cyber resiliency, per se.

- Does the control map to one or more of the 14 cyber resiliency techniques? The techniques characterize ways to achieve one or more cyber resiliency objectives. For some controls, mapping to a technique or an approach is trivial. For example, the control SI-14 (Non-Persistence) maps to the cyber resiliency technique of Non-Persistence as the control and cyber resiliency technique share the same name and achieve the same outcome. In other instances, the mapping is relatively straightforward, although not quite as trivial; for example, SC-29 (Heterogeneity) is about the use of diverse of information resources so it supports the cyber resiliency Diversity technique. In other instances, the mapping is not as straightforward, and the guidance listed below should be employed to help identify cyber resiliency controls.

- Does the control map to one of the cyber resiliency approaches that support the 14 cyber resiliency techniques? For example, SC-30(4) (Concealment and Misdirection | Misleading Information) maps to the Disinformation approach of the Deception technique. Since the approaches provide a finer granularity than the techniques, this question provides a more

---

[132] For the remainder of this appendix, the term *control* includes both controls and control enhancements.

[133] References to controls are taken from the latest draft of NIST Special Publication 800-53, Revision 5. The control references will be updated upon final publication.

[134] Note that the control baselines in [SP 800-53] are defined for levels of concern for confidentiality, integrity, and availability with respect to threats other than the advanced persistent threat.

detailed analysis of the controls and a control that maps to an approach is *likely* to be a resiliency control.

Many of the controls in [SP 800-53] address other important types of safeguards that are not necessarily related to cyber resiliency. Controls of this type are generally *not* included in the set of controls supporting cyber resiliency. These controls include:

- **Policy controls (the -1 controls)**

  The -1 controls (the policy and procedure controls) do not directly map to cyber resiliency techniques or approaches. Only a policy control that is specifically written to address the APT should be identified as a cyber resiliency control.

- **Training controls (largely confined to AT family)**

  In general, training-related controls do not satisfy the conditions listed above.

- **Documentation controls**

  Like the policy controls, documentation controls generally do not satisfy the conditions listed above. A documentation control would have to be narrowly focused (e.g., document how to respond to the presence of the advanced persistent threat) for it to be considered a cyber resiliency control.

- **Environmental controls (e.g., A/C, heating, found in PE family)**

  Environmental controls do not satisfy the conditions listed above unless they are narrowly focused (e.g., controls that address intentional power surges).

- **Personnel security controls**

  Personnel security controls do not satisfy the conditions listed above.

- **Compliance controls (e.g., those checking to ensure that all patches are up to date)**

  Cyber resiliency focuses primarily on evolving and adapting rather than compliance. Thus, unless a control is explicitly focused on ensuring that some specific (already established) cyber resiliency capability is implemented correctly and operating as intended, compliance controls generally are not considered part of cyber resiliency.

- **Vulnerability assessment controls**

  While adversaries take advantage of vulnerabilities, identifying such vulnerabilities is not the focus of cyber resiliency.

Some control families are more likely to support cyber resiliency than others. The Contingency Planning (CP), Incident Response (IR), System and Communications Protection (SC), and System and Information Integrity (SI) families have a high percentage of controls that are cyber resiliency-oriented. However, controls supporting cyber resiliency are not confined to these families nor are all controls in these families automatically controls supporting cyber resiliency.

After applying the above criteria, there may still be some ambiguity for some controls as to whether or not they are cyber resiliency in their focus. This is due in part to the overlap between aspects of cybersecurity and cyber resiliency. Delineation between the two is not easy to discern. To illustrate the distinction, it is useful to reference first principles.

*Cyber resiliency is essentially about ensuring continued mission operations despite the fact that an adversary has established a foothold in the organization's systems and cyber infrastructure.*

- Controls that are largely focused on keeping the adversary out of systems and infrastructure are generally not resiliency controls. For example, identification and authentication controls such as IA-4 (Identifier Management) are generally not focused on combating an adversary after they have achieved a foothold in an organizational system. Similarly, physical access controls (e.g., PE-2, PE-4) are generally considered basic information security measures, not cyber resiliency measures.

- One area where there is likely to be some confusion is between Auditing and Analytic Monitoring. Controls that are focused on correlation of collected information are more likely to be Analytic Monitoring-focused. Controls focused on storage capacity for audit trails, what information should be captured in an audit trail, or retention of the audit trail are more likely to fall into the Audit domain.

- In many instances, cyber resiliency capabilities are reflected in control enhancements instead of base controls. In those situations, [SP 800-53] requires that a parent control be selected if one or more of its control enhancements are selected. This means that for any cyber resiliency control enhancement selected, the associated base control is also selected and included in the security plan for the system.

Table G-1 identifies the controls and control enhancements in [SP 800-53] that support cyber resiliency using the criteria outlined above. For each of the selected "cyber resiliency controls or control enhancements" the table specifies the corresponding cyber resiliency technique and approach. In many instances, more than a single cyber resiliency technique or approach is provided. That is because many of the controls and enhancements support more than one cyber resiliency technique or approach. Where there are multiple corresponding cyber resiliency techniques, they are listed in a *prioritized* order where the technique with the strongest linkage is listed first. The table will be updated as new versions of [SP 800-53] are published.

### TABLE G-1: NIST CONTROLS SUPPORTING CYBER RESILIENCY TECHNIQUES

| CONTROL NO. | CONTROL NAME | RESILIENCY TECHNIQUE [APPROACHES] |
|---|---|---|
| Access Control | | |
| AC-2(6) | ACCOUNT MANAGEMENT \| DYNAMIC PRIVILEGE MANAGEMENT | Privilege Restriction [Dynamic Privileges] Adaptive Response [Dynamic Reconfiguration] |
| AC-2(8) | ACCOUNT MANAGEMENT \| DYNAMIC ACCOUNT MANAGEMENT | Adaptive Response [Dynamic Resource Allocation] Adaptive Response [Dynamic Reconfiguration] |
| AC-2(12) | ACCOUNT MANAGEMENT \| ACCOUNT MONITORING / ATYPICAL USAGE | Analytic Monitoring [Monitoring and Damage Assessment] |
| AC-3(2) | ACCESS ENFORCEMENT \| DUAL AUTHORIZATION | Privilege Restriction [Trust-Based Privilege Management] |
| AC-3(11) | ACCESS ENFORCEMENT \| RESTRICT ACCESS TO SPECIFIC INFORMATION TYPES | Privilege Restriction [Attribute-Based Usage Restriction] |
| AC-3(12) | ACCESS ENFORCEMENT \| ASSERT AND ENFORCE APPLICATION ACCESS | Privilege Restriction [Attribute-Based Usage Restriction] |
| AC-3(13) | ACCESS ENFORCEMENT \| ATTRIBUTE-BASED ACCESS CONTROL | Privilege Restriction [Attribute-Based Usage Restriction] |
| AC-4(2) | INFORMATION FLOW ENFORCEMENT \| PROCESSING DOMAINS | Segmentation [Predefined Segmentation] |
| AC-4(3) | INFORMATION FLOW ENFORCEMENT \| DYNAMIC INFORMATION FLOW CONTROL | Adaptive Response [Adaptive Management] |
| AC-4(8) | INFORMATION FLOW ENFORCEMENT \| SECURITY POLICY FILTERS | Substantiated Integrity [Integrity Checks] |
| AC-4(12) | INFORMATION FLOW ENFORCEMENT \| DATA TYPE IDENTIFIERS | Substantiated Integrity [Integrity Checks] |
| AC-4(17) | INFORMATION FLOW ENFORCEMENT \| DOMAIN AUTHENTICATION | Substantiated Integrity [Provenance Tracking] |
| AC-4(21) | INFORMATION FLOW ENFORCEMENT \| PHYSICAL OR LOGICAL SEPARATION OF INFORMATION FLOWS | Segmentation [Predefined Segmentation] |
| AC-6 | LEAST PRIVILEGE | Privilege Restriction [Attribute-Based Usage Restriction] |
| AC-6(1) | LEAST PRIVILEGE \| AUTHORIZE ACCESS TO SECURITY FUNCTIONS | Privilege Restriction [Attribute-Based Usage Restriction] |
| AC-6(2) | LEAST PRIVILEGE \| NON-PRIVILEGED ACCESS FOR NON-SECURITY FUNCTIONS | Privilege Restriction [Trust-Based Privilege Management] Realignment [Purposing] |
| AC-6(3) | LEAST PRIVILEGE \| NETWORK ACCESS TO PRIVILEGED COMMANDS | Privilege Restriction [Trust-Based Privilege Management] |
| AC-6(4) | LEAST PRIVILEGE \| SEPARATE PROCESSING DOMAINS | Privilege Restriction [Trust-Based Privilege Management, Attribute-Based Usage Restriction] Segmentation [Predefined Segmentation] |
| AC-6(5) | LEAST PRIVILEGE \| PRIVILEGED ACCOUNTS | Privilege Restriction [Trust-Based Privilege Management] |
| AC-6(6) | LEAST PRIVILEGE \| PRIVILEGED ACCESS BY NON-ORGANIZATIONAL USERS | Privilege Restriction [Trust-Based Privilege Management] |
| AC-6(7) | LEAST PRIVILEGE \| REVIEW OF USER PRIVILEGES | Coordinated Protection [Consistency Checking] Privilege Restriction [Trust-Based Privilege Management] |

| CONTROL NO. | CONTROL NAME | RESILIENCY TECHNIQUE [APPROACHES] |
|---|---|---|
| AC-6(8) | LEAST PRIVILEGE \| PRIVILEGE LEVELS FOR CODE EXECUTION | Privilege Restriction [Dynamic Privileges] |
| AC-6(10) | LEAST PRIVILEGE \| PROHIBIT NON-PRIVILEGED USERS FROM EXECUTING PRIVILEGED FUNCTIONS | Privilege Restriction [Attribute-Based Usage Restriction, Trust-Based Privilege Management] |
| AC-7(4) | UNSUCCESSFUL LOGON ATTEMPTS \| USE OF ALTERNATE FACTOR | Diversity [Path Diversity] |
| AC-12 | SESSION TERMINATION | Non-Persistence [Non-Persistent Services] |
| AC-23 | DATA MINING PROTECTION | Analytic Monitoring [Monitoring and Damage Assessment] Privilege Restriction [Trust-Based Privilege Management, Attribute-Based Usage Restriction, Dynamic Privileges] |
| **Audit and Accountability** | | |
| AU-5(3) | RESPONSE TO AUDIT PROCESSING FAILURES\| CONFIGURABLE TRAFFIC VOLUME THRESHOLDS | Adaptive Response [Dynamic Resource Allocation, Adaptive Management] |
| AU-6 | AUDIT REVIEW, ANALYSIS, AND REPORTING | Adaptive Response [Adaptive Management] Analytic Monitoring [Monitoring and Damage Assessment] |
| AU-6(3) | AUDIT REVIEW, ANALYSIS, AND REPORTING \| CORRELATE AUDIT REPOSITORIES | Analytic Monitoring [Sensor Fusion and Analysis] |
| AU-6(5) | AUDIT REVIEW, ANALYSIS, AND REPORTING \| INTEGRATED ANALYSIS OF AUDIT RECORDS | Analytic Monitoring [Sensor Fusion and Analysis] |
| AU-6(6) | AUDIT REVIEW, ANALYSIS, AND REPORTING \| CORRELATION WITH PHYSICAL MONITORING | Analytic Monitoring [Sensor Fusion and Analysis] |
| AU-6(8) | AUDIT REVIEW, ANALYSIS, AND REPORTING \| FULL TEXT ANALYSIS OF PRIVILEGED COMMANDS | Analytic Monitoring [Monitoring and Damage Assessment] Segmentation [Predefined Segmentation] |
| AU-6(9) | AUDIT REVIEW, ANALYSIS, AND REPORTING \| CORRELATION WITH INFORMATION FROM NONTECHNICAL SOURCES | Analytic Monitoring [Sensor Fusion and Analysis] |
| AU-9(1) | PROTECTION OF AUDIT INFORMATION \| HARDWARE WRITE-ONCE MEDIA | Substantiated Integrity [Integrity Checks] |
| AU-9(2) | PROTECTION OF AUDIT INFORMATION \| STORE ON SEPARATE PHYSICAL SYSTEMS AND COMPONENTS | Segmentation [Predefined Segmentation] |
| AU-9(3) | PROTECTION OF AUDIT INFORMATION \| CRYPTOGRAPHIC PROTECTION | Substantiated Integrity [Integrity Checks] |
| AU-9(5) | PROTECTION OF AUDIT INFORMATION \| DUAL AUTHORIZATION | Privilege Restriction [Trust-Based Privilege Management] |
| AU-9(6) | PROTECTION OF AUDIT INFORMATION \| READ-ONLY ACCESS | Privilege Restriction [Trust-Based Privilege Management, Attribute-Based Usage Restriction] Substantiated Integrity [Integrity Checks] |
| AU-9(7) | PROTECTION OF AUDIT INFORMATION \| STORE IN COMPONENT WITH DIFFERENT OPERATING SYSTEM | Diversity [Architectural Diversity] |
| AU-10 (2) | NON-REPUDIATION \| VALIDATE INFORMATION PRODUCER IDENTITY | Substantiated Integrity [Provenance Tracking] |
| **Assessment, Authorization, and Monitoring** | | |
| CA-7(3) | CONTINUOIUS MONITORING \| TREND ANALYSES | Contextual Analysis [Dynamic Resource Awareness, Dynamic Threat Awareness] |
| CA-7(5) | CONTINUOUS MONITORING \| CONSISTANCY ANALYSIS | Coordinated Protection [Consistency Analysis] |

| CONTROL NO. | CONTROL NAME | RESILIENCY TECHNIQUE [APPROACHES] |
|---|---|---|
| CA-8 | PENETRATION TESTING | Coordinated Protection [Self-Challenge] |
| CA-8(1) | PENETRATION TESTING \| INDEPENDENT PENETRATION AGENT OR TEAM | Coordinated Protection [Self-Challenge] |
| CA-8(2) | PENETRATION TESTING \| RED TEAM EXERCISES | Coordinated Protection [Self-Challenge] |
| CA-8(3) | PENETRATION TESTING \| FACILITY PENETRATION TESTING | Coordinated Protection [Self-Challenge] |
| **Configuration Management** | | |
| CM-2(7) | BASELINE CONFIGURATION \| CONFIGURE SYSTEMS AND COMPONENTS FOR HIGH-RISK AREAS | Analytic Monitoring [Monitoring and Damage Assessment, Forensic and Behavioral Analysis] |
| CM-4(1) | IMPACT ANALYSES\|SEPARATE TEST ENVIRONMENTS | Segmentation [Predefined Segmentation] |
| CM-5(3) | ACCESS RESTRICTIONS FOR CHANGE \| SIGNED COMPONENTS | Substantiated Integrity [Integrity Checks, Provenance Tracking] |
| CM-5(4) | ACCESS RESTRICTIONS FOR CHANGE \| DUAL AUTHORIZATION | Privilege Restriction [Trust-Based Privilege Management] |
| CM-5(5) | ACCESS RESTRICTIONS FOR CHANGE \| PRIVILEGE LIMITATION FOR PRODUCTION AND OPERATION | Privilege Restriction [Trust-Based Privilege Management] |
| CM-5(6) | ACCESS RESTRICTIONS FOR CHANGE \| LIMIT LIBRARY PRIVILEGES | Privilege Restriction Trust-Based Privilege Management] |
| CM-7(4) | LEAST FUNCTIONALITY \| UNAUTHORIZED SOFTWARE — BLACKLISTING | Realignment [Purposing] |
| CM-7(5) | LEAST FUNCTIONALITY \| AUTHORIZED SOFTWARE — WHITELISTING | Realignment [Purposing] |
| CM-8(3) | SYSTEM COMPONENT INVENTORY \| AUTOMATED UNAUTHORIZED COMPONENT DETECTION | Analytic Monitoring [Monitoring and Damage Assessment] |
| **Contingency Planning** | | |
| CP-2(1) | CONTINGENCY PLAN \| COORDINATE WITH RELATED PLANS | Coordinated Protection [Consistency Analysis] |
| CP-2(5) | CONTINGENCY PLAN \| CONTINUE MISSIONS AND BUSINESS FUNCTIONS | Coordinated Protection [Orchestration] Adaptive Response [Dynamic Reconfiguration] |
| CP-2(8) | CONTINGENCY PLAN \| IDENTIFY CRITICAL ASSETS | Contextual Awareness [Mission Dependency and Status Visualization] |
| CP-8(3) | TELECOMMUNICATIONS SERVICES \| SEPARATION OF PRIMARY / ALTERNATE PROVIDERS | Diversity [Architectural Diversity] |
| CP-9 | SYSTEM BACKUP | Redundancy [Protected Backup and Restore] |
| CP-9(6) | SYSTEM BACKUP \| REDUNDANT SECONDARY SYSTEM | Redundancy [Replication] |
| CP-9(7) | SYSTEM BACKUP \| DUAL AUTHORIZATION | Privilege Restriction [Trust-Based Privilege Management] |
| CP-11 | ALTERNATE COMMUNICATIONS PROTOCOLS | Diversity [Architectural Diversity, Design Diversity] |
| CP-12 | SAFE MODE | Adaptive Response [Adaptive Management] |
| CP-13 | ALTERNATIVE SECURITY MECHANISMS | Diversity [Architectural Diversity, Design Diversity] Adaptive Response [Adaptive Management] |
| CP-14 | SELF-CHALLENGE | Coordinated Protection [Self-Challenge] |

| CONTROL NO. | CONTROL NAME | RESILIENCY TECHNIQUE [APPROACHES] |
|---|---|---|
| **Identification and Authentication** | | |
| IA-2(6) | IDENTIFICATION AND AUTHENTICATION \| ACCESS TO PRIVILEGED ACCOUNTS - SEPARATE DEVICE | Diversity [Path Diversity] Coordinated Protection [Calibrated Defense-in-Depth, Orchestration] |
| IA-2(13) | IDENTIFICATION AND AUTHENTICATION \| OUT-OF-BAND AUTHENTICATION | Diversity [Path Diversity] Coordinated Protection [Calibrated Defense-in-Depth, Orchestration] Segmentation [Predefined Segmentation] |
| IA-3(1) | DEVICE IDENTIFICATION AND AUTHENTICATION \| CRYPTOGRAPHIC BIDIRECTIONAL AUTHENTICATION | Deception [Obfuscation] Substantiated Integrity [Integrity Checks] |
| IA-10 | ADAPTIVE AUTHENTICATION | Adaptive Response [Adaptive Management] Privilege Restriction [Dynamic Privileges] Coordinated Protection [Calibrated Defense-in-Depth] |
| **Incident Response** | | |
| IR-4(2) | INCIDENT HANDLING \| DYNAMIC RECONFIGURATION | Adaptive Response [Dynamic Reconfiguration] Dynamic Positioning [Functional Relocation of Sensors] |
| IR-4(3) | INCIDENT HANDLING \| CONTINUITY OF OPERATIONS | Adaptive Response [Dynamic Reconfiguration, Adaptive Management] Coordinated Protection [Orchestration] |
| IR-4(4) | INCIDENT HANDLING \| INFORMATION CORRELATION | Coordinated Protection [Orchestration] Analytic Monitoring [Sensor Fusion and Analysis] Contextual Awareness [Dynamic Threat Awareness] |
| IR-4(9) | INCIDENT HANDLING \| DYNAMIC RESPONSE CAPABILITY | Adaptive Response [Dynamic Reconfiguration] |
| IR-4(10) | INCIDENT HANDLING \| SUPPLY CHAIN COORDINATION | Coordinated Protection [Orchestration] |
| IR-4(11) | INCIDENT HANDLING \| INTEGRATED INCIDENT RESPONSE TEAM | Adaptive Response [Dynamic Reconfiguration, Adaptive Management] Analytic Monitoring [Forensic and Behavioral Analysis] Coordinated Protection [Orchestration] |
| IR-4(12) | INCIDENT HANDLING \| MALICIOUS CODE AND FORENSIC ANALYSIS | Analytic Monitoring [Forensic and Behavioral Analysis] |
| IR-4(13) | INCIDENT HANDLING \| BEHAVIOR ANALYSIS | Analytic Monitoring [Monitoring and Damage Assessment] |
| IR-5 | INCIDENT MONITORING | Analytic Monitoring [Monitoring and Damage Assessment, Forensic and Behavioral Analysis] |
| **Maintenance** | | |
| MA-4(4) | NONLOCAL MAINTENANCE \| AUTHENTICATION AND SEPARATION OF MAINTENANCE SESSIONS | Segmentation [Predefined Segmentation] |
| **Physical and Environmental Protection** | | |
| PE-3(5) | PHYSICAL ACCESS CONTROL \| TAMPER PROTECTION | Substantiated Integrity [Integrity Checks] |
| PE-6 | MONITORING PHYSICAL ACCESS | Analytic Monitoring [Monitoring and Damage Assessment] |

| CONTROL NO. | CONTROL NAME | RESILIENCY TECHNIQUE [APPROACHES] |
|---|---|---|
| PE-6(2) | MONITORING PHYSICAL ACCESS \| AUTOMATED INTRUSION RECOGNITION AND RESPONSES | Analytic Monitoring [Monitoring and Damage Assessment] Adaptive Response [Adaptive Management] Coordinated Protection [Orchestration] |
| PE-6(4) | MONITORING PHYSICAL ACCESS \| MONITORING PHYSICAL ACCESS TO SYSTEMS | Analytic Monitoring [Monitoring and Damage Assessment] Coordinated Protection [Calibrated Defense-in-Depth] |
| PE-9(1) | POWER EQUIPMENT AND CABLING \| REDUNDANT CABLING | Redundancy [Replication] |
| PE-11(1) | EMERGENCY POWER \| ALTERNATE POWER SUPPLY - MINIMAL OPERATIONAL CAPABILITY | Redundancy [Replication] |
| PE-11(2) | EMERGENCY POWER \| ALTERNATE POWER SUPPLY - SELF-CONTAINED | Redundancy [Replication] |
| PE-17 | ALTERNATE WORK SITE | Redundancy [Replication] |
| **Planning** | | |
| PL-8(1) | SECURITY AND PRIVACY ARCHITECTURE \| DEFENSE-IN-DEPTH | Coordinated Protection [Calibrated Defense-in-Depth] |
| PL-8(2) | SECURITY AND PRIVACY ARCHITECTURE \| SUPPLIER DIVERSITY | Diversity [Supply Chain Diversity] |
| **Program Management** | | |
| PM-7(1) | ENTERPRISE ARCHITECTURE \| OFFLOADING | Realignment [Offloading] |
| PM-16 | THREAT AWARENESS PROGRAM | Contextual Awareness [Dynamic Threat Awareness] |
| PM-16(1) | THREAT AWARENESS PROGRAM \| AUTOMATED MEANS FOR SHARING THREAT INTELLIGENCE | Contextual Awareness [Dynamic Threat Awareness] |
| PM-32 | CONTINUOUS MONITORING STRATEGY | Analytic Monitoring [Monitoring and Damage Assessment, Sensor Fusion and Analysis] |
| PM-33 | PURPOSING | Realignment [Purposing] |
| **Risk Assessment** | | |
| RA-3(3) | RISK ASSESSMENT \| DYNAMIC THREAT AWARENESS | Contextual Awareness [Dynamic Threat Awareness] Adaptive Response [Adaptive Management] |
| RA-5(5) | VULNERABILITY MONITORING AND SCANNING \| PRIVILEGED ACCESS | Analytic Monitoring [Monitoring and Damage Assessment] Privilege Restriction [Attribute-Based Usage Restriction] |
| RA-5(6) | VULNERABILITY MONITORING AND SCANNING \| AUTOMATED TREND ANALYSES | Analytic Monitoring [Sensor Fusion and Analysis] |
| RA-5(8) | VULNERABILITY MONITORING AND SCANNING \| REVIEW HISTORIC AUDIT LOGS | Analytic Monitoring [Sensor Fusion and Analysis] |
| RA-5(10) | VULNERABILITY MONITORING AND SCANNING \| CORRELATE SCANNING INFORMATION | Analytic Monitoring [Sensor Fusion and Analysis] |
| RA-9 | CRITICALITY ANALYSIS | Contextual Awareness [Mission Dependency and Status Visualization] Realignment [Offloading] |

| CONTROL NO. | CONTROL NAME | RESILIENCY TECHNIQUE [APPROACHES] |
|---|---|---|
| RA-10 | THREAT HUNTING | Analytic Monitoring [Monitoring and Damage Assessment] Contextual Awareness [Dynamic Threat Awareness] |
| **System and Services Acquisition** | | |
| SA-11(2) | DEVELOPER TESTING AND EVALUATION \| THREAT MODELING AND VULNERABILITY ANALYSIS | Contextual Awareness [Dynamic Threat Awareness] |
| SA-11(5) | DEVELOPER TESTING AND EVALUATION \| PENETRATION TESTING | Coordinated Protection [Self-Challenge] |
| SA-11(6) | DEVELOPER TESTING AND EVALUATION \| ATTACK SURFACE REVIEWS | Realignment [Replacement] |
| SA-15(5) | DEVELOPMENT PROCESS, STANDARDS, AND TOOLS \| ATTACK SURFACE REDUCTION | Realignment [Replacement] |
| SA-17(8) | DEVELOPER SECURITY ARCHITECTURE AND DESIGN \| ORCHESTRATION | Coordinated Protection [Orchestration] |
| SA-17(9) | DEVELOPER SECURITY ARCHITECTURE AND DESIGN \| DESIGN DIVERSITY | Diversity [Design Diversity] |
| SA-20 | CUSTOMIZED DEVELOPMENT OF CRITICAL COMPONENTS | Realignment [Specialization] |
| SA-23 | SPECIALIZATION | Realignment [Specialization] |
| **System and Communications Protection** | | |
| SC-2 | SEPARATION OF SYSTEM AND USER FUNCTIONALITY | Segmentation [Predefined Segmentation] |
| SC-2(1) | SEPARATION OF SYSTEM AND USER FUNCTIONALITY \| INTERFACES FOR NON-PRIVILEGED USERS | Segmentation [Predefined Segmentation] |
| SC-3 | SECURITY FUNCTION ISOLATION | Segmentation [Predefined Segmentation] |
| SC-3(1) | SECURITY FUNCTION ISOLATION \| HARDWARE SEPARATION | Segmentation [Predefined Segmentation] |
| SC-3(2) | SECURITY FUNCTION ISOLATION \| ACCESS AND FLOW CONTROL FUNCTIONS | Segmentation [Predefined Segmentation] |
| SC-3(3) | SECURITY FUNCTION ISOLATION \| MINIMIZE NONSECURITY FUNCTIONALITY | Realignment [Restriction] |
| SC-3(5) | SECURITY FUNCTION ISOLATION \| LAYERED STRUCTURES | Coordinated Protection [Orchestration] Segmentation [Predefined Segmentation] Realignment [Offloading] |
| SC-5(2) | DENIAL OF SERVICE PROTECTION \| CAPACITY, BANDWIDTH, AND REDUNDANCY | Adaptive Response [Dynamic Resource Allocation] Redundancy [Surplus Capacity] |
| SC-5(3) | DENIAL OF SERVICE PROTECTION \| DETECTION AND MONITORING | Analytic Monitoring [Monitoring and Damage Assessment] |
| SC-7 | BOUNDARY PROTECTION | Segmentation [Predefined Segmentation] |
| SC-7(10) | BOUNDARY PROTECTION \| PREVENT EXFILTRATION | Analytic Monitoring [Monitoring and Damage Assessment] Non-Persistence [Non-Persistent Information] Coordinate Protection [Self-Challenge] |
| SC-7(11) | BOUNDARY PROTECTION \| RESTRICT INCOMING COMMUNICATIONS TRAFFIC | Substantiated Integrity [Provenance Tracking] |
| SC-7(13) | BOUNDARY PROTECTION \| ISOLATION OF SECURITY TOOLS, MECHANISMS, AND SUPPORT COMPONENTS | Segmentation [Predefined Segmentation] |
| SC-7(15) | BOUNDARY PROTECTION NETWORK PRIVILEGED ACCESSES | Realignment [Offloading] Segmentation [Predefined Segmentation] |

| CONTROL NO. | CONTROL NAME | RESILIENCY TECHNIQUE [APPROACHES] |
|---|---|---|
| | | Privilege Restriction [Trust-Based Privileged Management] |
| SC-7(16) | BOUNDARY PROTECTION \| PREVENT DISCOVERY OF COMPONENTS AND DEVICES | Deception [Obfuscation] |
| SC-7(20) | BOUNDARY PROTECTION \| DYNAMIC ISOLATION AND SEGREGATION | Segmentation [Dynamic Segmentation and Isolation] <br> Adaptive Response [Dynamic Reconfiguration] |
| SC-7(21) | BOUNDARY PROTECTION \| ISOLATION OF SYSTEM COMPONENTS | Segmentation [Predefined Segmentation] |
| SC-7(22) | BOUNDARY PROTECTION \| SEPARATE SUBNETS FOR CONNECTING TO DIFFERENT SECURITY DOMAINS | Segmentation [Predefined Segmentation] |
| SC-8(1) | TRANSMISSION CONFIDENTIALITY AND INTEGRITY \| CRYPTOGRAPHIC PROTECTION | Substantiated Integrity [Integrity Checks] |
| SC-8(4) | TRANSMISSION CONFIDENTIALITY AND INTEGRITY \| CONCEAL OR RANDOMIZE COMMUNICATIONS | Deception [Obfuscation] <br> Unpredictability [Contextual Unpredictability] |
| SC-8(5) | TRANSMISSION CONFIDENTIALITY AND INTEGRITY \| PROTECTED DISTRIBUTION SYSTEM | Substantiated Integrity [Integrity Checks] <br> Segmentation [Predefined Segmentation] |
| SC-10 | NETWORK DISCONNECT | Non-Persistence [Non-Persistent Connectivity] |
| SC-18(5) | MOBILE CODE \| ALLOW EXECUTION ONLY IN CONFINED ENVIRONMENTS | Segmentation [Dynamic Segmentation and Isolation] |
| SC-22 | ARCHITECTURE AND PROVISIONING FOR NAME/ADDRESS RESOLUTION SERVICE | Redundancy [Replication] |
| SC-23(3) | SESSION AUTHENTICITY \| UNIQUE SYSTEM-GENERATED SESSION IDENTIFIERS | Unpredictability [Temporal Unpredictability] |
| SC-25 | THIN NODES | Realignment [Offloading, Restriction] <br> Non-Persistence [Non-Persistent Services, Non-Persistent Information] |
| SC-26 | DECOYS | Deception [Misdirection] <br> Analytic Monitoring [Monitoring and Damage Assessment, Forensic and Behavioral Analysis] |
| SC-28(1) | PROTECTION OF INFORMATION AT REST \| CRYPTOGRAPHIC PROTECTION | Deception [Obfuscation] <br> Substantiated Integrity [Integrity Checks] |
| SC-29 | HETEROGENEITY | Diversity [Architectural Diversity] |
| SC-29(1) | HETEROGENEITY \| VIRTUALIZATION TECHNIQUES | Diversity [Architectural Diversity] <br> Non-Persistence [Non-Persistent Services] |
| SC-30 | CONCEALMENT AND MISDIRECTION | Deception [Obfuscation, Misdirection] |
| SC-30(2) | CONCEALMENT AND MISDIRECTION \| RANDOMNESS | Unpredictability [Temporal Unpredictability, Contextual Unpredictability] |
| SC-30(3) | CONCEALMENT AND MISDIRECTION \| CHANGE PROCESSING AND STORAGE LOCATIONS | Dynamic Positioning [Functional Relocation of Cyber Resources] <br> Unpredictability [Temporal Unpredictability] |
| SC-30(4) | CONCEALMENT AND MISDIRECTION \| MISLEADING INFORMATION | Deception [Disinformation] |
| SC-30(5) | CONCEALMENT AND MISDIRECTION \| CONCEALMENT OF SYSTEM COMPONENTS | Deception [Obfuscation] |
| SC-32 | SYSTEM PARTITIONING | Segmentation [Predefined Segmentation] |
| SC-32(1) | SYSTEM PARTITIONING SEPARATE PHYSICAL DOMAINS FOR PRIVILEGED FUNCTIONS | Segmentation [Predefined Segmentation, Dynamic Segmentation and Isolation] |

| CONTROL NO. | CONTROL NAME | RESILIENCY TECHNIQUE [APPROACHES] |
|---|---|---|
| SC-34 | NON-MODIFIABLE EXECUTABLE PROGRAMS | Substantiated Integrity [Integrity Checks] |
| SC-34(1) | NON-MODIFIABLE EXECUTABLE PROGRAMS \| NO WRITABLE STORAGE | Non-Persistence [Non-Persistent Information] |
| SC-34(2) | NON-MODIFIABLE EXECUTABLE PROGRAMS \| INTEGRITY PROTECTION ON READ-ONLY MEDIA | Substantiated Integrity [Integrity Checks] |
| SC-34(3) | NON-MODIFIABLE EXECUTABLE PROGRAMS \| HARDWARE-BASED PROTECTION | Substantiated Integrity [Integrity Checks] |
| SC-35 | EXTERNAL MALICIOUS CODE IDENTIFICATION | Analytic Monitoring [Monitoring and Damage Assessment] Deception [Misdirection] |
| SC-36 | DISTRIBUTED PROCESSING AND STORAGE | Dynamic Positioning [Functional Relocation of Cyber Resources] Redundancy [Replication] |
| SC-36(1) | DISTRIBUTED PROCESSING AND STORAGE \| POLLING TECHNIQUES | Substantiated Integrity [Behavior Validation] |
| SC-36(2) | DISTRIBUTED PROCESSING AND STORAGE \| SYNCHRONIZATION | Redundancy [Replication] |
| SC-37 | OUT-OF-BAND CHANNELS | Diversity [Path Diversity] |
| SC-39 | PROCESS ISOLATION | Segmentation [Predefined Segmentation, Dynamic Segmentation and Isolation] |
| SC-39(1) | PROCESS ISOLATION \| HARDWARE SEPARATION | Segmentation [Predefined Segmentation, Dynamic Segmentation and Isolation] |
| SC-39(2) | PROCESS ISOLATION \| SEPARATION EXECUTION DOMAINS PER THREAD | Segmentation [Predefined Segmentation, Dynamic Segmentation and Isolation] |
| SC-40(2) | WIRELESS LINK PROTECTION \| REDUCE DETECTION POTENTIAL | Deception [Obfuscation] |
| SC-40(3) | WIRELESS LINK PROTECTION \| IMITATIVE OR MANIPULATIVE COMMUNICATIONS DECEPTION | Deception [Obfuscation] Unpredictability [Temporal Unpredictability, Contextual Unpredictability] |
| SC-44 | DETONATION CHAMBERS | Segmentation [Predefined Segmentation] Analytic Monitoring [Forensic and Behavioral Analysis] Deception [Misdirection] |
| SC-47 | COMMUNICATION PATH DIVERSITY | Diversity [Path Diversity] |
| SC-48 | SENSOR RELOCATION | Dynamic Positioning [Functional Relocation of Sensors] |
| SC-48(1) | SENSOR RELOCATION \| DYNAMIC RELOCATION OF SENSORS OR MONITORING CAPABILITIES | Dynamic Positioning [Functional Relocation of Sensors] |
| SC-49 | HARDWARE-ENFORCED SEPARATION AND POLICY ENFORCEMENT | Segmentation [Pre-Defined Segmentation] |
| SC-50 | SOFTWARE-ENFORCED SEPARATION AND POLICY ENFORCEMENT | Segmentation [Predefined Segmentation] |
| **System and Information Integrity** | | |
| SI-3(9) | MALICIOUS CODE PROTECTION \| MALICIOUS CODE ANALYSIS | Analytic Monitoring [Forensic and Behavioral Analysis] |
| SI-4(1) | SYSTEM MONITORING \| SYSTEM-WIDE INTRUSION DETECTION SYSTEM | Analytic Monitoring [Sensor Fusion and Analysis] Contextual Awareness [Mission Dependency and Status Visualization] |
| SI-4(2) | SYSTEM MONITORING \| AUTOMATED TOOLS AND MECHANISMS FOR REAL-TIME ANALYSIS | Analytic Monitoring [Monitoring and Damage Assessment] |

| CONTROL NO. | CONTROL NAME | RESILIENCY TECHNIQUE [APPROACHES] |
|---|---|---|
| | | Contextual Awareness [Mission Dependency and Status Visualization] |
| SI-4(3) | SYSTEM MONITORING \| AUTOMATED TOOL AND MECHANISM INTEGRATION | Analytic Monitoring [Sensor Fusion and Analysis] Adaptive Response [Adaptive Management] |
| SI-4(4) | SYSTEM MONITORING \| INBOUND AND OUTBOUND COMMUNICATIONS TRAFFIC | Analytic Monitoring [Monitoring and Damage Assessment] |
| SI-4(7) | SYSTEM MONITORING \| AUTOMATED RESPONSE TO SUSPICIOUS EVENTS | Analytic Monitoring [Monitoring and Damage Assessment] Adaptive Response [Adaptive Management] |
| SI-4(10) | SYSTEM MONITORING \| VISIBILITY OF ENCRYPTED COMMUNICATIONS | Analytic Monitoring [Monitoring and Damage Assessment] |
| SI-4(11) | SYSTEM MONITORING \| ANALYZE COMMUNICATIONS TRAFFIC ANOMALIES | Analytic Monitoring [Monitoring and Damage Assessment] |
| SI-4(16) | SYSTEM MONITORING \| CORRELATE MONITORING INFORMATION | Analytic Monitoring [Sensor Fusion and Analysis] Contextual Awareness [Dynamic Resource Awareness] |
| SI-4(17) | SYSTEM MONITORING \| INTEGRATED SITUATIONAL AWARENESS | Analytic Monitoring [Sensor Fusion and Analysis] Contextual Awareness [Dynamic Resource Awareness] |
| SI-4(18) | SYSTEM MONITORING \| ANALYZE TRAFFIC AND COVERT EXFILTRATION | Analytic Monitoring [Monitoring and Damage Assessment] |
| SI-4(24) | SYSTEM MONITORING \| INDICATORS OF COMPROMISE | Analytic Monitoring [Sensor Fusion and Analysis] |
| SI-4(25) | SYSTEM MONITORING \| OPTIMIZE NETWORK TRAFFIC ANALYSIS | Analytic Monitoring [Sensor Fusion and Analysis] |
| SI-6 | SECURITY AND PRIVACY FUNCTION VERIFICATION | Substantiated Integrity [Integrity Checks] |
| SI-7 | SOFTWARE, FIRMWARE, AND INFORMATION INTEGRITY | Substantiated Integrity [Integrity Checks] |
| SI-7(1) | SOFTWARE, FIRMWARE, AND INFORMATION INTEGRITY \| INTEGRITY CHECKS | Substantiated Integrity [Integrity Checks] |
| SI-7(5) | SOFTWARE, FIRMWARE, AND INFORMATION INTEGRITY \| AUTOMATED RESPONSE TO INTEGRITY VIOLATIONS | Substantiated Integrity [Integrity Checks] Adaptive Response [Adaptive Management] |
| SI-7(6) | SOFTWARE, FIRMWARE, AND INFORMATION INTEGRITY \| CRYPTOGRAPHIC PROTECTION | Substantiated Integrity [Integrity Checks] |
| SI-7(7) | SOFTWARE, FIRMWARE, AND INFORMATION INTEGRITY \| INTEGRATION OF DETECTION AND RESPONSE | Substantiated Integrity [Integrity Checks] Analytic Monitoring [Monitoring and Damage Assessment] |
| SI-7(9) | SOFTWARE, FIRMWARE, AND INFORMATION INTEGRITY \| VERIFY BOOT PROCESS | Substantiated Integrity [Integrity Checks] |
| SI-7(10) | SOFTWARE, FIRMWARE, AND INFORMATION INTEGRITY \| PROTECTION OF BOOT FIRMWARE | Substantiated Integrity [Integrity Checks] |
| SI-7(11) | SOFTWARE, FIRMWARE, AND INFORMATION INTEGRITY \| CONFINED ENVIRONMENTS WITH LIMITED PRIVILEGES | Privilege Restriction [Trust-Based Privilege Management] Segmentation [Predefined Segmentation, Dynamic Segmentation and Isolation] |
| SI-7(12) | SOFTWARE, FIRMWARE, AND INFORMATION INTEGRITY \| INTEGRITY VERIFICATION | Substantiated Integrity [Integrity Checks] |

| CONTROL NO. | CONTROL NAME | RESILIENCY TECHNIQUE [APPROACHES] |
|---|---|---|
| SI-10(3) | INFORMATION INPUT VALIDATION \|PREDICTABLE BEHAVIOR | Substantiated Integrity [Behavior Validation] |
| SI-10(5) | INFORMATION INPUT VALIDATION \| RESTRICT INPUTS TO TRUSTED SOURCES AND APPROVED FORMATS | Substantiated Integrity [Provenance Tracking] |
| SI-14 | NON-PERSISTENCE | Non-Persistence [Non-Persistent Services] |
| SI-14(1) | NON-PERSISTENCE \| REFRESH FROM TRUSTED SOURCES | Non-Persistence [Non-Persistent Services, Non-Persistent Information] Substantiated Integrity [Provenance Validation] |
| SI-14(2) | NON-PERSISTENCE \| NON-PERSISTENT INFORMATION | Non-Persistence [Non-Persistent Information] |
| SI-14(3) | NON-PERSISTENCE \| NON-PERSISTENT CONNCTIVITY | Non-Persistence [Non-Persistent Connectivity] |
| SI-15 | INFORMATION OUTPUT FILTERING | Substantiated Integrity [Integrity Checks] |
| SI-16 | MEMORY PROTECTION | Diversity [Synthetic Diversity] Unpredictability [Temporal Unpredictability] |
| SI-20 | TAINTING | Deception [Tainting] |
| SI-21 | INFORMATION REFRESH | Non-Persistence [Non-Persistent Information] |
| SI-22 | INFORMATION DIVERSITY | Diversity [Information Diversity] |
| SI-23 | INFORMATION FRAGMENTATION | Dynamic Positioning [Fragmentation] |
| **Supply Chain Risk Management** | | |
| SR-3(1) | SUPPLY CHAIN PROTECTION SAFEGUARDS AND PROCESSES \| DIVERSE SUPPLY CHAIN | Diversity [Supply Chain Diversity] |
| SR-3(2) | SUPPLY CHAIN PROTECTION SAFEGUARDS AND PROCESSES \| LIMITATION OF HARM | Diversity [Supply Chain Diversity] Deception [Obfuscation] |
| SR-4 | PROVENANCE | Substantiated Integrity [Provenance Tracking] |
| SR-4(1) | PROVENANCE \| IDENTITY | Substantiated Integrity [Provenance Tracking] |
| SR-4(2) | PROVENANCE \| TRACK AND TRACE | Substantiated Integrity [Provenance Tracking] |
| SR-4(3) | PROVENANCE \| VALIDATE AS GENUINE AND NOT ALTERED | Substantiated Integrity [Integrity Checks, Provenance Tracking] |
| SR-5 | ACQUISITION STRATEGIES, TOOLS, AND METHODS | Substantiated Integrity [Provenance Tracking] Deception [Obfuscation] |
| SR-5(1) | ACQUISITION STRATEGIES, TOOLS, AND METHODS \| ADEQUATE SUPPLY | Redundancy [Replication] Diversity [Supply Chain Diversity] |
| SR-6(1) | SUPPLIER REVIEWS \| PENETRATION TESTING AND ANALYSIS | Coordinated Protection [Self-Challenge] Analytic Monitoring [Monitoring and Damage Assessment] |
| SR-9 | TAMPER RESISTENCE AND DETECTION | Substantiated Integrity [Integrity Checks] |
| SR-9(1) | TAMPER RESISTENCE AND DETECTION \| MULTIPLE PHASES OF SYSTEM DEVELOPMENT LIFE CYCLE | Substantiated Integrity [Integrity Checks] Deception [Obfuscation] |
| SR-10 | INSPECTION OF SYSTEMS OR COMPONENTS | Substantiated Integrity [Integrity Checks] Analytic Monitoring [Monitoring and Damage Assessment, Forensic and Behavioral Analysis] |
| SR-11 | COMPONENT AUTHENTICITY | Substantiated Integrity [Integrity Checks] [Provenance Tracking] |

# ADVERSARY-ORIENTED ANALYSIS
APPROACHES FOR TAKING ADVERSARIAL ACTIVITIES INTO CONSIDERATION

This appendix supports adversary-oriented analysis of a system and applications of cyber resiliency, as discussed in Section 3.1.7, Section 3.2.3.2, and Section 3.2.4.3. Section H.1 provides a vocabulary to describe the current or potential effects a set of mitigations (i.e., risk-reducing actions or decisions such as the application of design principles, techniques, implementation approaches, requirements, controls, technologies, or solutions) could have on threat events (or classes of threat events).[135] Each intended effect is characterized in terms of its potential impact on risk and the expected changes in adversary behavior. Section H.2 describes the construct of a threat coverage analysis, which looks at potential effects of mitigations from the perspective of a given threat model and a vocabulary that defines potential effects. Section H.2 subsequently provides a representative cyber threat coverage analysis for cyber resiliency approaches. This involves mapping the 48 cyber resiliency approaches to classes of threat events in an existing adversarial cyber threat model using the provided vocabulary to identify the potential effects each cyber resiliency approach may have on the classes of adversary actions defined by the threat model.

## H.1  POTENTIAL EFFECTS ON THREAT EVENTS

Cyber resiliency solutions are relevant only if they have some effect on risk, specifically by reducing the likelihood of occurrence of threat events,[136] the ability of threat events to cause harm, and the extent of that harm.[137] The types of analysis of system architectures, designs, implementations, and operations indicated for cyber resiliency can include consideration of what effects alternatives could have on the threat events which are part of threat scenarios of concern to stakeholders.

From the perspective of protecting a system against adversarial threats, five high-level, desired effects on the adversary can be identified: *redirect, preclude, impede, limit,* and *expose.* These effects are useful for discussion but are often too general to facilitate the definition of specific measures of effectiveness. Therefore, more specific classes of effects are defined:

- Deter, divert, and deceive in support of redirect;

- Prevent, preempt, and expunge in support of preclude;

---

[135] While this appendix focuses on potential effects on adversary actions, most of the vocabulary applies to threat events caused by the full range of possible threat sources identified in [SP 800-30].

[136] The term *threat event* refers to an event or situation that has the potential for causing undesirable consequences or impacts. Threat events can be caused by either adversarial or non-adversarial threat sources. However, the emphasis in this section is on the effect on adversarial threats and specifically on the APT, for which threat events can be identified with adversary activities.

[137] While many different risk models are potentially valid and useful, three elements are common across most models. These are: the *likelihood of occurrence* (i.e., the likelihood that a threat event or a threat scenario consisting of a set of interdependent events will occur or be initiated by an adversary), the *likelihood of impact* (i.e., the likelihood that a threat event or scenario will result in an impact given vulnerabilities, weaknesses, and predisposing conditions), and the *level of the impact* [SP 800-30].

- Contain, degrade, delay, and exert in support of impede;

- Shorten and recover in support of limit; and

- Detect, reveal, and scrutinize in support of expose.

These effects are tactical (i.e., local to a specific threat event or scenario), although it is possible that their repeated achievement could have strategic effects as well. All effects except redirect (including deter, divert, and deceive) apply to non-adversarial and adversarial threat events; redirect (including deter, divert, and deceive) is applicable only to adversarial threat events.

Table H-1 defines the effects, indicates how each effect could reduce risk, and illustrates how the use of certain approaches to implementing cyber resiliency techniques for protection against attack could have the identified effect. The term *defender* refers to the organization or organizational staff responsible for providing or applying protections. It should be noted that likelihoods and impact can be reduced, but risk cannot be eliminated. Thus, no effect can be assumed to be complete, even those with names that suggest completeness, such as prevent, detect, or expunge. Table H-2 shows the potential effects of cyber resiliency techniques on risk factors.

**TABLE H-1: EFFECTS OF CYBER RESILIENCY TECHNIQUES ON ADVERSARIAL THREAT EVENTS**

| INTENDED EFFECT | IMPACT ON RISK | EXPECTED RESULTS |
|---|---|---|
| **Redirect (includes deter, divert, and deceive):** Direct threat events away from defender-chosen resources. | Reduce likelihood of occurrence and (to a lesser extent) reduce likelihood of impact. | • The adversary's efforts cease.<br>• The adversary actions are mistargeted or misinformed. |
| **Deter** Discourage the adversary from undertaking further activities by instilling fear (e.g., of attribution or retribution) or doubt that those activities would achieve intended effects (e.g., that targets exist). | Reduce likelihood of occurrence. | • The adversary ceases or suspends activities.<br>**Example:** The defender uses disinformation to make it appear that the organization is better able to detect attacks than it is and is willing to launch major counter-strikes. Therefore, the adversary chooses to not launch an attack due to fear of detection and reprisal. |
| **Divert** Direct the threat event toward defender-chosen resources. | Reduce likelihood of occurrence. | • The adversary refocuses activities on defender-chosen resources.<br>• The adversary directs activities toward targets beyond the defender's purview (e.g., other organizations).<br>• The adversary does not affect resources that the defender has not selected to be targets.<br>**Example:** The defender maintains an Internet-visible enclave with which untrusted external entities can interact and a private enclave accessible only via a VPN for trusted suppliers, partners, or customers (predefined segmentation).<br>**Example:** The defender uses non-persistent information and obfuscation to hide critical resources combined with functional relocation of cyber resources and disinformation to lure the adversary toward a sandboxed enclave where adversary actions cannot harm critical resources. |

| INTENDED EFFECT | IMPACT ON RISK | EXPECTED RESULTS |
|---|---|---|
| **Deceive**<br>Lead the adversary to believe false information about defended systems, missions, or organizations or about defender capabilities or TTPs. | Reduce likelihood of occurrence and/or reduce likelihood of impact. | • The adversary's efforts are wasted as the assumptions on which the adversary bases attacks are false.<br>• The adversary takes actions based on false information, thus revealing that they have obtained that information.<br>**Example:** The defender strategically places false information (disinformation) about the cybersecurity investments that it plans to make. As a result, the adversary's malware development is wasted by being focused on countering non-existent cybersecurity protections.<br>**Example:** The defender uses selectively planted false information (disinformation) and honeynets (misdirection) to cause an adversary to focus its malware at virtual sandboxes while at the same time employing obfuscation to hide the actual resources. |
| **Preclude (includes expunge, preempt, and negate)**<br>Ensure that the threat event does not have an impact. | Reduce likelihood of occurrence and/or reduce likelihood of impact. | • The adversary's efforts or resources cannot be applied or are wasted. |
| **Expunge**<br>Remove resources that are known to be or are suspected of being unsafe, incorrect, or corrupted. | Reduce likelihood of impact of subsequent events in the same threat scenario. | • A malfunctioning, misbehaving, or suspect resource is restored to normal operation.<br>• The adversary loses a capability for some period, as adversary-directed threat mechanisms (e.g., malicious code) are removed.<br>• Adversary-controlled resources are so badly damaged that they cannot perform any function or be restored to a usable condition without being entirely rebuilt.<br>**Example:** The defender uses virtualization to refresh critical software (non-persistent services) from a known good copy at random intervals (temporal unpredictability). As a result, malware that was implanted in the software is deleted. |
| **Preempt**<br>Forestall or avoid conditions under which the threat event could occur or on which an attack is predicated. | Reduce likelihood of occurrence. | • The adversary's resources cannot be applied or the adversary cannot perform activities (e.g., because resources adversary requires are destroyed or made inaccessible).<br>**Example:** An unneeded network connection is disabled (non-persistent connectivity) so that an attack via that interface cannot be made.<br>**Example:** A resource is repositioned (asset mobility) so that, in its new location, it cannot be affected by a threat event. |
| **Negate**<br>Create conditions under which the threat event cannot be expected to result in an impact. | Reduce likelihood of impact. | • The adversary can launch an attack, but it will not even partially succeed. The adversary's efforts are wasted as the assumptions on which the adversary based its attack are no longer valid, and as a result, the intended effects cannot be achieved.<br>**Example:** Subtle variations in critical software are implemented (synthetic diversity) with the result that the adversary's malware is no longer able to compromise the targeted software. |

| INTENDED EFFECT | IMPACT ON RISK | EXPECTED RESULTS |
|---|---|---|
| **Impede (includes contain, degrade, delay, and exert)** Make it more difficult for threat events to cause adverse impacts or consequences. | Reduce likelihood of impact and reduce level of impact. | • Adversary activities are restricted in scope, fail to achieve full effect, do not take place in accordance with adversary timeline, or require greater resources than adversary had planned. |
| **Contain** Restrict the effects of the threat event to a limited set of resources. | Reduce level of impact. | • The adversary can affect fewer resources than planned. The value of the activity to the adversary, in terms of achieving the adversary's goals, is reduced. **Example:** The defender organization makes changes to a combination of internal firewalls and logically separated networks (dynamic segmentation) to isolate enclaves in response to detection of malware with the result that the effects of the malware are limited to just initially infected enclaves. |
| **Degrade** Decrease the expected consequences of the threat event. | Reduce likelihood of impact and/or reduce level of impact. | • Not all the resources targeted by the adversary are affected, or the targeted resources are affected to a lesser degree than the adversary sought. **Example:** The defender uses multiple browsers and operating systems (architectural diversity) on both end-user systems and some critical servers. The result is that malware targeted at specific software can only compromise a subset of the targeted systems; a sufficient number continue to operate to complete the mission or business function. |
| **Delay** Increase the amount of time needed for the threat event to result in adverse impacts. | Reduce likelihood of impact and/or reduce level of impact. | • The adversary achieves the intended effects but not within the intended period. **Example:** The protection measures (e.g., access controls, encryption) allocated to resources increase in number and strength based on resource criticality (calibrated defense-in-depth). The frequency of authentication challenges varies randomly (temporal unpredictability) and with increased frequency for more critical resources. The result is that it takes the attacker more time to successfully compromise the targeted resources. |
| **Exert** Increase the level of effort or resources needed for an adversary to achieve a given result. | Reduce likelihood of impact. | • The adversary gives up planned or partially completed activities in response to finding that additional effort or resources are needed. • The adversary achieves the intended effects in their desired timeframe but only by applying more resources. Thus, the adversary's return on investment (ROI) is decreased. • The adversary reveals TTPs they had planned to reserve for future use. **Example:** The defender enhances defenses of moderate-criticality components with additional mitigations (calibrated defense-in-depth). To overcome these, the adversary must tailor and deploy TTPs that they were planning to reserve for use against higher value defender targets. **Example:** The defender adds a large amount of valid but useless information to a data store (obfuscation), requiring the adversary to exfiltrate and analyze more data before taking further actions. |

| INTENDED EFFECT | IMPACT ON RISK | EXPECTED RESULTS |
|---|---|---|
| **Limit (includes shorten and reduce)** Restrict the consequences of realized threat events by limiting the damage or effects they cause in terms of time, system resources, and/or mission or business impacts. | Reduce level of impact and reduce likelihood of impact of subsequent events in the same threat scenario. | • The adversary's effectiveness is restricted. |
| **Shorten** Limit the duration of adverse consequences of a threat event. | Reduce level of impact. | • The time period during which the adversary's activities affect defender resources is limited. **Example:** The defender employs a diverse set of suppliers (supply chain diversity) for time-critical components. As a result, when an adversary's attack on one supplier causes it to shut down, the defender can increase its use of the other suppliers, thus shortening the time when it is without the critical components. |
| **Reduce** Decrease the degree of damage from a threat event. Degree of damage can have two dimensions: breadth (i.e., number of affected resources) and depth (i.e., level of harm to a given resource). | Reduce level of impact. | • The level of damage to missions or business operations due to adversary activities is reduced, due to partial restoration or reconstitution of all affected resources. **Example:** Resources determined to be corrupted or suspect (integrity checks, behavior validation) are restored from older, uncorrupted resources (protected backup and restore) with reduced functionality. • The level of damage to missions or business operations due to adversary activities is reduced, due to full restoration or reconstitution of some of the affected resources. **Example:** The organization removes one of three compromised resources and provides a new resource (replacement, specialization) for the same or equivalent mission or business functionality. |
| **Expose (includes detect, scrutinize, and reveal)** Reduce risk due to ignorance of threat events and possible replicated or similar threat events in the same or similar environments. | Reduce likelihood of impact. | • The adversary loses the advantage of stealth as defenders are better prepared by developing and sharing threat intelligence. |
| **Detect** Identify threat events or their effects by discovering or discerning the fact that an event is occurring, has occurred, or (based on indicators, warnings, and precursor activities) is about to occur. | Reduce likelihood of impact and reduce level of impact (depending on responses). | • The adversary's activities become susceptible to defensive responses. **Example:** The defender continually moves its sensors (functional relocation of sensors), often at random times (temporal unpredictability), to common points of egress from the organization. They combine this with the use of beacon traps (tainting). The result is that the defender can quickly detect efforts by the adversary to exfiltrate sensitive information. |

| INTENDED EFFECT | IMPACT ON RISK | EXPECTED RESULTS |
|---|---|---|
| **Scrutinize** Analyze threat events and artifacts associated with threat events—particularly with respect to patterns of exploiting vulnerabilities, predisposing conditions, and weaknesses—to inform more effective detection and risk response. | Reduce likelihood of impact. | • The adversary loses the advantages of uncertainty, confusion, and doubt. • The defender understands the adversary better, based on analysis of adversary activities, including the artifacts (e.g., malicious code) and effects associated with those activities and on correlation of activity-specific observations with other activities (as feasible), and thus can recognize adversary TTPs. **Example**: The defender deploys honeynets (misdirection), inviting attacks by the defender and allowing the defender to apply their TTPs in a safe environment. The defender then analyzes (malware and forensic analysis) the malware captured in the honeynet to determine the nature of the attacker's TTPs, allowing it to develop appropriate defenses. |
| **Reveal** Increase awareness of risk factors and relative effectiveness of remediation approaches across the stakeholder community to support common, joint, or coordinated risk response. | Reduce likelihood of impact, particularly in the future. | • The adversary loses the advantage of surprise and possible deniability. • The adversary's ability to compromise one organization's systems to attack another organization is impaired as awareness of adversary characteristics and behavior across the stakeholder community (e.g., across all computer security incident response teams that support a given sector, which might be expected to be attacked by the same actor or actors) is increased. **Example**: The defender participates in threat information-sharing and uses dynamically updated threat intelligence data feeds (dynamic threat modeling) to inform actions (adaptive management). |

**TABLE H-2: EFFECTS OF CYBER RESILIENCY TECHNIQUES ON RISK FACTORS**

| | REDUCE IMPACT | REDUCE LIKELIHOOD OF IMPACT | REDUCE LIKELIHOOD OF OCCURENCE |
|---|---|---|---|
| Adaptive Response | X | X | |
| Analytic Monitoring | | X | |
| Contextual Awareness | X | X | |
| Coordinated Protection | X | X | |
| Deception | | X | X |
| Diversity | X | X | |
| Dynamic Positioning | X | X | X |
| Non-Persistence | X | X | X |
| Privilege Restriction | X | X | |
| Realignment | X | X | X |
| Redundancy | X | X | |
| Segmentation | X | X | |
| Substantiated Integrity | X | X | |
| Unpredictability | X | X | |

## H.2 COVERAGE ANALYSIS FOR CYBER RESILIENCY APPROACHES

The primary focus of cyber resiliency is on mitigating attacks on systems from the APT. A frequently asked question about any set of cybersecurity, cyber survivability, or cyber resiliency mitigations is: What effects would these have on cyber adversaries? Threat coverage analysis (i.e., mapping the current or potential effects of mitigations to a threat taxonomy) provides a structured way to answer this question. A threat coverage analysis identifies the current or potential effects of a set of mitigations (i.e., risk-reducing actions or decisions such as the application of foundational principles, requirements, controls, technologies, or solutions), using a threat model which identifies or characterizes threat events and a vocabulary that defines potential effects. A threat coverage analysis can also include quantitative or semi-quantitative assessments of the defined effects on the adversary as, for example, in the .gov Cybersecurity Architecture Review (.govCAR, [DHS18]). The analysis produces a notional map in which the number (or effectiveness score) of a set of mitigations is used to color, shade, or score each threat event. Threat coverage analysis can inform the selection of a set of mitigations which cover (i.e., produce at least one effect on each element of) a given a set of classes of threat events.

Two publicly accessible and broadly-adopted threat taxonomies are the NSA/CSS Technical Cyber Threat Framework (NTCTF) [NSA18] and the Adversarial Tactics, Techniques, and Common Knowledge (ATT&CK) [MITRE18] framework.[138] The two taxonomies are similar, especially at the higher levels of abstraction. As explained below, this similarity at higher levels of abstraction plays a key part in this appendix. The NTCTF is used in government and underlies the reviews of DoDCAR or .govCAR [DHS18], while ATT&CK is very popular in the private sector.

This appendix illustrates how cyber resiliency techniques and approaches can affect threat events using the NTCTF. This appendix uses the vocabulary for describing effects on adversary activities defined in Appendix H.1.

As illustrated in Table H-2, the NTCTF enables cyber campaigns by the APT to be described in terms of [Attack] *Stages*, [Adversary] *Objectives*, and [Adversary] *Actions*. The actions identified in the NTCTF are oriented toward enterprise IT architecture or an architecture for a command, control, and communications (C3) system or system-of-systems. However, the stages and adversary objectives are more general and can be applied to a broader range of system types. The six stages of a cyber campaign are Administration, Preparation, Engagement, Presence, Effect, and Ongoing Processes. Each of the stages consists of a series of adversary Objectives, and each adversary Objective is achieved by one or more Actions. The NTCTF currently identifies 21 adversary Objectives and over 200 Actions.

---

[138] The cyber kill chain defined in [Hutchins11] provides a framework but does not populate that framework.

**TABLE H-2:  STRUCTURE OF THE NSA TECHNICAL CYBER THREAT FRAMEWORK**

| STAGE | OBJECTIVE | ACTION |
|---|---|---|
| Administration | • Planning<br>• Resource Development<br>• Research | *Examples of Research Actions*<br>• Gather information<br>• Identify capability gaps<br>• Identify information gaps |
| Preparation | • Reconnaissance<br>• Staging | *Examples of Reconnaissance Actions*<br>• Conduct social engineering<br>• Scan devices<br>• Scrape websites |
| Engagement | • Delivery<br>• Exploitation | *Examples of Delivery Actions*<br>• Alter communications path<br>• Send malicious email<br>• Use legitimate remote access |
| Presence | • Execution<br>• Internal Recon<br>• Privilege Escalation<br>• Credential Access<br>• Lateral Movement<br>• Persistence | *Examples of Execution Actions*<br>• Create scheduled task<br>• Replace existing binary<br>• Write to disk |
| Effect | • Monitor<br>• Exfiltrate<br>• Modify<br>• Deny<br>• Destroy | *Examples of Monitor Actions*<br>• Activate recording<br>• Log keystrokes |
| Ongoing Processes | • Analysis, Evaluation, and Feedback<br>• Command and Control<br>• Evasion | *Examples of Evasion Actions*<br>• Block indicators on host<br>• Obfuscate data<br>• Remove toolkit |

This appendix focuses on the Stages and Objectives portions of the NCTCF. This level of abstraction can be applied when the technical details of the system-of-interest (e.g., legacy technologies or architectural commitments) are unknown or to be determined. A threat coverage analysis at the level of Stages and Objectives can thus be employed by organizations even before the specifics of systems are known. The same structure of analysis can be used when technical details are known and thus the defensive actions can be described in terms of those details; a more detailed analysis replaces adversary Objectives with adversary Actions (as in DoDCAR or .govCAR [DHS18]) or ATT&CK TTPs.

In this Appendix, each of the 21 NTCTF adversary Objectives is mapped against each of the 48 cyber resiliency approaches that are defined in Appendix E.4. The mapping identifies which, if any, of the 15 effects defined in Appendix H.1 that an approach could have on a given adversary objective (i.e., on one or more Actions under that Objective). The overall effectiveness will depend on how the approach is applied, as well as on the operational and threat environments, and can be determined by verification and validation processes. The greater the number of effects organizations can have on an adversary threat event, the greater the likelihood that the organization will be successful in countering the threat event.

## H.2.1  UTILITY OF THE TABLES

By seeing which effects a given approach could potentially have on a threat event, the systems engineer can determine which approaches (and corresponding controls) could maximize the system's chances of mitigating the adversary's actions. Thus, using the tables of this appendix may reveal to a systems engineer that the approaches (and correspondingly, the controls) that they are planning to invest in are largely focused on detecting an adversary, containing an adversary's assault, shortening the duration of a successful adversary attack, and reducing the damage from such an attack. Correspondingly, such an assessment would reveal to the system engineer that the organization's planned investments may be lacking in controls that have other effects, such as diverting or deceiving the adversary or preempting or negating the adversary's attempted assault. Such information can help the engineer and other stakeholders reconsider their cyber security investments so that they might be more balanced.

Also, the tables reveal which approaches (and correspondingly, which controls) have multiple potential effects on the adversary and which have only a few potential effects on the adversary. Such information might help guide investment decisions by guiding stakeholders to controls that have multiple effects, including those in which the organization has not previously invested.

Note that not all adversary objectives are affected by all approaches. Indeed, some objectives are affected only by one or two approaches. This is generally the case for adversary objectives in the early stages (e.g., Administration, Preparation) which largely involve adversary actions done prior to accessing a defender system.

## H.2.2  ORGANIZATION OF THE TABLES

The mapping is provided in four tables. Table H-3 includes two stages (i.e., Preparation and Engagement). Note that the Administration stage is omitted. The only cyber resiliency approach that could have an effect during that stage is Disinformation, which could have the effects Deceive and Deter against the Planning objective and the effects Deceive and Exert against the Resource Development and Research objectives. The remaining three tables (Table H-4, Table H-5, Table H-6) consist of one stage each. Some cyber resiliency approaches may have effects only under very narrowly constrained circumstances (e.g., approaches to Analytic Monitoring may detect Reconnaissance when a combination of technical and procedural solutions are used; Unpredictability can make another mechanism, such as Functional Relocation of Cyber Resources preempt Exploitation, more effective); these are indicated via *italics*.

## H.2.3  ASSUMPTIONS AND CAVEATS

Note that the mappings are done with the assumption that the adversary does not have any prior knowledge of the system-of-systems of interest. Any knowledge is gained through their actions (i.e., in the Administration, Preparation, and Engagement stages). Note also that this analysis simply *identifies* the potential effects of the implementation approaches. It does not and cannot assess how strongly any identified effect will be experienced by an APT actor.[139] In addition, this analysis identifies an effect on an adversary objective if it applies to at least one adversary action under that objective; it does not take into consideration the number of

---

[139] Any true measure of effectiveness will need to be defined and evaluated in a situated manner (i.e., by identifying assumptions about the architectural, technical, operational, and threat environments, as discussed in  Section 3.2.1).

possible actions under each objective. More detailed analysis, which could be reflected in scores rather than tallies, would require knowledge of the type of system (including its architecture and types of technologies) and the organization to which the requirements are to be applied. In addition, more detailed analysis could map not to adversary objectives but to adversary actions or even individual adversary TTPs (e.g., as defined by the ATT&CK framework). Finally, some effects are beyond what can be designed and implemented in a technical system and/or the system's supporting processes and practices. For example, detection of adversary Resource Development actions requires (not necessarily cyber) intelligence gathering and analysis, which is beyond the scope of cyber resiliency. Similarly, the Reveal effect involves use of cyber threat intelligence by other organizations.

**TABLE H-3: POTENTIAL EFFECTS ON ADVERSARY ACTIVITIES FOR THE OBJECTIVES IN THE PREPARATION AND ENGAGEMENT STAGES**

| TECHNIQUE | STAGE → | PREPARATION | | ENGAGEMENT | |
|---|---|---|---|---|---|
| | OBJECTIVE → / APPROACH | Reconnaissance | Staging | Delivery | Exploitation |
| Adaptive Response | Dynamic Reconfiguration | Shorten Exert Negate | No effect | Shorten Negate | Negate |
| | Dynamic Resource Allocation | No effect | No effect | No effect | No effect |
| | Adaptive Management | No effect | No effect | Exert | Preempt |
| Analytic Monitoring | Monitoring and Damage Assessment | Detect | No effect | Detect | Detect |
| | Sensor Fusion and Analysis | Detect | No effect | Detect | Detect |
| | Forensic and Behavioral Analysis | No effect | No effect | Scrutinize Reveal | Scrutinize Reveal |
| Contextual Awareness | Dynamic Resource Awareness | No effect | No effect | No effect | No effect |
| | Dynamic Threat Awareness | Exert | Detect | Detect | Detect |
| | Mission Dependency & Status Visualization | No effect | No effect | No effect | No effect |
| Coordinated Protection | Calibrated Defense-in-Depth | Exert | No effect | No effect | No effect |
| | Consistency Analysis | No effect | No effect | No effect | No effect |
| | Orchestration | No effect | No effect | No effect | No effect |
| | Self-Challenge | No effect | No effect | No effect | Detect Exert |
| Deception | Obfuscation | Preempt Delay Exert | Preempt Exert | No effect | Preempt |
| | Disinformation | Deceive Preempt Deter Exert | Deceive | Preempt Divert Exert | Deceive Negate |
| | Misdirection | Deceive | No effect | Divert Deceive Preempt | Preempt |
| | Tainting | Exert | No effect | Deceive Detect | No effect |

| TECHNIQUE | STAGE → | PREPARATION | | ENGAGEMENT | |
|---|---|---|---|---|---|
| | OBJECTIVE → | Reconnaissance | Staging | Delivery | Exploitation |
| | APPROACH | | | | |
| Diversity | Architectural Diversity | No effect | No effect | No effect | No effect |
| | Design Diversity | Exert | No effect | No effect | Delay<br>Exert |
| | Synthetic Diversity | No effect | No effect | No effect | Negate |
| | Information Diversity | No effect | No effect | No effect | No effect |
| | Path Diversity | No effect | No effect | No effect | No effect |
| | Supply Chain Diversity | No effect | No effect | Exert | No effect |
| Dynamic Positioning | Functional Relocation of Sensors | No effect | No effect | Detect | Detect |
| | Functional Relocation Cyber Resources | Negate<br>Exert<br>Delay<br>Degrade<br>Shorten | No effect | Preempt | Preempt<br>Delay |
| | Asset Mobility | Negate<br>Degrade<br>Shorten | No effect | Preempt | Negate<br>Preempt |
| | Fragmentation | No effect | No effect | No effect | No effect |
| | Distributed Functionality | No effect | No effect | No effect | No effect |
| Non-Persistence | Non-Persistent Information | No effect | No effect | No effect | No effect |
| | Non-Persistent Services | Degrade<br>Exert<br>Shorten<br>Reduce | No effect | Preempt<br>Shorten | Expunge |
| | Non-Persistent Connectivity | Degrade<br>Exert<br>Shorten<br>Reduce | No effect | Degrade<br>Preempt | Preempt |
| Privilege Restriction | Trust-Based Privilege Management | No effect | No effect | Preempt | Negate |
| | Attribute-Based Usage Restrictions | No effect | No effect | Preempt | Negate |
| | Dynamic Privileges | No effect | No effect | No effect | No effect |
| Realignment | Purposing | No effect | No effect | No effect | No effect |
| | Offloading | No effect | No effect | Preempt | Preempt |
| | Restriction | No effect | No effect | Preempt | Preempt<br>Negate |
| | Replacement | No effect | No effect | Preempt | Negate |
| | Specialization | No effect | No effect | Preempt | No effect |
| Redundancy | Protected Backup | No effect | No effect | No effect | No effect |
| | Surplus Capacity | No effect | No effect | No effect | No effect |
| | Replication | No effect | No effect | No effect | No effect |
| Segmentation | Predefined Segmentation | Contain<br>Delay<br>Exert | No effect | Contain | No effect |
| | Dynamic Segmentation | No effect | No effect | Contain | No effect |
| Substantiated Integrity | Integrity Checks | No effect | Exert | Detect<br>Negate | Detect |
| | Provenance Tracking | No effect | Delay<br>Exert | Detect<br>Delay<br>Exert | No effect |
| | Behavior Validation | Detect | No effect | Detect | Detect |

| TECHNIQUE | STAGE → | PREPARATION | | ENGAGEMENT | |
|---|---|---|---|---|---|
| | OBJECTIVE → | Reconnaissance | Staging | Delivery | Exploitation |
| | APPROACH | | | | |
| Unpredict-ability | Temporal Unpredictability | No effect | No effect | No effect | Preempt |
| | Contextual Unpredictability | Negate | No effect | No effect | Preempt |

**TABLE H-4: POTENTIAL EFFECTS ON ADVERSARY ACTIVITIES FOR THE OBJECTIVES IN THE PRESENCE STAGE**

| TECHNIQUE | STAGE → OBJECTIVE → APPROACH | Execution | Internal Recon | Privilege Escalation | Credential Access | Lateral Movement | Persistence |
|---|---|---|---|---|---|---|---|
| Adaptive Response | Dynamic Reconfiguration | Negate Delay Exert | Exert Shorten | No effect | No effect | Contain | No effect |
| | Dynamic Resource Allocation | No effect | Delay Exert Shorten | No effect | No effect | No effect | No effect |
| | Adaptive Management | Delay Preempt Shorten Reduce | No effect | Shorten Reduce | No effect | No effect | Preempt Negate |
| Analytic Monitoring | Monitoring and Damage Assessment | Detect | Detect | Detect | Detect | Detect | Detect |
| | Sensor Fusion and Analysis | Detect | Detect | Detect | Detect | Detect | Detect |
| | Forensic and Behavioral Analysis | Detect Scrutinize Reveal | Detect Scrutinize Reveal | Detect Scrutinize Reveal | Detect Scrutinize Reveal | Detect Scrutinize Reveal | Detect Scrutinize Reveal |
| Contextual Awareness | Dynamic Resource Awareness | No effect | No effect | No effect | No effect | No effect | No effect |
| | Dynamic Threat Awareness | Detect | Detect | No effect | No effect | Detect | Detect |
| | Mission Dependency and Status Visualization | No effect | No effect | No effect | No effect | No effect | No effect |
| Coordinated Protection | Calibrated Defense-in-Depth | Delay Exert | Delay Exert | Delay Exert | Delay Exert | Delay Exert Contain | No effect |
| | Consistency Analysis | No effect | No effect | Degrade Exert | Degrade Exert | No effect | Detect |
| | Orchestration | No effect | No effect | No effect | No effect | No effect | No effect |
| | Self-Challenge | Detect | Detect | Detect | Detect | Detect | No effect |
| Deception | Obfuscation | Preempt Exert | Delay Exert | Delay Exert | Delay Exert | Delay Exert | No effect |
| | Disinformation | Preempt Deter Deceive Delay | Deceive Delay Degrade | Delay Exert Deceive | Delay Deter Deceive Exert | Deter Deceive Delay | Deceive Delay |
| | Misdirection | Divert Contain Delay | Divert Delay | Delay Deceive Scrutinize | Delay Divert Scrutinize | Contain | Deceive Negate Scrutinize |
| | Tainting | No effect | Exert | No effect | No effect | No effect | No effect |
| Diversity | Architectural Diversity | Delay Exert | Delay Exert | No effect | No effect | Degrade Delay | No effect |
| | Design Diversity | No effect | Delay Exert | Delay Degrade | Delay Exert | Contain Delay | Degrade |

| TECHNIQUE | STAGE → OBJECTIVE → APPROACH | PRESENCE | | | | | |
|---|---|---|---|---|---|---|---|
| | | Execution | Internal Recon | Privilege Escalation | Credential Access | Lateral Movement | Persistence |
| | Synthetic Diversity | Delay Exert | Delay Exert | Delay Degrade | Delay Exert | Contain Delay | Degrade |
| | Information Diversity | No effect | No effect | No effect | No effect | No effect | No effect |
| | Path Diversity | No effect | No effect | No effect | No effect | No effect | No effect |
| | Supply Chain Diversity | No effect | No effect | No effect | No effect | No effect | No effect |
| Dynamic Positioning | Functional Relocation of Sensors | Detect | Detect | No effect | No effect | Detect | Detect |
| | Functional Relocation of Cyber Resources | Delay Exert | Delay Exert | Delay Exert | Delay Exert | Delay Exert | No effect |
| | Asset Mobility | Delay Exert | Delay Exert | No effect | No effect | No effect | No effect |
| | Fragmentation | Delay Exert | Delay Exert | No effect | Delay Exert | Contain | No effect |
| | Distributed Functionality | Delay Exert | Exert | No effect | No effect | Exert | Exert |
| Non-Persistence | Non-Persistent Information | No effect | Delay Exert | Preempt Exert | Preempt Exert | No effect | Preempt Exert |
| | Non-Persistent Services | Expunge Preempt Delay | Expunge Preempt Delay Exert | Expunge Delay | No effect | Expunge Delay Exert | Negate Expunge |
| | Non-Persistent Connectivity | Preempt Delay | Delay Exert Preempt | No effect | No effect | Delay Preempt | Preempt |
| Privilege Restriction | Trust-Based Privilege Management | Negate Degrade Delay | Degrade | Negate Delay Degrade Exert | Negate Delay Degrade Exert | Delay Exert Preempt Contain | Degrade Exert |
| | Attribute-Based Usage Restrictions | Negate Degrade Delay | Degrade | Negate Delay Degrade Exert | Negate Delay Degrade Exert | Delay Exert Preempt Contain | Degrade Exert |
| | Dynamic Privileges | Degrade Delay | Degrade | Delay Degrade Exert Shorten | Delay Degrade Exert Shorten | Delay Exert Preempt Contain | No effect |
| Realignment | Purposing | No effect | No effect | No effect | No effect | No effect | No effect |
| | Offloading | Preempt, Exert | No effect | No effect | No effect | No effect | No effect |
| | Restriction | Preempt Exert | No effect | No effect | No effect | Preempt Exert | No effect |
| | Replacement | No effect | No effect | No effect | No effect | Negate Exert | Negate Exert Expunge |
| | Specialization | No effect | No effect | No effect | Negate Exert | Negate Exert | Negate Exert |

| TECHNIQUE | STAGE → | PRESENCE | | | | | |
|-----------|---------|----------|---|---|---|---|---|
| | OBJECTIVE → | Execution | Internal Recon | Privilege Escalation | Credential Access | Lateral Movement | Persistence |
| | APPROACH | | | | | | |
| **Redundancy** | Protected Backup | No effect | No effect | No effect | No effect | No effect | No effect |
| | Surplus Capacity | No effect | No effect | No effect | No effect | No effect | No effect |
| | Replication | No effect | No effect | No effect | No effect | No effect | No effect |
| **Segmentation** | Predefined Segmentation | Contain Delay | Contain Delay | Delay Negate Contain | Contain Delay Preempt | Delay Contain | No effect |
| | Dynamic Segmentation | Contain Delay | Contain Delay | Delay Negate Contain | Contain Delay Preempt | Delay Contain | No effect |
| **Substantiated Integrity** | Integrity Checks | Detect | No effect | No effect | No effect | No effect | Detect |
| | Provenance Tracking | No effect | No effect | No effect | No effect | No effect | No effect |
| | Behavior Validation | Detect | No effect | Detect | Detect | No effect | Detect |
| **Unpredict-ability** | Temporal Unpredictability | Preempt Detect Delay | Delay Preempt | Delay Preempt | Delay Preempt | Delay Preempt | Delay Preempt |
| | Contextual Unpredictability | Preempt Detect Delay Exert | Delay Exert Preempt | Delay Exert Preempt | Delay Exert Preempt | Delay Exert Preempt | Delay Exert Preempt |

**TABLE H-5: POTENTIAL EFFECTS ON ADVERSARY ACTIVITIES FOR THE OBJECTIVES IN THE EFFECT STAGE**

| TECHNIQUE | STAGE → OBJECTIVE → APPROACH | EFFECT | | | | |
|---|---|---|---|---|---|---|
| | | Monitor | Exfiltrate | Modify | Deny | Destroy |
| **Adaptive Response** | Dynamic Reconfiguration | Contain Shorten | Delay Preempt Shorten Reduce | Delay Preempt Contain Shorten Reduce | Delay Preempt Contain Shorten Reduce | Delay Degrade Preempt Contain Shorten Reduce |
| | Dynamic Resource Allocation | No effect | No effect | No effect | Shorten Reduce | Shorten Reduce |
| | Adaptive Management | Delay Degrade Preempt | Delay, Preempt | Delay Preempt | Delay Preempt Shorten Reduce | Delay Degrade Preempt |
| **Analytic Monitoring** | Monitoring and Damage Assessment | No effect | Detect Scrutinize | Detect Scrutinize | Detect Scrutinize | Scrutinize |
| | Sensor Fusion and Analysis | No effect | Detect | Detect | No effect | No effect |
| | Forensic and Behavioral Analysis | No effect | No effect | Detect | No effect | No effect |
| **Contextual Awareness** | Dynamic Resource Awareness | No effect | Detect | Detect | Detect | Detect |
| | Dynamic Threat Awareness | Detect | Detect | Detect | Detect | Detect |
| | Mission Dependency and Status Visualization | No effect | Detect | Detect | Detect | Detect |
| **Coordinated Protection** | Calibrated Defense-in-Depth | No effect | Delay Exert | Delay Exert Preempt | Delay Exert Preempt | Delay Exert Preempt |
| | Consistency Analysis | No effect | No effect | No effect | No effect | No effect |
| | Orchestration | No effect | No effect | Shorten Reduce | Shorten Reduce | Shorten Reduce |
| | Self-Challenge | No effect | Detect | Detect | Detect | Detect |
| **Deception** | Obfuscation | Delay Degrade Preempt | Delay Degrade Preempt | Delay Degrade Preempt | Preempt | Preempt |
| | Disinformation | Deceive | Deter Deceive Delay Degrade | Preempt Deter Deceive | Preempt Deter Deceive | Preempt Deceive |
| | Misdirection | Deceive Divert | No effect | Divert Deceive Scrutinize | Divert Deceive Scrutinize | Divert Deceive Scrutinize |

| TECHNIQUE | STAGE → | EFFECT | | | | |
|---|---|---|---|---|---|---|
| | OBJECTIVE → | Monitor | Exfiltrate | Modify | Deny | Destroy |
| | APPROACH | | | | | |
| | Tainting | No effect | Deter Detect Preempt Scrutinize Reveal | No effect | No effect | No effect |
| **Diversity** | Architectural Diversity | Delay Exert Preempt | No effect | Preempt Delay Exert | Preempt Delay Exert | Preempt Delay Exert |
| | Design Diversity | Delay Exert Preempt | No effect | Preempt Delay Exert | Preempt Delay Exert | Preempt Delay Exert |
| | Synthetic Diversity | Delay Preempt | No effect | Preempt Negate | Preempt Negate | Preempt Negate |
| | Information Diversity | No effect | No effect | Contain Detect Shorten Reduce | Preempt Negate Delay Exert | Preempt Negate Delay Exert Reduce |
| | Path Diversity | No effect | No effect | No effect | Preempt Negate Delay Exert Shorten Reduce | Preempt Negate Delay Exert Shorten Reduce |
| | Supply Chain Diversity | No effect | No effect | No effect | No effect | Shorten Reduce |
| **Dynamic Positioning** | Functional Relocation of Sensors | Detect | Detect | Detect | Detect | Detect |
| | Functional Relocation of Cyber Resources | Delay Exert Degrade | Delay Exert | Delay Exert Degrade | Delay Preempt Shorten Reduce | Delay Preempt |
| | Asset Mobility | No effect | No effect | No effect | Delay Preempt | Delay Preempt |
| | Fragmentation | Delay Degrade Exert | Delay Exert | Delay Degrade Exert | Delay Degrade Exert | Delay Degrade Exert |
| | Distributed Functionality | No effect | No effect | Delay Degrade Exert | Delay Degrade Exert | Delay Degrade Exert |
| **Non-Persistence** | Non-Persistent Information | Preempt | Delay Preempt | Delay Preempt | No effect | No effect |
| | Non-Persistent Services | Expunge Preempt | Delay Preempt | Delay Preempt | No effect | No effect |
| | Non-Persistent Connectivity | Preempt | Delay Preempt | Delay Preempt | Delay | Delay |
| **Privilege Restriction** | Trust-Based Privilege Management | No effect | Exert Delay | Exert Delay Negate | Exert Delay Negate | Exert Delay Negate |
| | Attribute-Based Usage Restrictions | No effect | Exert Delay | Exert Delay Negate | Exert Delay Negate | Exert Delay Negate |

| TECHNIQUE | STAGE → | EFFECT | | | | |
|---|---|---|---|---|---|---|
| | OBJECTIVE → APPROACH | Monitor | Exfiltrate | Modify | Deny | Destroy |
| | Dynamic Privileges | No effect | Exert Delay | Exert Delay Negate | Exert Delay Negate | Exert Delay Negate |
| **Realignment** | Purposing | No effect | No effect | No effect | No effect | No effect |
| | Offloading | No effect | No effect | Preempt Negate | Preempt Negate | Preempt Negate |
| | Restriction | Preempt Exert | Preempt Exert | Preempt Negate | Preempt Negate | Preempt Negate |
| | Replacement | No effect | No effect | Negate | Negate | Negate |
| | Specialization | Negate Exert | No effect | Negate | Negate | Negate |
| **Redundancy** | Protected Backup | No effect | No effect | Shorten Reduce | Shorten Reduce | Shorten Reduce |
| | Surplus Capacity | No effect | No effect | No effect | Shorten Reduce | Shorten |
| | Replication | No effect | No effect | Reduce Shorten | Shorten Reduce | Negate |
| **Segmentation** | Predefined Segmentation | Negate | Delay Degrade Exert | Contain | Degrade Exert Contain | Contain |
| | Dynamic Segmentation | Negate | Delay Degrade Exert | Contain | Degrade Exert Contain | Contain |
| **Substantiated Integrity** | Integrity Checks | No effect | No effect | Detect | Detect | Detect |
| | Provenance Tracking | No effect | No effect | Detect | No effect | No effect |
| | Behavior Validation | No effect | No effect | Detect | Detect | Detect |
| **Unpredict-ability** | Temporal Unpredictability | Preempt | Preempt Exert | Preempt Exert | Preempt Exert | Preempt Exert |
| | Contextual Unpredictability | Preempt | Preempt Exert | Preempt Exert | Preempt Exert | Preempt Exert |

**TABLE H-6: POTENTIAL EFFECTS ON ADVERSARY ACTIVITIES FOR THE OBJECTIVES IN THE ONGOING PROCESSES STAGE**

| TECHNIQUE | STAGE → | ONGOING PROCESSES | | |
|---|---|---|---|---|
| | OBJECTIVE → <br> APPROACH | Analysis, Evaluation, and Feedback | Command and Control | Evasion |
| Adaptive Response | Dynamic Reconfiguration | Delay <br> Exert | Shorten | No effect |
| | Dynamic Resource Allocation | No effect | Shorten <br> Expunge | No effect |
| | Adaptive Management | Deter <br> Delay <br> Exert | Shorten <br> Expunge | No effect |
| Analytic Monitoring | Monitoring and Damage Assessment | No effect | Detect <br> Scrutinize | Detect <br> Scrutinize |
| | Sensor Fusion and Analysis | No effect | Detect | Detect |
| | Forensic and Behavioral Analysis | No effect | Detect <br> Scrutinize <br> Reveal | Detect <br> Scrutinize <br> Reveal |
| Contextual Awareness | Dynamic Resource Awareness | No effect | Detect | Detect |
| | Dynamic Threat Awareness | No effect | Detect | Detect |
| | Mission Dependency and Status Visualization | No effect | No effect | No effect |
| Coordinated Protection | Calibrated Defense-in-Depth | No effect | Delay <br> Degrade <br> Exert <br> Negate | Delay <br> Degrade <br> Exert |
| | Consistency Analysis | No effect | Detect | Detect |
| | Orchestration | No effect | No effect | No effect |
| | Self-Challenge | No effect | No effect | No effect |
| Deception | Obfuscation | Delay <br> Exert | Negate | Exert |
| | Disinformation | Deter <br> Divert <br> Deceive <br> Exert | Deceive <br> Detect <br> Exert | Detect |
| | Misdirection | Deter <br> Divert <br> Deceive <br> Delay <br> Exert | Delay <br> Exert <br> Detect | Deceive <br> Exert |
| | Tainting | Deter | No effect | No effect |
| Diversity | Architectural Diversity | Deter <br> Delay <br> Exert | Delay <br> Exert | Delay <br> Exert |
| | Design Diversity | Deter <br> Delay <br> Exert | Delay <br> Exert | Delay <br> Exert |
| | Synthetic Diversity | Deter <br> Delay <br> Exert | Delay <br> Exert | Delay <br> Exert |
| | Information Diversity | No effect | No effect | No effect |
| | Path Diversity | No effect | No effect | No effect |
| | Supply Chain Diversity | No effect | No effect | No effect |

| TECHNIQUE | STAGE → | ONGOING PROCESSES | | |
| | OBJECTIVE → | Analysis, Evaluation, and Feedback | Command and Control | Evasion |
| | APPROACH | | | |
| Dynamic Positioning | Functional Relocation of Sensors | No effect | Detect | Detect |
| | Functional Relocation of Cyber Resources | Delay Exert | Delay Exert | Delay Exert |
| | Asset Mobility | No effect | No effect | No effect |
| | Fragmentation | Delay Exert | No effect | No effect |
| | Distributed Functionality | Delay Exert | No effect | No effect |
| Non-Persistence | Non-Persistent Information | Delay Exert | No effect | Delay Exert Preempt Expunge |
| | Non-Persistent Services | No effect | Delay Exert Preempt Expunge Shorten | Delay Exert Preempt Expunge |
| | Non-Persistent Connectivity | No effect | Delay, Exert Expunge Shorten | Delay Exert Preempt |
| Privilege Restriction | Trust-Based Privilege Management | No effect | No effect | Delay Exert Contain |
| | Attribute-Based Usage Restrictions | No effect | Exert | No effect |
| | Dynamic Privileges | No effect | Exert | Exert |
| Realignment | Purposing | No effect | No effect | No effect |
| | Offloading | No effect | No effect | No effect |
| | Restriction | No effect | No effect | No effect |
| | Replacement | Preempt | Preempt Expunge | Preempt Expunge |
| | Specialization | Exert | No effect | Exert Preempt |
| Redundancy | Protected Backup | No effect | No effect | No effect |
| | Surplus Capacity | No effect | No effect | No effect |
| | Replication | No effect | No effect | No effect |

# CYBER RESILIENCY USE CASES

APPLYING CYBER RESILIENCY ENGINEERING—REPRESENTATIVE EXAMPLES

This appendix provides a structured presentation of some of the examples throughout this document, presenting them as cyber resiliency use cases. A cyber resiliency use case describes a representative situation in which cyber resiliency should be considered by systems security engineering and security risk management.[140] It discusses how cyber resiliency concepts and constructs can be interpreted and applied to that situation. It illustrates how cyber resiliency solutions can be defined for, or a specific solution or set of solutions can be applied to, that situation and how those solutions can be analyzed to support systems security engineering and risk management tasks.

The use cases were developed by identifying a system, describing its context in enough detail that cyber resiliency constructs can be interpreted and constraints on alternative mitigations can be identified, describing a motivating threat scenario, identifying one or more alternative mitigations, and describing the potential effects of those mitigations on the system's cyber resiliency and on adversary objectives. Thus, the development of a use case follows the process described in Section 3.2 with a narrow focus on the motivating threat scenario and without the level of detail that would be afforded for a system in a real-world context. While the use cases in this appendix draw from published sources, they are fictional and lack the specific details which would inform analysis and decision-making in real-world situations.

Each use case is described in one or two pages with supporting details in sub-sections. The summary description identifies the motivating threat scenario, summarizes the results of the analysis of which cyber resiliency constructs are most applicable to the system, and describes alternative or complementary solutions under consideration. The sub-sections describe the context, which is used to determine the applicability of cyber resiliency constructs and constrains the set of potential solutions; restate cyber resiliency constructs in terms of the system and its context and illustrate how those constructs could be prioritized to support identification and analysis of potential solutions; and describe how potential solutions can be defined and analyzed.

## I.1  SELF-DRIVING CAR

In this use case, an organization seeks to build on existing and emerging technologies to produce a high-assurance self-driving car, recognizing that autonomous technology could be subverted by an adversary to divert and potentially crash the vehicle.[141] The organization intends to sell the vehicle to fleet operators and other organizations (e.g., for moving material around a campus). As this use case illustrates, safety and cyber resiliency are mutually supportive. This

---

[140] The scenarios described in this appendix are hypothetical in nature and are not based on actual threat events or cyber-attacks. The scenarios described in Appendix J are based on actual cyber-attacks on existing industrial control systems.

[141] A self-driving car provides high or full automation as defined by the Society of Automotive Engineers (SAE). See [NHTSA].

use case treats the vehicle as an autonomous system; it does not address the vehicle as a constituent sub-system of a larger system-of-systems, such as a Smart City.[142] The vehicle will evolve from existing automotive technologies and will apply established standards and guidelines for cybersecurity.[143] These include guidance on performing risk assessments, which enable the development of threat scenarios.

### I.1.1 MOTIVATING THREAT SCENARIO

The motivating threat scenario in this use case involves an adversary taking over key vehicle systems to cause a crash, steal the vehicle, or abduct its passengers. To do so, the adversary exploits a weakness in the infotainment and telematics system to command it to download malware, thus establishing a foothold in that system. The adversary-installed malware injects data and commands onto the controller access network (CAN) bus, achieving such adversary objectives as Command and Control, Internal Reconnaissance, and Execution[144] to extend its presence. The adversary uses malware in the telematics system (and possibly in other sub-systems, such as a collision avoidance system) to track the vehicle's location. By remotely directing its installed malware, the adversary achieves the intended cyber effects (e.g., Data Alteration, Denial of Service, Data Deletion) and thereby achieves the intended physical effects (e.g., crash, theft).

### I.1.2 APPLICABILITY OF CYBER RESILIENCY CONSTRUCTS

Many of the structural cyber resiliency design principles are consistent with and supportive of safety engineering. These include Limit the need for trust, Contain and exclude behaviors, Leverage health and status data, and Maintain situational awareness. By applying these design principles, safety can also be improved. In the context of the vehicle, situational awareness focuses on performance and behavior of vehicle sub-systems; threat awareness and tracking of cyber courses of action are out of scope.

Many of the cyber resiliency approaches are applied as part of safety and reliability engineering, using health and status data to identify indications of faults and failures and taking corrective actions (in particular, by failing safely). These include Monitoring and Damage Assessment, Orchestration, Self-Challenge, Dynamic Resource Awareness, Mission Dependency and Status Visualization, Trust-Based Privilege Management, and Attribute-Based Usage Restriction. Other cyber resiliency approaches, while applicable and consistent with safety and reliability engineering, cannot be implemented in the vehicle itself; they must be applied via enabling systems during manufacturing or assembly. These include Consistency Analysis, Purposing, Offloading, Restriction, and Specialization.

### I.1.3 SOLUTIONS CONSIDERED

Solutions considered in this use case are summarized in Table I-1. These solutions constitute a representative subset of possible alternatives within the constraints imposed by the operational and programmatic context and by the single illustrative threat scenario. For each identified

---

[142] See [ICFPWG18].

[143] These include [SAEJ3061], [ISO 26262], the forthcoming [SAEJ3101], and the forthcoming consolidation of SAE J3061 and ISO 26262 into ISO/SAE 21434. Note that these publications do not address autonomous vehicles.

[144] These adversary objectives are taken from the NTCTF. See Appendix H.2.

solution or mitigation, the second column identifies the cyber resiliency design principles, techniques, and approaches the solution or mitigation applies, and the third column identifies the potential *effects* the solution or mitigation could have on adversary objectives, as defined in the NTCTF.[145]

**TABLE I-1: SUMMARY OF ALTERNATIVES AND ANALYSIS**

| SOLUTION OR MITIGATION | CYBER RESILIENCY CONSTRUCTS APPLIED | POTENTIAL EFFECTS ON ADVERSARY OBJECTIVES |
|---|---|---|
| **Validate data sent to or from the infotainment and telematics system.** | Structural design principles:<br>Limit the need for trust<br>Techniques and Approaches:<br>Substantiated Integrity:<br>Integrity Checks<br>Provenance Tracking | Delivery, Lateral Movement, Command and Control: *Negate*<br>Modify: *Degrade* |
| **Control interfaces between embedded systems.** | Structural design principles:<br>Contain and exclude behaviors<br>Techniques and Approaches:<br>Segmentation:<br>Predefined Segmentation<br>Substantiated Integrity:<br>Integrity Checks<br>Provenance Tracking | Lateral Movement, Command and Control: *Negate, Contain* |
| **Refresh software, configuration data, and connections to the infotainment and telematics system.** | Structural design principles:<br>Limit the need for trust<br>Maximize transience<br>Techniques and Approaches:<br>Non-Persistence:<br>Non-Persistent Information<br>Non-Persistent Services<br>Non-Persistent Connectivity<br>Substantiated Integrity:<br>Integrity Checks | Persistence, Modify: *Shorten* |

The following subsections provide additional details.

## I.1.4 CONTEXT DETAILS

**Architectural Concept.** The architecture of an automated vehicle involves multiple embedded systems: powertrain (e.g., engine management, braking), chassis and safety (e.g., tire pressure monitoring, adaptive anti-lock braking system, adaptive cruise control), cabin and comfort (e.g., HVAC), and telematics and infotainment (e.g., radio, cellular communications, Global Positioning System [GPS] navigation). These embedded systems integrate components from multiple manufacturers (e.g., sensors, controllers, communications) and are, in turn, integrated by the organization.[146]

---

[145] See Appendix H.2.

[146] See [RAND18] for a discussion of the spectrum from components at the micro level to a smart transportation system at the macro level.

**Operational Environment.** The organization intends to sell the vehicle to fleet operators and other organizations (e.g., for moving material around a campus).[147] The vehicle passenger (if any) can be assumed to be competent as a driver and able to take control or trigger any fail-safe mechanisms based on that competence, but must be assumed to be ignorant of cyber threats to the vehicle. Similarly, vehicle maintenance staff are not assumed to understand or be able to address cyber threats.

**Mission Context.** The mission of a self-driving car is to provide safe and timely transportation to an operator-specified location. Human safety is a concern not only for the operator and other passengers but also for individuals in the operating environment (e.g., occupants of other vehicles, pedestrians, occupants of buildings near roadways). In addition, any damage to the physical environment (e.g., collision damage to lighting, traffic signals, or barriers; fuel spills) is a safety concern. Other mission concerns relate to the potential failure to reach the intended destination (or to reach it by the required or predicted time), theft of the vehicle, and the potential for kidnapping.

**Programmatic Context.** The development will be performed in-house in development spirals. Programmatic risk management prioritizes risk that safety requirements will be met over other forms of risk. Technical, cost, and schedule risk are closely monitored since the system-of-interest integrates systems and components from a wide range of sources. Due to its concern simply to develop a working automated vehicle, the organization might choose to discount adversarial threats. However, industry guidance increasingly treats cybersecurity as a risk area. In addition, the organization seeks a differentiator from others also working on self-driving cars. Thus, the organization includes adversarial threats in its risk-framing for the system-of-interest, reasoning that a demonstration that its vehicle can withstand adversarial threats that disable or crash a competitor's vehicle will be compelling.

**Threat Context.** Development considers risks due to multiple threat sources, as reflected in system requirements. These include non-adversarial threats such as component faults and failures within safety-critical embedded systems; faults, failures, and resource contention from different sub-systems resulting in degradation of internal communications over the Controller Access Network (CAN) bus, which can cause a master control unit (MCU) or vehicle control unit (VCU) to act on incorrect information; and erratic or unpredictable behavior in the operating environment, which the vehicle's systems have not learned to address.

Development explicitly considers adversarial threats, noting that an adversary that has compromised a component or sub-system can emulate faults or failures, simulate observations of unpredictable behavior, or launch denial-of-service attacks on internal communications or sub-systems. Examples of adversary motives related to safety concerns include terrorism (e.g., using the vehicle as a weapon) and causing physical harm (i.e., killing or maiming) to identifiable passengers. In addition, adversaries may be motivated by financial gain directly (e.g., kidnapping passengers by rerouting the vehicle, vehicle theft) or indirectly (e.g., by obtaining PII from occupant devices that interface with the vehicle, usually through the infotainment system; by listening in to occupant conversations).

---

[147] Therefore, many of the solutions identified in [Miller18], which could be implemented if the organization maintained control of the vehicle, are not applicable to the intended operational environment.

Based on its risk-framing, the organization assumes that all adversaries have a high degree of persistence and moderate-to-high capabilities. The primary scenarios related to causing the vehicle to fail in its safety and transportation mission involve exploiting a foothold established by compromising a component via the supply chain or exploiting a weakness in the vehicle infotainment and telematics system to establish a foothold in that system; using a variety of TTPs in such categories as Command and Control, Internal Reconnaissance, and Execution to extend its presence; achieving the intended cyber effects (e.g., Data Alteration, Data Deletion, Denial of Service); and thereby achieving the intended physical effects (e.g., crash, theft).

Based on these scenarios, developers determine that the infotainment and telematics system is a critical element on multiple attack paths. While ECUs, MCUs, and VCUs can be compromised via supply chain attacks, these are less attractive attack surfaces.

### I.1.5  RESTATEMENT AND APPLICATION OF CYBER RESILIENCY CONSTRUCTS

As illustrated in Table I-2 and Table I-3, cyber resiliency objectives and strategic design principles are restated or interpreted in the context described above to make them more understandable to stakeholders. These restatements enable stakeholders to provide input to assessments of the relative priority of these constructs. The priorities for this use case are also included in Tables I-2 and I-3.

#### TABLE I-2: RESTATEMENTS OF CYBER RESILIENCY OBJECTIVES FOR SELF-DRIVING CARS

| OBJECTIVE | RESTATEMENT AND PRIORITY |
|---|---|
| Prevent or Avoid | Prevent false geolocation, driving directions, and operating instructions from causing unsafe conditions. (**Priority: Very High**) |
| Prepare | Provide fail-safe mechanisms and supporting alerting mechanisms. (**Priority: High**) |
| Continue | Enable the passenger (or other designated operator) to take control of the vehicle or to engage fail-safe mechanisms. (**Priority: High**) |
| Constrain | Ensure that the car can fail safely despite cyber-attack, disruption, or interference. (**Priority: Very High**) |
| Reconstitute | Ensure that in the absence of physical damage, the car's cyber resources can be restored to a known good state. (**Priority: Low**) |
| Understand | Provide health and status data and, as available, security-related information to external systems responsible for the security and safety of transportation. (Not prioritized. The relevance and priority of this objective will depend on larger operational and governance concepts for smart transportation and critical infrastructure protection.) |
| Transform | Track emerging operational concepts, governance structures and processes, and adoption and usage patterns to ensure that the car's concept of use is or can be made compatible. (**Priority: Low**) |
| Re-Architect | Track emerging standards, technologies, and processes related to Smart Cities to ensure that the car's architecture is or can be made compatible. (Not prioritized. The relevance and priority of this objective will depend on larger operational and governance concepts for smart transportation and critical infrastructure protection.) |

The relative priorities of strategic design principles reflect the organizational risk-framing.

**TABLE I-3: RESTATEMENTS OF STRATEGIC CYBER RESILIENCY DESIGN PRINCIPLES FOR SELF-DRIVING CARS**

| STRATEGIC DESIGN PRINCIPLES | RESTATEMENT AND RELATIVE PRIORITY |
|---|---|
| Focus on common critical assets. | Prevent false geolocation, driving directions, and operating instructions from causing unsafe conditions. (**Priority: Very High**) |
| Support agility and architect for adaptability. | Provide fail-safe mechanisms and supporting alerting mechanisms; accommodate future interfaces to external sensors and controls. (**Priority: High**) |
| Reduce attack surfaces. | Enable the operator to take control of the vehicle or to engage fail-safe mechanisms. (**Priority: High**) |
| Assume compromised resources. | Ensure that the car can fail safely despite cyber-attack, disruption, or interference. (**Priority: Very High**) |
| Expect adversaries to adapt. | Ensure that in the absence of physical damage, the car's cyber resources can be restored to a known good state. (**Priority: Low**) |

Consideration of the relative priorities of the cyber resiliency objectives and strategic design principles, along with the architectural context, enables the applicability of the structural cyber resiliency design principles to be determined as illustrated in Table I-4.

**TABLE I-4: APPLICABILITY OF STRUCTURAL CYBER RESILIENCY DESIGN PRINCIPLES TO SELF-DRIVING CARS**

| STRUCTURAL DESIGN PRINCIPLE | APPLICABILITY |
|---|---|
| Limit the need for trust. | Applicable; consistent with and reinforcing of safety. |
| Control visibility and use. | Applicable in principle but may be infeasible depending on needs and capability limitations of constituent sub-systems. |
| Contain and exclude behaviors. | Applicable; consistent with and reinforcing of safety. |
| Layer defenses and partition resources. | Applicable in principle but may be infeasible due to added complexity. |
| Plan and manage diversity. | Not applicable; diversity in components restricted by limited number of original equipment manufacturers (OEMs). |
| Maintain redundancy. | Applicable in principle but may be infeasible due to added complexity or size, weight, and power concerns. |
| Make resources location-versatile. | Not applicable. |
| Leverage health and status data. | Applicable; consistent with and reinforcing of safety. |
| Maintain situational awareness. | Applicable; consistent with and reinforcing of safety. |
| Manage resources (risk-) adaptively. | Not applicable. |
| Maximize transience. | Potentially applicable to infotainment and telematics. |
| Determine ongoing trustworthiness. | Applicable in principle but may be infeasible depending on capability limitations of constituent sub-systems. |
| Change or disrupt the attack surface. | Not applicable. |
| Make the effects of deception and unpredictability user-transparent. | Applicable; given the assumption about the operator and maintenance communities, this is crucial. |

Similarly, the relative applicability of the structural design principles, in conjunction with the architectural context, enables the applicability of the cyber resiliency techniques and approaches to be determined as illustrated in Table I-5.

**TABLE I-5:  APPLICABILITY OF CYBER RESILIENCY TECHNIQUES AND APPROACHES TO SELF-DRIVING CARS**

| TECHNIQUES | APPROACHES | APPLICABILITY |
|---|---|---|
| Adaptive Response | Dynamic Reconfiguration | Not applicable. |
| | Dynamic Resource Allocation | Not applicable. |
| | Adaptive Management | Applicable to situations in which the operator must take over. |
| Analytic Monitoring | Monitoring and Damage Assessment | Applicable with restricted focus on indicators of anomalous and potentially adverse behavior, which could affect vehicle safety using health and status data. |
| | Sensor Fusion and Analysis | Not applicable. May be applicable to the larger system-of-systems of which the vehicle is a part (e.g., Smart Transportation, Smart City); if so, imposes requirements for data collection and provision. |
| | Forensic and Behavioral Analysis | Not applicable. May be applicable to the larger system-of-systems of which the vehicle is a part but not expected to impose requirements on the vehicle. |
| Contextual Awareness | Dynamic Resource Awareness | Applicable via health and status data. |
| | Dynamic Threat Awareness | Not applicable. May be highly applicable to the larger system-of-systems of which the vehicle is a part, but no requirements will be imposed on the vehicle. |
| | Mission Dependency and Status Visualization | Applicable, via health and status data. |
| Coordinated Protection | Calibrated Defense-in-Depth | Applicable but may be undesirable due to size, weight, and power considerations. |
| | Consistency Analysis | Applicable; applied via enabling systems, during design, development, implementation, and maintenance. |
| | Orchestration | Applicable. |
| | Self-Challenge | Applicable in the form of self-diagnostics. |
| Deception | Obfuscation | Encryption of control traffic is technically feasible, but may be undesirable due to size, weight, and power considerations. |
| | Disinformation | Not applicable to commodity vehicle. May be highly applicable to the system-of-systems of which the vehicle is a part. |
| | Misdirection | Not applicable. |
| | Tainting | Not applicable. |
| Diversity | Architectural Diversity | Not applicable to the commodity vehicle. May be incidental to the larger system-of-systems of which the vehicle is a part. |
| | Design Diversity | Technically feasible but unlikely to be deemed applicable. |
| | Synthetic Diversity | Not applicable. |
| | Information Diversity | Not applicable. |
| | Path Diversity | Not applicable to vehicle-internal systems. May be applicable to the larger system-of-systems of which the vehicle is a part. However, use of multiple paths (e.g., Wi-Fi, cell, satellite), which require different comms devices, may be infeasible due to size, weight, and power considerations. |
| | Supply Chain Diversity | Potentially applicable to enabling systems (manufacture and assembly) but limited by number of OEMs; not applicable to individual vehicle. |
| Dynamic Positioning | Functional Relocation of Sensors | Not applicable. |
| | Functional Relocation of Cyber Resources | Not applicable. |
| | Asset Mobility | Applicable to vehicle as a whole. Not applicable to vehicle sub-systems. |
| | Fragmentation | Not applicable. |

| TECHNIQUES | APPROACHES | APPLICABILITY |
|---|---|---|
| | Distributed Functionality | Not applicable. |
| Non-Persistence | Non-Persistent Information | Potentially applicable to infotainment and telematics system. May refresh configuration data upon vehicle startup. |
| | Non-Persistent Services | Potentially applicable to infotainment and telematics system. May refresh services upon vehicle startup. |
| | Non-Persistent Connectivity | Not applicable to connectivity within the vehicle. Applicable to the larger system-of-systems of which the vehicle is a part as a side effect of the vehicle transiting between different cells or Wi-Fi regions. |
| Privilege Restriction | Trust-Based Privilege Management | Applicable. |
| | Attribute-Based Usage Restriction | Applicable. |
| | Dynamic Privileges | Not applicable. |
| Realignment | Purposing | Applicable; implemented via enabling systems (manufacture and assembly). |
| | Offloading | Not applicable to individual vehicle; applicable to enabling systems (manufacture and assembly). |
| | Restriction | Applicable (with special attention paid to connectivity related to the infotainment system); implemented via enabling systems. May fail to be applied by OEMs. |
| | Replacement | Not applicable. |
| | Specialization | Applicable; implemented via enabling systems. |
| Redundancy | Protected Backup and Restore | Not applicable. |
| | Surplus Capacity | Not applicable. |
| | Replication | Not applicable. |
| Segmentation | Predefined Segmentation | Potentially applicable. Can cryptographically separate sub-systems (in particular, isolate the infotainment system from vehicle control systems). However, size, weight, power, and cost considerations may make this programmatically infeasible. |
| | Dynamic Segmentation and Isolation | Not applicable. |
| Substantiated Integrity | Integrity Checks | Applicable to data on the CAN bus and to data from an external system. Potentially applicable to Embedded Control Unit (ECU) software. |
| | Provenance Tracking | Applicable to data on the CAN bus and to data from an external system. Potentially applicable to Embedded Control Unit (ECU) software. |
| | Behavior Validation | Applicable; implemented as self-diagnostics, and recorded internally. |
| Unpredictability | Temporal Unpredictability | Not applicable. |
| | Contextual Unpredictability | Not applicable. |

## I.1.6  DEFINITION AND ANALYSIS OF SOLUTION CHARACTERISTICS

As Table I-5 indicates, many of the cyber resiliency approaches are applied as part of safety and reliability engineering using health and status data to identify indications of faults and failures and taking corrective actions (in particular, by failing safely). These include Monitoring and

Damage Assessment, Orchestration, Self-Challenge, Dynamic Resource Awareness, Mission Dependency and Status Visualization, Trust-Based Privilege Management, and Attribute-Based Usage Restriction. Other cyber resiliency approaches, while applicable and consistent with safety and reliability engineering, cannot be implemented in the vehicle itself; they must be applied via enabling systems during manufacturing or assembly. These include Consistency Analysis, Purposing, Offloading, Restriction, and Specialization.

Analysis reveals that data sent to and from the infotainment and telematics system should be validated against multiple criteria, applying Integrity Checks and Provenance Tracking:

- Data sent from the system using the CAN bus can only be sent to operator displays.

- Data sent from the system using Wi-Fi or radio to external systems can only take the form of telematics (e.g., speed, location).

- Values of geolocation or directional data received by the system are checked against recent values; significant differences are treated as indicators of a fault or failure.

Information from a subsystem of one embedded system (e.g., the engine management subsystem of the powertrain system) should only be received by that system's MCU and (if the architecture uses a central VCU) by the VCU. This applies Predefined Segmentation together with Provenance Tracking. Additional mitigation can be provided via Integrity Checks and Behavior Validation.

Finally, because the connections between the infotainment and telematics system and external systems present an attractive attack vector, that system is a good candidate for the application of Non-Persistence and Integrity Checks. Software and configuration data can be refreshed from a "gold copy" upon vehicle start-up; external connections can be set to time out and require validation upon re-initiation.

Potential cyber resiliency improvements can be analyzed with respect to the motivating scenario using an adversary objective coverage analysis. Adversary objectives identified in the NTCTF[148] relevant to that scenario are selected; these include Delivery, Execution, Lateral Movement, Persistence, Command and Control, and Modify. Examples of specific actions to achieve these objectives are identified since the actions in the NTCTF are oriented toward enterprise IT rather than CPS. For a CPS, two additional adversary objectives in the Effect stage can be defined: Destroy physical objects and Deceive the system.[149] None of the alternatives considered above address these adversary objectives directly; their intent is to interrupt the attack before actions to achieve those objectives can be taken.

## I.2  ENTERPRISE IT SYSTEM

In this use case, an organization seeks to acquire a workflow system to support a new public-facing business function for which the organization is responsible. The organization is primarily

---

[148] See Appendix H.2.

[149] The NTCTF Destroy objective covers actions to destroy data and ICT hardware but does not include physical destruction of non-cyber resources. For systems with some degree of autonomy, Deceive is also a concern: an adversary can cause the system to take actions based on false information by manipulating the physical environment or the behaviors of other systems.

concerned with the possibility of fraud. However, the potential for breaches of personally identifiable information (PII) and denial-of-service are also concerns. This use case illustrates how cyber resiliency concepts, properties, characteristics, functions, behavior, or constraints can be allocated to different elements in the enterprise architecture.[150] Many of the aspects of cyber resiliency which apply to the workflow system will be addressed by the enterprise architecture and such enterprise services as security and performance monitoring, security services, and contingency operations. This use case also illustrates ways in which an organization's risk management strategies, both for cybersecurity and for information and communications technology (ICT) investments, affect the consideration of potential cybersecurity solutions.

### I.2.1 MOTIVATING THREAT SCENARIO

The motivating threat scenario in this use case involves an adversary creating a set of fraudulent transactions. To do so, the adversary exploits a weakness in the infrastructure of the enterprise to obtain the credentials of an organizational user authorized to perform tasks within the workflow. The adversary exploits that user's privileges to create new tasks or modify data related to existing tasks to execute fraudulent transactions. The adversary escalates the user's privileges to install malware into the workflow system so that even if the activities taken in the identity of the user are detected and remediated, the adversary can maintain a presence, create or usurp credentials, and continue to operate.

### I.2.2 APPLICABILITY OF CYBER RESILIENCY CONSTRUCTS

In an enterprise IT environment, all cyber resiliency constructs are potentially applicable, subject to the organization's ICT strategy. However, the responsibility for following a cyber resiliency design principle or implementing a cyber resiliency technique can be allocated to different system elements in the enterprise architecture. For example, responsibilities for such security services as identity and access management (IdAM) or intrusion detection can be allocated to the enterprise rather than to individual applications. While the workflow system will inherit capabilities and use functionality from enterprise services, the allocation of responsibilities makes some cyber resiliency techniques (e.g., Contextual Awareness) inapplicable to the workflow system itself. Rather, the workflow system must apply cyber resiliency constructs in a manner consistent with the larger enterprise application in order to interface and interact with enterprise services correctly.

### I.2.3 SOLUTIONS CONSIDERED

The organization is particularly interested in the benefits offered by microservice architectures and how microservices could help support or leverage other cybersecurity or cyber resiliency capabilities. Solutions for this use case consistent with this interest are summarized in Table I-6. These constitute a representative subset of possible alternatives within the constraints imposed by the architectural, operational, and programmatic context. For each identified solution or mitigation, the second column identifies the cyber resiliency design principles, techniques, and

---

[150] See Appendix F.2.4.

approaches the solution or mitigation applies, and the third column identifies the potential effects the solution or mitigation could have on adversary objectives, as defined in the NTCTF.[151]

**TABLE I-6:  CYBER RESILIENCY ANALYSIS FOR WORKFLOW SYSTEM**

| SOLUTION OR MITIGATION | CYBER RESILIENCY CONSTRUCTS APPLIED | POTENTIAL EFFECTS ON ADVERSARY OBJECTIVES |
|---|---|---|
| **Microservice architecture** | Structural design principles:<br>  Contain and exclude behaviors<br>  Layer defenses and partition<br>  resources<br>Techniques and Approaches:<br>  Segmentation:<br>    Predefined Segmentation<br>  Realignment:<br>    Purposing<br>  Dynamic Positioning:<br>    Fragmentation | Lateral Movement, Internal Reconnaissance: *Impede (Delay, Degrade, Exert)*<br>Deny: *Impede (Delay, Degrade, Exert), Limit (Shorten, Reduce)* |
| **Granular privileges** | Structural design principles:<br>  Limit the need for trust<br>  Control visibility and use<br>  Contain and exclude behaviors<br>Techniques and Approaches:<br>  Privilege Restriction:<br>    Trust-Based Privilege<br>    Management<br>    Attribute-Based Usage Restriction | Credential Access, Privilege Escalation: *Impede (Delay, Degrade, Exert)* |
| **Frequent data validation** | Structural design principles:<br>  Determine ongoing trustworthiness<br>Techniques and Approaches:<br>  Analytic Monitoring:<br>    Monitoring and Damage<br>    Assessment (indirect)<br>  Substantiated Integrity:<br>    Integrity Checks<br>    Provenance Tracking | Modify: *Detect, Shorten, Reduce* |
| **Virtualization and non-persistence** | Structural design principles:<br>  Maximize transience<br>  Change or disrupt the attack surface<br>Techniques and Approaches:<br>  Adaptive Management (all)<br>Dynamic Positioning:<br>  Functional Relocation of Cyber<br>  Resources<br>Non-Persistence:<br>  Non-Persistent Services<br>  Non-Persistent Connectivity | Persistence, Internal Reconnaissance: *Impede (Delay, Degrade, Exert)*<br>Execution, Command and Control: *Limit (Shorten, Reduce)* |
| **Synthetic diversity** | Structural design principles:<br>  Change or disrupt the attack surface<br>Techniques and Approaches:<br>  Diversity:<br>    Synthetic Diversity | Lateral Movement, Internal Reconnaissance: *Impede (Delay, Degrade, Exert)* |

---

[151] See Appendix H.2.

| SOLUTION OR MITIGATION | CYBER RESILIENCY CONSTRUCTS APPLIED | POTENTIAL EFFECTS ON ADVERSARY OBJECTIVES |
|---|---|---|
| | | |

## I.2.4  CONTEXT DETAILS

**Architectural Concept.** The workflow system will consist of applications for executing business function tasks in a prescribed order, a browser client to interact with end-users, workflow tracking and analytics, and interactions with enterprise databases. This system-of-interest depends on several other systems provided as part of the enterprise architecture, including security services (e.g., identity and access management, or IdAM; auditing; continuous diagnostics and mitigation, or CDM), resource provisioning (e.g., cloud services), networking (a common infrastructure), enterprise services to support external end-users, and enterprise-provided storage and data management systems. At the enterprise level, the security risk management strategy highlights defense-in-depth and support for a relatively mature Security Operations Center (SOC). Due to resource limitations and a strong preference for commercial off-the-shelf (COTS) products in the enterprise information and communications technology (ICT) strategy, some cyber resiliency approaches (e.g., many of the approaches to Diversity, Specialization) are excluded from consideration. The organization is particularly interested in the benefits offered by microservice architectures and how microservices could support or leverage other cybersecurity or cyber resiliency capabilities. Procurement of the workflow system is viewed as a test case for microservices.

**Operational Environment.** The organization is sufficiently large and aware of cybersecurity to maintain a Security Operations Center (SOC), provide cybersecurity training and awareness to its staff, and provide tailored training to administrative staff. The organization complements the SOC with an insider threat program; SOC staff and staff responsible for that program collaborate frequently.[152] The organization is beginning to include Deception into its operational concept; however, this is a nascent capability. The staff who interact with the workflow system will have basic cybersecurity training and awareness.

**Mission Context.** The new function is of moderate criticality to the organization. Its malfunction or unavailability for more than 12 hours can be expected to damage the organization's reputation with the general public and with its partner organizations. The function handles personally identifiable information (PII). Consequences of concern relate to denial of, reduced effectiveness of, or loss of confidence in the business function supported by the workflow system; injection of bogus tasks (which could cause the organization to provide goods, services, or money to an unauthorized recipient); and exfiltration or exposure of sensitive information the system handles. Of these, fraud via injection of bogus tasks is of highest concern.

**Programmatic Context.** The workflow system will be procured incrementally in development spirals. The procurement will be consistent with the enterprise ICT strategy, strongly favoring COTS products and deprecating special-purpose development. As noted above, strong organizational interest in microservice architectures will inform the procurement of the workflow system, which will be treated as a test case. Programmatic risk management

---

[152] That is, the organization applies enhancements (6) and (7) to IR-4 in [SP 800-53].

prioritizes schedule risk over other forms of risk; rapid delivery of initial functionality to the public is of high importance. Additional functionality will be provided in later spirals. The organization ensures that security is represented in its procurement processes, maintains security standards for internal software development which are shared with its contractors, and has internal processes and procedures for applying the RMF process. For threat modeling, the organization uses the .govCAR methodology [DHS18] and the NSA Technical Cyber Threat Framework [NSA18].[153] For existing organizational systems, the organization also uses ATT&CK, which identifies adversary TTPs in more technology-specific terms.

**Threat Context.** Development of the workflow system considers risks due to multiple threat sources, which are reflected in system requirements. The workflow system must be capable of detecting and responding to indications of human error on the part of organizational users (human resources performing tasks in the workflow), as well as administrators of systems and services on which the workflow system depends. (Note that from the viewpoint of the workflow system, these are indistinguishable from attacks by an adversary that has established a presence on another enterprise service.) Threats related to structural failure or natural disaster are managed at the organizational level; the workflow system must conform to requirements related to continuity of operations defined by organizational policy.

Adversaries could be motivated by direct gain (e.g., obtaining goods, services, or money from the public-facing function), indirect gain (e.g., obtaining PII which can be sold or exploited), or the goal of damaging the organization's reputation. Based on its risk-framing and threat intelligence, the organization assumes that adversaries have a high degree of persistence and moderate-to-high capabilities. Adversaries motivated by gain are highly concerned about stealth. The concern for stealth of adversaries motivated by damaging the organization's reputation depends on the TTPs they use. The primary scenarios of concern involve exploiting commonplace weaknesses to establish a foothold within the enterprise infrastructure and attacking the workflow system from another enterprise service; exploiting a weakness within the browser client to establish a foothold within the workflow system; using a variety of TTPs (in such categories as Persistence, Lateral Movement, Privilege Escalation, Command and Control, Internal Reconnaissance, and Execution) to maintain and extend the foothold; and achieving the intended effects (e.g., Exfiltrate, Deny, or Modify).

## I.2.5  RESTATEMENT AND APPLICATION OF CYBER RESILIENCY CONSTRUCTS

Cyber resiliency objectives and strategic design principles are restated or interpreted in the context described above to make them understandable to stakeholders. These restatements enable stakeholders to provide input to assessments of the relative priority of these constructs, as illustrated in Table I-7 and Table I-8.

**TABLE I-7: RESTATEMENTS OF CYBER RESILIENCY OBJECTIVES FOR NOTIONAL WORKFLOW SYSTEM**

| OBJECTIVE | RESTATEMENT AND PRIORITY |
|---|---|
| Prevent or Avoid | Prevent adversaries from obtaining credentials, escalating privileges, modifying data managed by the system, or disrupting the system. (**Priority: High**, to protect against fraud) |
| Prepare | Provide error detection, error correction, and interfaces with supporting services for continuity of operations. (Priority: Medium, to protect against fraud and operator error) |

[153] See Appendix H.2.

| OBJECTIVE | RESTATEMENT AND PRIORITY |
|---|---|
| Continue | Minimize periods of outage or degraded service. (**Priority: Medium**; outages up to 12 hours are acceptable) |
| Constrain | Limit damage from disruption and erroneous information. (**Priority: High**, to protect against fraud) |
| Reconstitute | Restore workflow functionality, based on valid data, subsequent to adversity. (**Priority: High**, to maintain public confidence) |
| Understand | (Same as Prepare, above. Responsibility for achieving this objective is allocated to the supporting systems.) |
| Transform | Ensure that workflow functionality can accommodate expected changes in staffing (e.g., staffing level, expertise) and workload. (**Priority: Low**) |
| Re-Architect | Ensure that interfaces to workflow system elements are compatible with existing and emerging technical standards, including standards for reporting health and status and security information. (**Priority: Low**) |

The relative priorities of strategic design principles reflect the overall organizational risk management strategy. At the enterprise level, the organization places high priority on Focus on common critical assets, Assume compromised resources, and Expect the adversary to evolve.

**TABLE I-8: RESTATEMENTS OF STRATEGIC CYBER RESILIENCY DESIGN PRINCIPLES FOR WORKFLOW SYSTEM**

| STRATEGIC DESIGN PRINCIPLES | RESTATEMENT AND RELATIVE PRIORITY |
|---|---|
| Focus on common critical assets. | No change. (**Priority: Low** for the workflow application. This principle applies at the enterprise level where it is High priority.) |
| Support agility and architect for adaptability. | Apply modular design to enable the workflow system to be reconfigured and system elements to be replaced easily. (**Priority: High** for the workflow system, consistent with agile or spiral development) |
| Reduce attack surfaces. | Disable or remove unnecessary interfaces to workflow system elements. (**Priority: Medium** for the workflow system; at each spiral, systems engineers need to analyze interfaces and data or control flows.) |
| Assume compromised resources. | Build in behavioral checks to identify compromised system elements and data quality checks to reduce risks of ill-formed or malicious data. (**Priority: High** for the workflow system, consistent with the enterprise risk management strategy. The assumption for the workflow system is not only of compromised end-users but also of an adversary presence in enterprise systems.) |
| Expect adversaries to adapt. | Support other systems which detect, predict, or proactively compensate for unexpected behavior. (**Priority: Medium** for the workflow system, based on the need to support application of the principle at the enterprise level where it is High priority.) |

Consideration of the relative priorities of the cyber resiliency objectives and strategic design principles, in conjunction with the architectural context, enables the applicability of the structural cyber resiliency design principles to be determined as illustrated in Table I-9. Some principles are applicable to both the workflow system and the enterprise as they support the application of the Assume compromised resources strategic design principle. Others are applicable to the enterprise architecture, and their application could impose requirements on the workflow system.

**TABLE I-9: APPLICABILITY OF STRUCTURAL CYBER RESILIENCY DESIGN PRINCIPLES TO WORKFLOW SYSTEM**

| STRUCTURAL DESIGN PRINCIPLE | APPLICABILITY TO WORKFLOW SYSTEM |
|---|---|
| Limit the need for trust. | Applicable, both to the system-of-interest and to the enterprise. |
| Control visibility and use. | Applicable, both to the system-of-interest and to the enterprise. |
| Contain and exclude behaviors. | Applicable, both to the system-of-interest and to the enterprise. |
| Layer defenses and partition resources. | Applicable, both to the system-of-interest and to the enterprise. |
| Plan and manage diversity. | Not applicable, due to the enterprise ICT strategy. |
| Maintain redundancy. | Applicable to the enterprise (and implemented in support of contingency planning); may impose requirements on the system-of-interest. |
| Make resources location-versatile. | Not applicable, due to the enterprise ICT strategy. |
| Leverage health and status data. | Applicable to the enterprise (and implemented via SOC functionality); may impose requirements on the system-of-interest. |
| Maintain situational awareness. | Applicable to the enterprise (and implemented via SOC functionality); may impose requirements on the system-of-interest. |
| Manage resources (risk-) adaptively. | Applicable to the enterprise (and implemented in support of contingency planning); may impose requirements on the system-of-interest. |
| Maximize transience. | Applicable, both to the system-of-interest and to the enterprise. |
| Determine ongoing trustworthiness. | Applicable, both to the system-of-interest and to the enterprise. |
| Change or disrupt the attack surface. | Applicable, both to the system-of-interest and to the enterprise. |
| Make the effects of deception and unpredictability user-transparent. | Applicable, both to the system-of-interest and to the enterprise. |

Similarly, the relative applicability of the structural design principles in conjunction with the architectural context enables the applicability of cyber resiliency techniques and approaches to be determined as illustrated in Table I-10. The applicability (i.e., not applicable, potentially applicable depending on identified circumstances, applicable, or highly applicable) of each approach to the workflow system is assessed. In addition, because the cyber resiliency of the workflow system depends on enterprise services, the assumptions that systems engineers can make about the applicability of each approach and allocations of corresponding requirements to such services are identified.

**TABLE I-10: APPLICABILITY OF CYBER RESILIENCY TECHNIQUES AND APPROACHES TO WORKFLOW SYSTEM**

| TECHNIQUES | APPROACHES | APPLICABILITY TO WORKFLOW SYSTEM | APPLICABILITY TO ENTERPRISE SERVICES |
|---|---|---|---|
| Adaptive Response | Dynamic Reconfiguration | Applicable. | Highly applicable to enterprise-supplied resources; workflow design assumes these capabilities. |
| | Dynamic Resource Allocation | Applicable. | Highly applicable to enterprise-supplied resources; workflow design assumes these capabilities. |

| TECHNIQUES | APPROACHES | APPLICABILITY TO WORKFLOW SYSTEM | APPLICABILITY TO ENTERPRISE SERVICES |
|---|---|---|---|
| | Adaptive Management | Not applicable. | Applicable to enterprise-supplied resources; workflow design assumes these capabilities. |
| Analytic Monitoring | Monitoring and Damage Assessment | While it is desirable for the workflow system to provide self-monitoring/audit and initial analysis of monitored data to enterprise CDM and insider threat monitoring services, this approach is determined to be not applicable due to resource limitations. | Highly applicable at the enterprise level via CDM, performance monitoring and assessment, and insider threat monitoring; workflow design assumes these capabilities. |
| | Sensor Fusion and Analysis | Not applicable. However, the enterprise architecture imposes requirements for data collection and provision on the workflow system. | Applicable, in support of SOC activities. |
| | Forensic and Behavioral Analysis | Not applicable. | Highly applicable, in support of SOC and insider threat program activities. |
| Contextual Awareness | Dynamic Resource Awareness | Not applicable. However, the enterprise architecture imposes requirements for data collection and provision on the workflow system. | Highly applicable, in support of SOC activities. |
| | Dynamic Threat Awareness | Not applicable. The enterprise architecture is not expected to impose requirements on the workflow system. | Highly applicable, in support of SOC activities. |
| | Mission Dependency and Status Visualization | Not applicable. However, the enterprise architecture imposes requirements for data collection and provision on the workflow system. | Highly applicable, in support of SOC activities. |
| Coordinated Protection | Calibrated Defense-in-Depth | Not applicable. However, the enterprise architecture may impose requirements on the workflow system. | Highly applicable, consistent with the enterprise security risk management strategy. |
| | Consistency Analysis | Applicable to the enterprise; may impose requirements on the system-of-interest. | Applicable, in support of SOC and insider threat program activities. |
| | Orchestration | Applicable to the enterprise; may impose requirements on the system-of-interest to support coordination. | Applicable, in support of contingency planning and insider threat program activities. |
| | Self-Challenge | Not applicable. Capabilities at the enterprise level are not expected to impose requirements on the workflow system. | Applicable, in support of contingency planning. |
| Deception | Obfuscation | Applicability depends on the sensitivity of the data. | Applicability depends on the sensitivity of the data. |

| TECHNIQUES | APPROACHES | APPLICABILITY TO WORKFLOW SYSTEM | APPLICABILITY TO ENTERPRISE SERVICES |
|---|---|---|---|
| | Disinformation | Not applicable. Capabilities at the enterprise level are not expected to impose requirements on the workflow system. | Applicable, but nascent. |
| | Misdirection | Not applicable; the nascent capability at the enterprise level is not expected to impose requirements on the workflow system. | Applicable, but nascent. |
| | Tainting | Application at the enterprise level may result in the workflow system handling false data. | Applicable, but nascent. |
| Diversity | Architectural Diversity | Not applicable. | Not applicable, based on the enterprise ICT strategy. |
| | Design Diversity | Technically feasible but not applicable given the programmatic context and the enterprise strategy. | Not applicable, based on the enterprise ICT strategy. |
| | Synthetic Diversity | Potentially applicable. | Applicable, as technically feasible and as long as costs and performance reduction are within acceptable limits. |
| | Information Diversity | Not applicable. | Not applicable, based on the enterprise ITC strategy. |
| | Path Diversity | Potentially applicable, depending on the architecture of the workflow system. | Applicable, as technically feasible and as long as costs and performance reduction are within acceptable limits. |
| | Supply Chain Diversity | Potentially applicable to the enterprise; not expected to impose requirements on the system-of-interest. | Not applicable, based on the enterprise ICT strategy. |
| Dynamic Positioning | Functional Relocation of Sensors | Not applicable. Capabilities at the enterprise level are not expected to impose requirements on the workflow system. | Applicable, in support of SOC activities. |
| | Functional Relocation of Cyber Resources | Applicable, supported by enterprise services providing virtualization. | Highly applicable, primarily in support of performance management. |
| | Asset Mobility | Not applicable. | Not applicable. |
| | Fragmentation | Potentially applicable, depending on capabilities of enterprise storage and data management services. | Applicable, as technically feasible and as long as costs and performance reduction are within acceptable limits. |
| | Distributed Functionality | Potentially applicable, depending on the enterprise architecture. | Applicable, as technically feasible and as long as costs and performance reduction are within acceptable limits. |
| Non-Persistence | Non-Persistent Information | Potentially applicable. Must be aligned with privacy requirements. | Applicability varies depending on the type of information. |

| TECHNIQUES | APPROACHES | APPLICABILITY TO WORKFLOW SYSTEM | APPLICABILITY TO ENTERPRISE SERVICES |
|---|---|---|---|
| | Non-Persistent Services | Applicable; closely aligned with performance optimization. | Applicable. |
| | Non-Persistent Connectivity | Applicable; closely aligned with performance optimization. | Applicable. |
| Privilege Restriction | Trust-Based Privilege Management | Applicable; relies on other enterprise systems. | Applicable. |
| | Attribute-Based Usage Restriction | Applicable; relies on other enterprise systems. | Applicable. |
| | Dynamic Privileges | Applicable; relies on other enterprise systems. | Applicable. |
| Realignment | Purposing | Applicable. | Applicable. |
| | Offloading | Not applicable; implementation at the enterprise level is not expected to impose requirements on the workflow system. | Applicable. |
| | Restriction | Applicable. | Applicable. |
| | Replacement | Not applicable; however, implementation at the enterprise level may impose requirements on the workflow system. | Applicable. |
| | Specialization | Not applicable. | Not applicable, based on the enterprise ITC strategy. |
| Redundancy | Protected Backup and Restore | Not applicable; however, implementation at the enterprise level may impose requirements on the workflow system. | Highly applicable, in support of contingency planning. |
| | Surplus Capacity | Not applicable; implementation at the enterprise level is not expected to impose requirements on the workflow system. | Highly applicable, in support of contingency planning. |
| | Replication | Not applicable; however, implementation at the enterprise level may impose requirements on the workflow system. | Highly applicable, in support of contingency planning. |
| Segmentation | Predefined Segmentation | Potentially applicable, via micro-segmentation of the functions within the workflow system.\nHighly applicable to the enterprise; may impose requirements on the system-of-interest. | Highly applicable. |
| | Dynamic Segmentation and Isolation | Applicable to the enterprise; may impose requirements on the system-of-interest. | Applicable, as long as performance reduction is within acceptable limits. |
| Substantiated Integrity | Integrity Checks | Highly applicable. | Applicable. |
| | Provenance Tracking | Applicable, as applied to data and commands. | Applicable, as applied to network traffic. |

| TECHNIQUES | APPROACHES | APPLICABILITY TO WORKFLOW SYSTEM | APPLICABILITY TO ENTERPRISE SERVICES |
|---|---|---|---|
| | Behavior Validation | Highly applicable. | Applicable, in support of SOC and insider threat program activities. |
| Unpredictability | Temporal Unpredictability | Not applicable; however, capabilities at the enterprise level may impose requirements on the workflow system. | Applicable, in support of SOC and insider threat program activities. |
| | Contextual Unpredictability | Not applicable; however, capabilities at the enterprise level may impose requirements on the workflow system. | Applicable, in support of SOC and insider threat program activities. |
| | | | |

### I.2.6 DEFINITION AND ANALYSIS OF SOLUTION CHARACTERISTICS

To define and analyze characteristics of possible solutions, systems engineers consider available COTS products and technologies with a focus on microservice architectures; applicable design principles, techniques, and approaches identified above; and threat-modeling, focused primarily on the Presence stage and on selected adversary actions in the Effect stage of the NTCTF.[154] This analysis indicates that the following characteristics will enable the workflow system to meet its cyber resiliency objectives and apply its relevant strategic design principles:

- The system is constructed as a set of microservices, both to support cyber resiliency and to enable replacement or enhancement in development spirals.

- The system defines granular privileges and restricts their uses. (This is facilitated by the microservice architecture.)

- The system validates data repeatedly throughout the workflow. (This may involve checksums, cryptographic hashes and signatures, and data quality cross-checking.)

- The system uses virtualization and non-persistence, both to optimize performance and to reduce the duration any given instance of a workflow service is exposed. (This is facilitated by the microservice architecture.)

- The system uses Synthetic Diversity for its services.

These desired characteristics can be mapped to controls in [SP 800-53] and used to define system requirements.

## I.3 CAMPUS MICROGRID

An organization desires to upgrade the microgrid for its campus, which houses a critical facility.[155] A microgrid includes an industrial control system (ICS) with safety-critical sub-systems. The organization has nominally made a commitment to conform with the Sandia Microgrid

---

[154] See Table I-6.

[155] Microgrids are used in a variety of environments, including military bases, facilities, or campuses which have extremely high reliability/power quality requirements (e.g., data centers, hospitals or medical centers, correctional institutions), office parks, and high-cost supply areas. Microgrids can be islands (stand-alone microgrids) or tied to the larger power grid (grid-tied microgrids).

Cyber Security Reference Architecture [Sandia15] for automated grid management and control (AGMC) operations and maintenance. Therefore, the existing microgrid already applies numerous security and system resilience measures. However, the organization has not committed to investing in the microgrid cybersecurity situational awareness (CSSA) or the cybersecurity configuration management (CSCM) functions identified in [Sandia15], nor is the organization willing to invest in the use of Deception or Unpredictability.

### I.3.1  MOTIVATING THREAT SCENARIO

The motivating threat scenario in this use case involves an adversary disrupting or denying power to a campus that houses critical operations. To do so, the adversary takes advantage of the campus microgrid's connections to external systems (i.e., the systems of the electrical power utility for the geographic area in which the campus is located) by compromising the information exchange between the centralized campus energy management system (EMS) and building management systems (BMS). By manipulating the microgrid operational metrics transmitted to the EMS, the adversary elicits EMS control signals that demand large power curtailments within or islanding of the microgrid. Thus, critical mission operations or business functions are denied or disrupted.[156]

### I.3.2  APPLICABILITY OF CYBER RESILIENCY CONSTRUCTS

Many of the cyber resiliency design principles are consistent with the Sandia Microgrid Cyber Security Reference Architecture. Similarly, many of the techniques and approaches are relevant to the constituent sub-systems of the microgrid. The discussion identifies the applicability of specific design principles, techniques, and approaches. Some cyber resiliency design principles and techniques are not applicable due to the organization's policy and investment strategy rather than for technical reasons. These are related to Deception, Unpredictability, and approaches to Analytic Monitoring and Contextual Awareness that relate to CSSA or CSCM.

### I.3.3  SOLUTIONS CONSIDERED

The organization's commitment to the Sandia Microgrid Cyber Security Reference Architecture has provided a foundation for cyber resiliency. However, the concern that the critical facility will be targeted raises the possibility of applying several additional alternatives, as indicated in Table I-11.[157] Note that the set of alternatives is constrained by the organization's determination not to invest in CSSA/CSCM functionality in the near term.

**TABLE I-11:  SUMMARY OF ALTERNATIVES AND ANALYSIS**

---

[156] In order to maintain a cyber focus, on-site (physical) access threats are not addressed in this use case.

[157] Adversary objectives are defined in the NSA/CSS Technical Cyber Threat Framework [NSA18].

| SOLUTION OR MITIGATION | CYBER RESILIENCY CONSTRUCTS APPLIED | POTENTIAL EFFECTS ON ADVERSARY OBJECTIVES |
|---|---|---|
| **Isolate the components of the critical facility from the microgrid (i.e., nested islanding), making such components dependent on its internal Uninterruptible Power Supply (UPS).** | Structural design principles:<br>  Contain and exclude behaviors<br>  Layer defenses and partition resources<br>Techniques and Approaches:<br>  Segmentation:<br>    Predefined Segmentation<br>    Dynamic Segmentation and Isolation<br>  Substantiated Integrity:<br>    Integrity Checks | Lateral Movement, Command and Control: *Negate, Contain*<br>Deny: *Shorten* |
| **Make the campus Energy Management System (EMS) distributed and decentralized rather than centralized.** | Strategic design principle:<br>  Support agility and architect for adaptability<br>Structural design principles:<br>  Layer defenses and partition resources<br>  Manage resources (risk-)adaptively<br>Techniques and Approaches:<br>  Dynamic Positioning:<br>    Distributed Functionality<br>  Redundancy:<br>    Replication | Deny, Destroy: *Degrade, Delay, Exert, Shorten, Reduce* |
| **Harden devices (e.g., controllers, relays, switches, meters) by removing unnecessary software and services and disabling unneeded communications and data ports.** | Strategic design principle:<br>  Reduce attack surfaces<br>Structural design principle:<br>  Contain and exclude behaviors<br>Techniques and Approaches:<br>  Realignment:<br>    Restriction | Delivery, Exploitation: *Preempt* |

## I.3.4 CONTEXT DETAILS

**Architectural Concept.** The organization has acquired a microgrid for its main campus, which consists of power generation systems (e.g., solar panel arrays, gas-fired generators), a limited amount of power storage (e.g., battery arrays), power delivery systems, power transfer systems (e.g., transformers between the microgrid and the larger regional electrical grid), and a campus power management system. The microgrid interfaces with building automation systems (BAS) or building management systems (BMS) for the buildings on the campus. The organization has used the Energy Surety Microgrid (ESM) methodology developed by Sandia National Laboratories (SNL) and adopted the Sandia Microgrid Reference Architecture [Sandia15] but has focused solely on providing AGMC operations and maintenance. Key constituent systems include the Energy Management System (EMS), the Human-Machine Interface (HMI) and its server, remote terminal units (RTUs), the utility data connection, energy generation and storage sub-systems, smart meters, breakers, BMS, relays or intelligent electronic devices (IEDs), and an engineering workstation for maintenance. Currently, the only external interface for the campus microgrid is the larger regional electrical grid, but ultimately, it will be integrated into the emerging Smart Grid. Thus, the organization is tracking the adoption of the NIST Guidelines for Smart Grid Cybersecurity [IR 7628] [CSFSGP] and seeks to be consistent with those guidelines.

**Operational Environment.** Microgrid power provided to the buildings and other facilities (e.g., street lighting, traffic lights) is primarily supplied by the larger regional electrical grid, but is complemented by on-site power generation and storage systems (e.g., solar panels, battery arrays). It provides emergency power (e.g., from gas-fired generators) if the regional grid cannot supply adequate power. The microgrid is operated by the organization's physical plant sub-organization. While the staff in the sub-organization receives basic cybersecurity training and awareness, they are largely unaware of cyber threats against energy systems, and the organization does not plan to invest in CSSA or CSCM functions in the near term. While most of the buildings on the campus are operated by the organization, some are operated by tenants; tenants have access to BAS.

**Mission Context.** The mission of the microgrid is twofold: First, the microgrid ensures that critical operations can continue in situations where the larger power grid is degraded or unavailable (e.g., in case of natural disaster). Second, the microgrid enables the organization to manage its electrical power costs, power quality requirements, and environmental goals by generating power (thereby reducing consumption from the larger power grid) and by storing power, as appropriate.

Some microgrid sub-systems are safety-critical. Consequences of greatest concern relate to the safety of those sub-systems physically near distribution and transfer systems (and, depending on the generation type, possibly also those near generation systems) and potential failure of power to critical systems or buildings.

**Programmatic Context.** The organization's physical plant sub-organization procures new sub-systems, replaces existing ones (e.g., acquiring a new generator or replacing an old one), and integrates these into its existing microgrid. Programmatic risk management prioritizes safety risk over other forms of risk. One of those safety risks is the physical destruction of the gas-fired generator, for example, through a cyber-attack. Cost is the next priority.

**Threat Context.** The organization receives a U.S. Government threat briefing and realizes that the most critical mission operations or business functions at this campus are targeted by highly sophisticated, persistent, and stealthy adversaries. One high-concern threat scenario involves exploitation of cyber-vulnerabilities to destroy the gas-fired generator [Swearingen13]. The other threat scenarios of greatest concern to the organization are those in which an adversary gains a foothold in the microgrid EMS via interactions with the larger power grid, via physical access to a device (e.g., a remote terminal unit or RTU, a controller, a relay device) and its ports (e.g., USB) or via interactions between the EMS and BAS systems to which building tenants have access. Using that foothold, the adversary extends its control over local EMS functions, and possibly also the human-machine interface (HMI), so that operators can be deceived about EMS behavior. The adversary then either transmits a command to malware installed on the EMS or has ensured that installed malware can look for triggering conditions (e.g., islanding of the microgrid) to cut power to the facility housing critical operations.

The organization recognizes a variety of other threat scenarios or specific adversary actions are possible. For example, threat scenarios involving operator error can result in significant adverse consequences. Some devices, such as RTUs or controllers, may be compromised due to supply chain attacks. Man-in-the-middle attacks can also be launched against communications between the EMS and controllers or relays. The adversary can cause devices to overheat, overvolt, or otherwise become damaged. The organization recognizes that integration with the Smart Grid will change its attack surfaces. However, for purposes of this analysis, the focus is on denial-of-electrical-service to the critical facility.

## I.3.5 RESTATEMENT AND APPLICATION OF CYBER RESILIENCY CONSTRUCTS

Cyber resiliency objectives and strategic design principles are restated or interpreted in the context described above to make them understandable to stakeholders. These restatements enable stakeholders to provide input to assessments of the relative priority of these constructs, as illustrated in Table I-12 and Table I-13.

**TABLE I-12: RESTATEMENTS OF CYBER RESILIENCY OBJECTIVES FOR CAMPUS MICROGRID**

| OBJECTIVE | RESTATEMENT AND PRIORITY |
|---|---|
| Prevent or Avoid | Prevent failure or degradation of power generation, transfer, and delivery; prevent destruction of equipment. (**Priority: High**) |
| Prepare | Maintain procedures, resources, and processes to address a range of disruptions, hazards, and threats to power generation, transfer, and delivery. (**Priority: High**) |
| Continue | Ensure that power is delivered to systems or buildings based on criticality. (**Priority: Very High**) |
| Constrain | Ensure graceful degradation and safe failure of system elements to limit potential cascading failures. (**Priority: High**) |
| Reconstitute | Restore power generation, transfer, and delivery capabilities as quickly and completely as possible subsequent to disruption. (**Priority: High**) |
| Understand | Maintain situational awareness of the status of system elements, patterns and predictions of use, and status of external systems (e.g., regional power grid). (**Priority: High**) |
| Transform | Track emerging operational concepts, governance structures and processes, and adoption and usage patterns for Smart Grid systems to ensure that the microgrid's concept of use is or can be made compatible. (**Priority: Very Low**) |
| Re-Architect | Assure uninterrupted power delivery to the critical facility by adding distribution connections from the microgrid's energy storage and gas-fired generator directly to the critical facility as backups. (**Priority: High**) |

The relative priorities of *strategic* design principles reflect the overall organizational risk management strategy.

**TABLE I-13: RESTATEMENTS OF STRATEGIC CYBER RESILIENCY DESIGN PRINCIPLES FOR CAMPUS MICROGRID**

| STRATEGIC DESIGN PRINCIPLES | RESTATEMENT AND RELATIVE PRIORITY |
|---|---|
| Focus on common critical assets. | Prioritize protections based first on the criticality of the buildings, mission operations, and business functions requiring power, and then on the criticality of microgrid system elements. (**Priority: Very High**) |
| Support agility and architect for adaptability. | Design microgrid constituent systems in a modular way to accommodate technologies, both available and emerging, and use concepts which change at different rates. (**Priority: Medium**) |
| Reduce attack surfaces. | Minimize interfaces and information flows between microgrid control and other campus management systems (e.g., building access control systems); resist the all-systems convergence impulse. (**Priority: High**) |
| Assume compromised resources. | Design the microgrid so that constituent systems can be monitored closely for indications of adverse behavior and so that the effects of adversity can be limited. (**Priority: Medium**) |

| STRATEGIC DESIGN PRINCIPLES | RESTATEMENT AND RELATIVE PRIORITY |
|---|---|
| Expect adversaries to adapt. | (Not prioritized. Deemed to be applicable to the larger Smart Grid.) |

Consideration of the relative priorities of cyber resiliency objectives and strategic design principles, in conjunction with the architectural context, enables the applicability of the *structural* cyber resiliency design principles to be determined as illustrated in Table I-14.

TABLE I-14: APPLICABILITY OF STRUCTURAL CYBER RESILIENCY DESIGN PRINCIPLES TO CAMPUS MICROGRID

| STRUCTURAL DESIGN PRINCIPLE | APPLICABILITY |
|---|---|
| Limit the need for trust. | Applicable to the EMS, its interfaces with other sub-systems, and its interfaces with BMS. |
| Control visibility and use. | Applicable to the EMS, its interfaces with other sub-systems, and its interfaces with BMS. |
| Contain and exclude behaviors. | Applicable to the EMS, its interfaces with other sub-systems, and its interfaces with BMS. |
| Layer defenses and partition resources. | Applicable. |
| Plan and manage diversity. | Partially applicable, by supporting multiple forms of generation. |
| Maintain redundancy. | Applicable, by providing multiple sub-systems and multiple sources of power supply and distribution. |
| Make resources location-versatile. | Partially applicable, insofar as some devices could be physically relocated; not applicable to functionality, which is tightly bound to devices. |
| Leverage health and status data. | Applicable to the EMS. |
| Maintain situational awareness. | Applicable to the EMS. |
| Manage resources (risk-) adaptively. | Highly applicable in order to provide assured power to critical operations. |
| Maximize transience. | Not applicable. |
| Determine ongoing trustworthiness. | Applicable to and applied to the EMS. |
| Change or disrupt the attack surface. | Partially applicable, in that the microgrid could be islanded (i.e., cut off from the larger electrical grid) and that individual devices or buildings could be cut off from the microgrid. Also applicable to protection and safety-related subsystems within the microgrid. |
| Make the effects of deception and unpredictability user-transparent. | Not applicable, since the organization has chosen not to consider deception or unpredictability. |

Similarly, the relative applicability of the structural design principles, in conjunction with the architectural context, enables the applicability of the cyber resiliency techniques and approaches to be determined as illustrated in Table I-15.

TABLE I-15: APPLICABILITY OF CYBER RESILIENCY TECHNIQUES AND APPROACHES TO CAMPUS MICROGRID

| TECHNIQUES | APPROACHES | APPLICABILITY |
|---|---|---|
| Adaptive Response | Dynamic Reconfiguration | Applicable, consistent with [Sandia15]. |
| | Dynamic Resource Allocation | Applicable to the microgrid as a whole; implemented via the EMS. |
| | Adaptive Management | Applicable to the system-of-interest as a whole; implemented via the EMS. |

| TECHNIQUES | APPROACHES | APPLICABILITY |
|---|---|---|
| Analytic Monitoring | Monitoring and Damage Assessment | Applicable, consistent with [Sandia15]. For ICS, focus is on indicators of anomalous and potentially adverse behavior using H&S data; for power management, can also look for adversarial activities. |
| | Sensor Fusion and Analysis | Potentially applicable, consistent with [Sandia15]. However, the organization has not made a commitment to CSSA/CSCM. |
| | Forensic and Behavioral Analysis | Currently not applicable since the organization has not made a commitment to CSSA/CSCM. Potentially applicable in the future, depending on changes in the organization's governance and risk management strategy. |
| Contextual Awareness | Dynamic Resource Awareness | Currently not applicable since the organization has not made a commitment to CSSA/CSCM. Potentially applicable in the future, depending on changes in the organization's governance and risk management strategy. |
| | Dynamic Threat Awareness | Currently not applicable since the organization has not made a commitment to CSSA/CSCM. Potentially applicable in the future, depending on changes in the organization's governance and risk management strategy. |
| | Mission Dependency and Status Visualization | Applicable, consistent with [Sandia15]. |
| Coordinated Protection | Calibrated Defense-in-Depth | Applicable, consistent with [Sandia15]. |
| | Consistency Analysis | Applicable, consistent with [Sandia15]. |
| | Orchestration | Applicable, consistent with [Sandia15]. |
| | Self-Challenge | Applicable in the form of self-diagnostics, penetration testing, and Red Team exercises. |
| Deception | Obfuscation | Applicable, consistent with [Sandia15], via encryption of control data between power management system and other constituent systems; may also be applied to reporting of H&S data from other constituent systems to power management system. |
| | Disinformation | Currently not applicable. Applicability depends on the risk management strategy of the owning organization; that strategy must ensure that Disinformation does not interfere with correct operations or with situational awareness. |
| | Misdirection | Currently not applicable. Applicability depends on the risk management strategy of the owning organization; that strategy must ensure that Misdirection does not interfere with situational awareness. |
| | Tainting | Currently not applicable. Technically feasible, at least for the EMS and HMI, but unlikely to be deemed applicable. |
| Diversity | Architectural Diversity | Applicable to the critical facility. Ensure critical facility receives power from three diverse power sources: the regional grid; the microgrid; and energy storage subsystem within the microgrid. |
| | Design Diversity | Technically feasible, but unlikely to be deemed applicable. |
| | Synthetic Diversity | Technically feasible, but unlikely to be deemed applicable. |
| | Information Diversity | Potentially applicable to performance or H&S data. |
| | Path Diversity | Partially applicable. If normal communications between constituent systems is unreliable, operators may be able to go to those systems physically and communicate via cell phone. |
| | Supply Chain Diversity | Potentially applicable, but may be programmatically infeasible due to cost. |
| Dynamic Positioning | Functional Relocation of Sensors | Potentially applicable. |
| | Functional Relocation of Cyber Resources | Applicability depends on the size and complexity of the power management system. |

| TECHNIQUES | APPROACHES | APPLICABILITY |
|---|---|---|
| | Asset Mobility | Potentially applicable to constituent systems under restricted circumstances; for example, some generators can be physically moved. |
| | Fragmentation | Not applicable. |
| | Distributed Functionality | Applicable to the EMS. |
| Non-Persistence | Non-Persistent Information | Applicable (and inherent to the type of device) for many devices, which overwrite data on an ongoing basis; potentially applicable to the EMS and HMI servers. |
| | Non-Persistent Services | Applicable solely to AGMC maintenance and to some processes on the EMS and HMI servers; not applicable to services on Intelligent Electronic Devices (IEDs), such as relays, which require continuous processing. . |
| | Non-Persistent Connectivity | Applicable solely to AGMC maintenance; not applicable to AMGC operations, which require continuous connectivity. . |
| Privilege Restriction | Trust-Based Privilege Management | Applicable, consistent with [Sandia15]. |
| | Attribute-Based Usage Restriction | Applicable, consistent with [Sandia15]. |
| | Dynamic Privileges | Potentially applicable, solely within the EMS and HMI, but unlikely to be selected due to lack of commitment to CSSA / CSCM. |
| Realignment | Purposing | Applicable (and inherent in the type of system). |
| | Offloading | Not applicable; no functionality in the microgrid is unnecessary to its operations. |
| | Restriction | Applicable, in the form of device hardening. |
| | Replacement | Potentially applicable, but may be precluded by cost. |
| | Specialization | Potentially applicable, but may be precluded by cost. |
| Redundancy | Protected Backup and Restore | Applicable to EMS. |
| | Surplus Capacity | Applicable to generation, storage, and distribution systems. |
| | Replication | Applicable to generation, storage, and distribution systems. |
| Segmentation | Predefined Segmentation | Applicable, consistent with [Sandia15]. |
| | Dynamic Segmentation and Isolation | Applicable, consistent with [Sandia15]. |
| Substantiated Integrity | Integrity Checks | Applicable to data exchange, consistent with [Sandia15]. |
| | Provenance Tracking | Applicable to data exchange, consistent with [Sandia15]. |
| | Behavior Validation | Applicable at the sub-system level and to the power management system; can use health and status data. |
| Unpredictability | Temporal Unpredictability | Potentially applicable, to selected functions or capabilities, but not considered due to the organization's risk management strategy. |
| | Contextual Unpredictability | Potentially applicable, to selected functions or capabilities, but not considered due to the organization's risk management strategy. |

## I.3.6  DEFINITION AND ANALYSIS OF SOLUTION CHARACTERISTICS

As noted above, the organization has at least nominally adopted the Sandia Microgrid Reference Architecture and seeks to be consistent with the NIST Guidelines for Smart Grid Cybersecurity [IR 7628] [CSFSGP]. Therefore, the campus microgrid already applies multiple cyber resiliency techniques and implementation approaches, including Adaptive Response, Monitoring and Damage Assessment, Coordinated Protection, Obfuscation, Segmentation, and Substantiated

Integrity. However, the organization has not invested in an internal cyber defense capability for its microgrid (i.e., in the CSSA and CSCM functions), and thus has not applied Sensor Fusion and Analysis or Contextual Awareness. The organization currently prioritizes solutions which require minimal additional investment. Additional solutions that could be considered include:

- **Nested islanding:** Enable the critical facility to be isolated from the rest of the microgrid, dependent on its internal UPS.

- **Decentralization:** Make the EMS distributed rather than centralized.[158]

- **Device hardening:** Harden devices (e.g., controllers, relays, switches, meters) by removing unnecessary software and services and disabling unneeded communications and data ports. Protect the gas-fired generator by replacing the existing digital relay with an analog, non-networked relay.[159]

- **Supply chain risk management:** Monitor and manage risks of compromise via the supply chain for microgrid devices (e.g., relays, RTUs, switches).

- **Deception:** Create a deception environment, emulating a portion of the campus microgrid, to lure and detect attacker activities. Implement additional cyber defenses against those attacker activities in the real microgrid.

Note that nested islanding and decentralization could be implemented together to ensure separable energy management at the critical facility. Note also that implementing supply chain risk management and deception would require expertise and commitment that the organization currently lacks, and therefore, its potential effects on the motivating threat scenario are not considered further. The most likely choice given the organization's current lack of commitment to an internal cyber defense capability is device hardening.

---

[158] In this context, "decentralization" refers to planned decentralization, not decentralization that may occur through a lack of consistent architectural planning.

[159] Roxey's "Aurora disruptor" is briefly described in [Fairley19].

# CYBER RESILIENCY IN A REAL-WORLD EXAMPLE

ANALYSIS OF AN ATTACK ON A CRITICAL INFRASTRUCTURE

This appendix provides an example of how cyber resiliency could be applied in a real-world critical infrastructure use case.[160] The example is based on publicly available descriptions of the cyber-attacks on the Ukrainian power grid in 2015 [SANS16] [BAH16] and then in 2016 [ESET17] [Dragos17] [SANS17].

## J.1  POWER GRID ATTACK—2015

In December 2015, three power distribution companies in the Ukraine were unable to provide electrical power to approximately 225,000 customers due to coordinated cyber-attacks. The cyber campaigns, of which the outages were the culmination, involved two phases. In the first phase, the attackers compromised the enterprise IT of each company. This phase followed a conventional cyber kill chain [Hutchins11], using a set of ATT&CK tactics [MITRE18] to achieve adversary objectives [NSA18]. In the second phase, attackers exploited connectivity between each company's IT and operational technology (OT). Attackers then used a set of tactics specific to industrial control systems (ICS) following an ICS kill chain [Assante15] and using a set of tactics for ICS rather than IT [Alexander17].

To achieve their desired effects, the attacker used stolen credentials to open breakers, disrupting power distribution; delivered a malicious firmware update to Ethernet-to-serial converters to sever communications between the control station and substations; initiated a DoS attack on a telephone call center; triggered an outage of the Uninterruptible Power Supply (UPS) to the call center and to data centers; locked operators out of the human-machine interface (HMI) on the OT network; and ran the KillDisk wiper software, which erases master boot records and deletes system log records, to destroy critical system data. While the Ukrainian operators were able to restore power to customers using manual procedures within six hours, they were left without automated control for more than a year in some locations.

For ease of exposition, the steps the attacker took on the OT network can be summarized as follows:

- Establish remote connection to OT network. This initially was via a compromised Domain Controller on the IT network and subsequently via a VPN connection using compromised credentials;

- Maintain communications back to the adversary;

- Perform internal reconnaissance of the OT network;

- Stage and schedule the KillDisk malware;

- Reconfigure the UPS to schedule an outage;

---

[160] This appendix is derived from [Steiger18].

- Upload malicious firmware to the Ethernet-to-serial bridges, thus severing connections between control stations;

- Issue the command to open the substation breakers;

- Lock the operators out of the HMI; and

- Initiate the DoS attack on telephone communications.

Table J-1 identifies steps in the attacker's operations on the OT network. For each step, the second column identifies potential applications of cyber resiliency techniques to redirect, preclude, impede, limit, or expose the attacker's actions in the step. A growing number of products that apply those techniques are available. Some of the potential mitigations can be implemented procedurally. For a few potential mitigations, custom solutions may be needed.

**TABLE J-1:  ATTACKER AND DEFENDER USES OF CYBER RESILIENCY FOR 2015 ATTACK**

| ATTACK STEP | POTENTIAL MITIGATIONS | REPRESENTATIVE TECHNOLOGIES |
|---|---|---|
| **Establish remote connection to OT network** | • Non-Persistence of the connection between the IT and OT networks [preclude, limit]<br>• Analytic Monitoring for anomalous connections to the OT network [expose]<br>• Segmentation of the OT network [preclude, limit]<br>• Substantiated Integrity on communications to OT network [preclude, impede]<br>• Privilege Restriction to force more stringent authentication (802.1x) for crossing network zones [preclude, impede] | • Custom process to close and re-establish connections<br>• Intrusion detection system (IDS) for OT, ICS, or Supervisory Control and Data Acquisition (SCADA)<br>• Software Defined Networking (SDN) for network segmentation<br>• Step-up authentication |
| **Maintain communications back to adversary** | • Analytic Monitoring to look for C2 (anomalous message traffic) [expose]<br>• Segmentation to make C2 require multiple hops [impede]<br>• Non-Persistence of communications forcing re-establishment of connections [limit] | • IDS for OT, ICS, or SCADA<br>• Software Defined Networking (SDN) for network segmentation<br>• Custom process to close and re-establish connections |
| **Perform internal reconnaissance of the OT network** | • Deception to obfuscate traffic [impede]<br>• Deception to create false targets together with Analytic Monitoring to detect traffic to those targets [misdirect, expose] | • Encryption for OT, ICS, or SCADA<br>• Deception technology for OT, ICS, or SCADA |
| **Stage KillDisk malware and schedule KillDisk execution** | • Non-Persistence – Non-Persistent Information (delete staged malware) [preclude]<br>• Redundancy – Protected Backup and Restore [limit]<br>• Analytic Monitoring (detect unauthorized or unexpected commands in scheduler) [expose] | • Procedures to periodically wipe and reinstate schedules for tasks<br>• Tune IDS to monitor scheduled tasks and alert on destructive actions<br>• Tune IDS to use behavioral analysis tools for HMIs and scheduled tasks |

| ATTACK STEP | POTENTIAL MITIGATIONS | REPRESENTATIVE TECHNOLOGIES |
|---|---|---|
| **Reconfigure UPS to schedule outage** | • Analytic Monitoring of UPS configuration changes [expose]<br>• Privilege Restriction on configuration changes [impede]<br>• Substantiated Integrity using multi-factor authentication (MFA) configuration changes [impede] | • IDS for OT, ICS, or SCADA<br>• Change processes and procedures to rotate credentials<br>• Use an OT security management platform to restrict privileges and require MFA for configuration changes |
| **Upload malicious firmware to Ethernet/serial bridge** | • Substantiated Integrity (signing, voting) on firmware upload [impede]<br>• Deception to create false targets together with Analytic Monitoring to detect traffic to those targets [misdirect, expose]<br>• Analytic Monitoring on changes to firmware together with Adaptive Response to respond to changes [expose, limit]<br>• Privilege Restriction – require MFA on all firmware updates [impede] | • Change processes and procedures to inject signing, hashing, and voting on firmware upload<br>• Inject purposeful mistakes into code to create code canaries on firmware uploads<br>• Run planned uploads through signing and code scanning environments to detect code manipulation |
| **Open substation breakers** | • Deception to create false targets together with Analytic Monitoring to detect traffic to those targets [misdirect, expose]<br>• Substantiated Integrity together with Privilege Restriction on commands with destructive potential [preclude, impede] | • Deception technology to create honeypot HMI screens integrated with IDS for OT, ICS, or SCADA<br>• Use an OT security management platform to restrict privileges and require MFA or step-up authentication |
| **Lock out operators from HMI** | • Diversity with Redundancy to provide multiple HMIs [impede] | • Make architectural changes to use existing technologies in a diverse and redundant way |
| **Initiate DoS on telephone communications** | • Diversity with Redundancy – Path Diversity [impede, limit]<br>• Dynamic Positioning of communications capabilities [limit]<br>• Realignment to restrict or replace key communications [preclude, impede] | • Maintain multiple communications paths to include courier as well as network, enterprise, and cellular telephone communications<br>• Use a critical alerting and incident response service |

In addition to the cyber resiliency techniques identified in the second column of Table J-1, potential mitigations that apply across multiple attack steps can include Self-Challenge via Red Teaming and tabletop exercises and Consistency Analysis of incident response plans for different types of incidents to ensure that cyber-attacks are considered as the source of or a complicating factor in system outages [BAH16].

## J.2  POWER GRID ATTACK—2016

In December 2016, a more narrowly targeted cyber-attack impacted a single transmission-level substation in Ukraine. The malware involved (referred to as CRASHOVERRIDE [Dragos17] [ICS-CERT17] or Industroyer [ESET17]) used a modular design with payloads that target several industrial communication protocols widely used outside of the U.S. and are capable of directly controlling switches and circuit breakers.

Table J-2 identifies the functionality in the CRASHOVERRIDE malware used in the attacker's operations on the OT network. For each step, the second column identifies potential mitigations to redirect, preclude, impede, limit, or expose the malware functionality in the step.

**TABLE J-2:  ATTACKER AND DEFENDER USES OF CYBER RESILIENCY FOR MALWARE USED IN 2016 ATTACK**

| MALWARE FUNCTIONALITY | POTENTIAL MITIGATIONS | REPRESENTATIVE TECHNOLOGIES |
|---|---|---|
| **Launcher & Scanner tool scans OT network (serial, protocols, HMIs)** | • Analytic Monitoring of OT environment for specific protocol scans across networks, programmable logic controllers (PLCs), and HMIs; Analytic Monitoring for unexpected traffic [expose]<br>• Segmentation of relatively flat networks to increase compartmentalization of OT spaces [preclude, impede, limit] | • IDS for OT, ICS, or SCADA; monitoring for firmware, ladder logic, or PLC code writing to unexpected network locations<br>• SDN for network segmentation |
| **Define variables for OT payloads** | • Substantiated Integrity to validate provenance of applications [preclude, impede]<br>• Analytic Monitoring to look for changes to local programs, such as the launcher behavior adding variables [expose] | • Code signing<br>• IDS for OT, ICS, or SCADA; looking for unsigned code or monitoring for changes in local programs |
| **Provide command line interface (CLI) and interactive services on HMIs** | • Substantiated Integrity (signing, voting) on instantiating new services [preclude, impede]<br>• Deception in application programming interfaces (APIs), CLIs, and possibly HMI screens [redirect, expose]<br>• Analytic Monitoring to detect changes to interactive services [expose]<br>• Privilege Restriction – require MFA on all service updates [preclude, impede] | • Deception technology to create honeypot HMI screens, integrated with IDS for OT, ICS, or SCADA<br>• Use an OT security management platform to restrict privileges, require MFA on service updates, and require code signature verification on instantiation of new services |
| **Provide payloads for different protocols: IEC 101, IEC 104, IEC 61850, Open Platform Communication (OPC) DA (Data Access)** | • Deception to create false targets together with Analytic Monitoring to detect traffic to those targets [misdirect, expose]<br>• Analytic Monitoring to detect anomalous traffic for different protocols [expose] | • Deception technology to create honeypot HMI screens integrated with IDS for OT, ICS, or SCADA<br>• IDS for OT, ICS, or SCADA |
| **Execute CLI and interactive services on HMIs** | • Analytic Monitoring on execution of newly instantiated services or of commands from CLI [expose]<br>• Privilege Restriction on service and CLI execution and on HMI interaction to prove that the interaction is human-initiated [impede, preclude]<br>• Substantiated Integrity for significant process execution | • IDS for OT, ICS, or SCADA<br>• Use an OT security management platform to restrict service and CLI execution, constrain HMI interaction, and require MFA to authenticate commands for execution of significant processes |

| MALWARE FUNCTIONALITY | POTENTIAL MITIGATIONS | REPRESENTATIVE TECHNOLOGIES |
|---|---|---|
| **Execute SIPROTEC DoS, HMI switch toggle, Amplify, Data Wiper attacks** | • Redundancy with Diversity of HMIs [impede]<br>• Analytic Monitoring of HMI interactions with operators and to detect Wiper commands and derivatives in the scheduler [expose]<br>• Adaptive Response (e.g., run notepad to remove Wiper commands and derivatives) [impede, limit] | • Make architectural changes to use existing technologies in a diverse and redundant way<br>• IDS for OT, ICS, or SCADA |
| **Future Payloads** | • Redundancy with Diversity of OT procedures and protocols [impede]<br>• Redundancy of actions/logins on HMIs [impede] | • Make architectural changes to use existing technologies in a diverse and redundant way<br>• Use an OT security management platform to require redundant actions via HMIs |

www.ingramcontent.com/pod-product-compliance
Lightning Source LLC
LaVergne TN
LVHW081657050326
832903LV00026B/1794